NO TO
YOU CAN D

MW00928668

AN ALTERNATIVE
TO THE ESCORTED TOUR

BOB KAUFMAN

The Gelato Press
thegelatopress.com
thegelatopress@gmail.com
PO BOX 110725
NAPLES, FL, USA

ITALY NO TOUR NEEDED
YOU CAN DO IT YOURSELF
An Alternative to the Escorted Tour

ISBN: 9798864645536

65432

Other books by Bob Kaufman:

ITALY Made Easy for Seniors
  An Alternative to the Escorted Tour
  ISBN: 9798374018103

ITALY The Best Places to See by Rail
  An Alternative to the Escorted Tour
  ISBN: 9781985276802

ITALY Over 300 Critical Tips You Need to Know Before You Go
  ISBN: 9781677189281

ITALY Skip the Hotel and Stay at a Palace
  For the Same Price Live like Royalty
  ISBN: 9781792795626

ITALY The Stocking Stuffer Edition
  Over 300 Trivia Questions
  ISBN: 9798395896667

SPAIN The Best Places to See by Rail
  An Alternative to the Escorted Tour
  ISBN: 9798684495076

Back cover photos and thank you for:

The Gladiators at the Colosseum
Lenore Brownstein and the Author

Gondola ride in Venice
The Dolens, Gary, Sandy,
Jennie and Paul

Antipasto in Cortona
Al and Sharon Tunkel,
Joseph and Cindy Maloney,
Michael and Marge Panice,
William and Roberta Haag,
Don and Liz Russell

Acknowledgements:
Lenore Brownstein, for being sequestered with me for six months while I wrote this book, and for her assisted editing of the entire book in addition to coming up with the title. Kudos to Sarah Lummus, Dan Paradis, Donald French, Manny Suarez Graphic Design, and Suzzette Freedlander of the DSPOT for the cover layout. In addition, Al Tunkel, Gail Linden, and Gary Dolen for their assistance with photos. And finally, I would also like to thank Stephen Roth of Orleans, Massachusetts, who is no longer with us. Steve gave me the idea of the "hopoff" in 2008 over dinner at "Alberto's" restaurant in Hyannis, Mass.

WIKIPEDIA
Wikipedia, the free encyclopedia, has been the source of historical information, facts and figures, etc. All information is in the public domain. The writer has made a generous contribution to the Wikipedia Foundation.

Reviews on back cover

INSPIRATION
FOR MY LOVE OF ITALY

"I find other countries have this or this, but Italy is the only one that has it all for me. The culture, the cuisine, the people, the landscape, the history. Just everything to me comes together there."

FRANCES MAYES, AUTHOR
"UNDER THE TUSCAN SUN"

There is no other country in the world with more UNESCO World Heritage Sites (58) than Italy. Italy is **HISTORY**.

"The world is a book, and those who don't travel only read one page."– St. Augustine

---

And finally,
You will never learn from people who say
"I coulda, I woulda, I shoulda"
You only pass by here once,
So visit Italy!

MEET THE AUTHOR

Bob Kaufman has a passion for travel in Italy and Spain. While not Italy, he wrote his first book in 1983. He thought he would write his eighth book on Italy since few know there is an alternative to the escorted tour. Bob should know. He ran those escorted tours for over 35 years.

What Bob does in this book is convert those escorted tours into a "Do it Yourself" option. He takes the fear out of seeing this fabulous country without an escorted tour. Bob makes it easy with planned itineraries which result in far less money than a tour and absolutely no regimentation. The author takes all the mystery out of "doing it yourself." It's also a great way to stop and smell the roses, or better smell the olives. the grapes and taste Italy's great wines.

Bob's an Eagle Scout; loves travelling to Italy (he has made over 30 trips) and when he is not digging clams in the summer on Cape Cod, he is enjoying the beautiful Florida Gulf Coast in the winter with his travelling companion partner Lenore and their little Maltese "Milo." Bob and Lenore love Italian food and of course, gelato.

TABLE OF CONTENTS

MAP OF ITALY AND SICILY EXPLAINED

The map following this page is intended to give the reader a sense of the general location of cities and towns with respect to each other. It does not show distance. If you are an AAA Plus or Premier member you can obtain the AAA map of Italy, Austria & Switzerland, Florence, Milan, Naples, Rome at no cost. All you need do is contact your local AAA office. Also, feel free to make copies of my hand-drawn maps and use a highlighter yellow or pink pen to layout your trip.

APPENDIX MAPS:
Note: Maps are "logical maps" with no scale. See page x.

Distances and times are approximate.

ROME-FLORENCE-VENICE-MILAN
Note, from Florence to Pisa you can take the road "SGC" or the A11 Autostrada. Both roads will get you to Pisa.

AMALFI & NAPLES AREA

TUSCANY/UMBRIA HILLTOP TOWNS

APULIA & SALENTO

SICILY- AROUND THE ISLAND

REPETITION- Since this book is a reference, I do not know where you have entered or started reading. You may have skipped a few chapters which did not pertain to your plans. Therefore, I repeat many facts and give you reference for additional information in other chapters.

ITALY & SICILY
Not to any scale

SAMPLE OF LOGICAL MAPS

ROME – FLORENCE – VENICE – MILAN

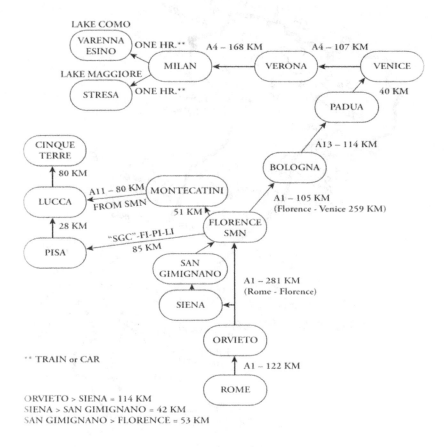

** TRAIN or CAR

ORVIETO > SIENA = 114 KM
SIENA > SAN GIMIGNANO = 42 KM
SAN GIMIGNANO > FLORENCE = 53 KM

CHAPTER 1

INTRODUCTION
&
ORGANIZATION

WHAT THIS BOOK IS ABOUT AND WHAT IT IS NOT

This book is about seeing Italy for the first time (and subsequent visits) by doing it yourself (DIY). In other words, you are not taking one of those escorted tours. If, after reading this book, you decide, "I think I will take an escorted tour," too much for me to handle, that's fine. At least you looked at the DIY option.

Don't expect this book to offer you lots of details on each place to visit, hotels, restaurants to dine in, or colorful pictures. It won't. It's intended to tell you how to do it—"It" means planning your trip and then experiencing it. However, details are discussed, like where to park the car, how not to get into a ZTL (I'll explain later), and more.

Throughout my book, I will also try to weave as much history as I can into the places you will see or traverse. However, *Italy No Tour Needed You Can Do It Yourself* is not a history book. To describe the history of the country, you would need several dozen encyclopedias the size of the Encyclopedia Britannica.

OBJECTIVE OF THIS BOOK

This book is very different than all my other books. It's about planning a trip to Italy and then doing it yourself, just as the title states. Doing it yourself does not mean going on an escorted tour. What it does mean is renting a car and visiting all those places you have seen pictures of, or heard about, and it's pretty easy to do if you follow the information I have provided in this book. Just don't think of it as driving all over the place and coming home exhausted. I also allow you to combine parts of your road trips with rail. It's called a hop-off. The objective of your vacation should be relaxing with minimal stress. For years, travel agents have called

An Alternative to the Escorted Tour

this "FIT," or foreign independent travel. I call it DIY. Here is a comparison of the DIY visit compared with the escorted tour.

DIY COMPARED TO ESCORTED TOURS

If you visit some of the few remaining "real" travel agents and ask about a 10-14 day trip to Italy for first timers, they will likely suggest an escorted tour. I can't share the name of these tour operators. However, they run the gamut from the deluxe, top-of-the-line tours to the bottom bare-bones tours. Just what do these tours have in common? First, they all use beautiful coaches, we don't call them buses. Buses are usually yellow or orange and take the kids to school. Coaches are like an airline and are typically complete with a restroom (for emergencies). Some even have snack bars with refrigerators, Cappuccino machines, and more. Tour directors are on every coach. These are not tour guides. Most admissions, i.e., Colosseum, etc., are included. Many of the high-end operators will provide you with complimentary drinks during the day. Where possible, "step-on tour guides" board the coach for the detailed history of each historical site. All tour participants are issued headsets with radio receivers required by Italian law.

Hotels and breakfasts are included. These range from usually three-star to five-star hotels. As you probably know, the high-end five-star hotels will provide those slippers and robes, turn down service, and chocolates before you retire. Likewise, the high-end five-star hotels will have fantastic breakfasts, while the three-star hotels will have a basic European breakfast of mostly cold items with several hot dishes included e.g. scrambled eggs.

All escorted tours, whether basic or high-end, have one thing in common: They are all highly regimented! What this means, on a typical day, departing for an over-the-road, overnight stop from Rome to Florence:

7:00A - Wakeup call – "But I want to sleep late, NO can do."
7:30A - Bags outside your room for pickup by the porter
8:00A - Breakfast in the breakfast room
8:45A - All aboard the coach
9:00A - Departure from Rome hotel
11:00A - Arrive in Florence – lunch on your own

2

ITALY NO TOUR NEEDED
You Can Do It Yourself

3:00P - Depart Florence – for Montecatini hotel.
But I want to shop some more, NO can do.
Would you please get on the coach?

What all this boils down to is cost. This is a true "you pay for what you get" experience. Exclusive of airfare, you can expect to pay for ten days (excluding your fly days):

Cost for a couple:
High-end tour $10,000 - 14,000   Basic Tour $6,000-$8,000
Cost for a single:
High-end tour $8,000 - $12,000   Basic Tour $3,000-$4,500

Also, remember that there will be some upcharges on basic tours. For example, what will you do on that free day in Rome after you have walked your feet off? You can sit and relax on our coach for a day trip to Pompeii (including lunch and admission) for $249 per person. And what about that optional "Rome by Night with Dinner" for $169 per person? Oh, did I forget to tell you about tipping your tour directors? You can usually figure a couple of hundred dollars here.

By now, I hope I have convinced you that the escorted tours are pricey and highly regimented compared to the DIY vacation.

Here is what you can expect to pay for a DIY visit to Italy for ten days, once again, excluding your fly days:

Item of Cost	Dble	Sgl
3-Star Hotel 10 nights w/breakfast (see note below)	1500	1200
Lunch for 10 days (light lunch, panini, pizza etc.)	300	150
Dinners includes wine Tourist Menu	400	200
Auto Rental (see note on upgrade to automatic trans)	400	400
Petrol/Tolls	400	400
Taxi/Limos/Metro/some rail	400	200
Admissions	300	150
Snacks	200	100
Total for 10 nights	3900	2800

Notes:
Rental is manual transmission; add $300 for automatic.

An Alternative to the Escorted Tour

Two star hotels, AirBnB, etc., will lower your cost per day. However, be advised that you will probably have to spend 6Euros per person for a pastry and a coffee at a standup bar.

By now I hope I have convinced you that "Doing It Yourself" will save you a bundle. However, you need to consider all those negatives that your Mom, Dad, or friends told you about:

THE NEGATIVES OF A DO-IT-YOURSELF VISIT

By now, I hope you realize that an escorted tour costs much more than an FIT or a Do It Yourself visit to Italy. You are also being swayed (bamboozled) by your parents and friends not to rent a car and drive around Italy for your vacation; you don't need all that stress and aggravation. Here are some of the reasons:

1. You will have difficulty. You can't speak the language or understand those Italians, even if they speak with their hands. *Most of the people in the major tourist areas speak English. In many of the smaller towns, they do understand you. Make sure you bring your GPS with that Italy map in it.*

2. It's dangerous driving on those Italian roads. *It's no different driving on our interstate roads, e.g., I-40, I-95.*

3. The Italian drivers are crazy. *Stay out of the far left-hand lane. You will be fine.*

4. All the people in Italy drive very fast on all the highways. *Yes, the speed limit on the major Autostrada highways is 80 MPH. I suggest you stay in the right-hand slower lane and avoid the high-speed inside lane. You will be fine.*

5. You don't know what those symbols mean on all those signs. You will probably get lots of parking tickets. *You need to go to the internet and look at all those signs, mainly Parking, No Parking, and No Entry.*

6. You can't drive in Venice. *No kidding!*

ITALY NO TOUR NEEDED
You Can Do It Yourself

However, you can park your rental in the garages once you arrive at the end of the roadway (in the lagoon area) or keep it on the land side of Venice, known as Venice Mestre.

7. Don't attempt to drive down what "choo" call it, the Amalfi Drive. You will kill yourself and Jen. Jason, you are crazy!
Mom, I think I can drive it. Otherwise, I will have a driver take us down the Amalfi Drive. It's all in Bob Kaufman's book.

8. It's a lot of work and very stressful driving in unfamiliar places.
I read Bob Kaufman's book, and it seems quite easy.

9. You won't know what to order on the menu.
Most of the wait people speak a little English, and many restaurants have English menus. They speak with their hands.

10. Jason, you are only 27 and just too young to rent a car and drive around a country that you know nothing about.
Mom, did I not drive to California with Jen last year?

11. Finally, those Italian cars are too small, and if you get into an accident… forget it.
They are all small to compact. And we will be fully insured.

12. Now, is there anything else we can say to convince Jen and you that an escorted tour is really the best option?
Mom, don't worry, I read Kaufman's books; I'm all set!

And one more thing. Don't expect that everything on an escorted tour runs without a hitch. You would expect so. However, things do happen. My cousin recently came back from a two-week escorted tour of Italy. After parting with $14,000 for him and his wife, he had significant complaints. Here are some of his comments: "First, we did not get three choices for dinner (as stated in the tour participant agreement) on the menu each night; we could not understand the poor English of our tour guide and the step-on guides. The hotels were not what the tour operator had said they would be, and the bus rides were very long. And finally, when we reached Venice, the tour guide came down with COVID,

An Alternative to the Escorted Tour

Oy, Oy, Oy. We aborted the last four days of the tour when we arrived in Venice and flew home. We asked for a partial refund, and the tour operator refused," all is true.

THE BENEFITS OF THE DIY ITALIAN VACATION

If you are financially well off and don't mind a highly regimented tour, or should I say "day," you need not read any further. Call your friendly travel agent and book a tour from one of those tour companies. However, if money and regimentation bother you, then read on. Here are the positive reasons for choosing a DIY Italian vacation.

As a tour operator for many years, I can tell you emphatically that this is one item you will "pay for what you get." Book a budget escorted tour or book a high-end expensive tour. Most of the difference will be in the hotels and the meals provided. After all, a tour of the Colosseum will be the same if you book an escorted tour or if you book yourself for the day on a tour of Rome and the Colosseum with the Grayline (booked on Tripadvisor as Gray Line – I Love Rome Tours and Tickets). It is also available through Viator, one of the Tripadvisor companies.

Throughout this book, I recommend the "Hop-On-Hop-Off" city bus tours to enhance your experience in each city. Now, getting back to the benefits of a DIY tour of Italy:

1. As stated, it's a fraction of the cost of the escort tours.

2. There is no regimentation. Don't even take an iPhone watch.

3. You can choose your own hotels, Airbnbs, or whatever your preferences are, from simple hostels to five-star hotels.

4. You can sleep late every morning.

5. You can have breakfast in the hotel (it is usually included) or enjoy a cappuccino and a croissant at a café or a standup bar on the street with all the locals.

ITALY NO TOUR NEEDED
You Can Do It Yourself

6. You can shop to your heart's content without needing to keep looking at your watch.

7. You can stop at off-the-road locations for wine tasting, vineyard tours, souvenirs, or a dip in the Med. You can even pull off the road and help locals pick olives. I did it in Spoletto!

8. You can have lunch and dinner anywhere you want.

9. You can schedule your visits to specific towns to coincide with street markets and fairs.

10. On arrival at your hotel, you can take a snooze before dinner or a dip in the pool, in season, assuming they have one.

11. You won't have to wait for your luggage to be delivered to your room, and you won't have to wait for a bellman to bring your bags down to the lobby. And, yes, you can call the front desk anytime and have a bellman bring your bags to your room.

12. Finally, you can order anything off the menu or eat as much pizza as you like.

I hope by now, you have been convinced to see Italy on your own (the objective of this book). So, let's read on and see how you plan your trip. But, first, some more basics on this book:

A WORD ABOUT THE FORMAT OF THIS BOOK
By now, you may have realized that this book uses larger-than-normal bold print. Why? It's just easier to read. Hopefully, the fonts used in this book will make it easier to read than all those other books with tiny print. I don't provide colorful pictures of sites you will visit or pretty hotel lobbies. Hopefully, you can bring back your own.

From time to time, I provide TIPS, which may be outside the content of the item discussed. You may find highlighting these tips with one of those yellow or pink markers is a good idea.

An Alternative to the Escorted Tour

CHICAGO MANUAL OF STYLE (CMOS)
I call it Bob's Manual of Style. Throughout this book, you will notice I don't adhere to what is known as the Chicago Manual of Style. For example, according to CMOS, the time would be 10 a.m. In Bob's style, it is 10AM. I use BC and AD right up against the numeric. So, it would be 476AD, not 476 A.D. I spell Century with a capital "C." So, expect to see the 4th Century and not the 4th century. Some words are spelled either of two accepted forms, e.g., Amphitheatre and Amphitheater. Also, some numbers are not spelled out. For example, instead of writing, "it is a little over one and a half miles to the ruins," I write it as "a little over 1.5 miles to the ruins." Just easier to read. I spell many words in Italian and English, so you get a feel for the Italian. For example, I use Roma for Rome, Pranzo for lunch, etc.

I try to make this book as palatable as possible. Many times, I weave my sense of humor into the pages. Many readers of my other books have stated, "I love your style. It's so easy to read and very enjoyable. I can't wait to make plans."

THE LANGUAGE PROBLEM
What problem? There is NO problem. Most of the people speak some English. Don't forget you can always use your hands when conversing with Italians. My favorite hand gesture in a restaurant is to imitate an octopus or a squid. It is best you pick up a copy of *Italian Without Words* by Cangelosi and Carpini, available on Amazon.com. It costs about $7.00. There are other books on this subject. Below, I have included some common words you may want to learn. You might want to pick up a small book on conversational Italian that you can keep in your pocket. The best one on the market is "*Italian Phrases for DUMMIES.*" It is also available on Amazon.com and in many bookstores.

TERMINOLOGY
Here are the terms, definitions, and whatever you want to call it, I regularly use in my books:
Automobile rent-a-car – Auto a noleggio
Grazie- thank you or Prego- Don't mention it (not the sauce)
Bin- The track number in the rail station
Campanile- A tower   Stazione- The rail station

8

ITALY NO TOUR NEEDED
You Can Do It Yourself

Carrozza- the carriage or coach number on a train
Cena – Dinner   Pranzo-Lunch
Centro Storico- the central historic district
Colazione- Breakfast (Cola-Zee-Oh-knee)
Crenellated Roof- It's those large notches on the top of
    the medieval castles where they shoot arrows.
Duomo- The church, many times it's a cathedral or basilica
Ferrovia- the rail station in Venice
Firenze- The Italian word for Florence
Frecci xxxx - the high-speed trains of Trenitalia.
    Frecci is short for "Arrow." Freccirosa would mean red
    arrow, since rosa is red.
Funicular –It's a cable car system. Ascensore- Elevator/Lift
Scala Mobile-Escalato
Parcheggio-Parking Lot

THE TIME PROBLEM
Once again, there is NO problem if you know what you are doing. Most times are written using the 24-hour clock (sometimes called military or 24-hour clock time). This eliminates all problems with AM and PM. If you purchase rail tickets for 0600, this does not mean 6PM. It means 6AM. A six o'clock PM train is 1800. Just remember to add 1200. Railways, bus companies, and venues will not refund your money if you goof; however, most will try to accommodate you. One of my good friends showed up at the Termini train station in Rome at 4PM to get her 6PM train to Naples, only to be told by the security people that her train left the station at 6AM that morning. The Trenitalia people were good enough to put her on a train at 1900 (7PM).

THE DATE PROBLEM
Europeans, especially Italians, use the format for the date as Day/Month/Year instead of our system of Month/Day/Year. If you are booking October 8, 2024, it is written in European format as 8/10/2024. I always suggest writing it as:
Arriving Thursday, Oct 24, 2024, and not 24/10/2024
Always include the day of the week. And double-check all.
I might note Oct 8, 2024, is also World Octopus Day; it's true.

An Alternative to the Escorted Tour

I suggest you read this book, cover to cover, before making any plans. Many people will buy their air tickets, then realize about three months before their trip that friends have suggested they go to Lake Como and the Lakes District for three days, instead of flying out of Rome, fly home from Milan. Good idea, but they are now locked into their airline schedule with a round-trip from Chicago to Rome when they now need an additional three days with a return from Milan back to Chicago. Here are points you need to know in your planning phase of your trip:

CRITICAL PLANNING DATES

Air—It can only be booked 330 days before the RETURN DATE. If you book using airline points, there is usually no penalty for changing, canceling, or rebooking. If paying cash (i.e., not using any type of frequent flyer points), penalties usually apply. You should check the airline's official website.

Rental cars can usually be booked 330 days before your pickup date. I will explain the options, i.e., pre-pays, cancellations, age requirements, insurance, etc.

Trains in Italy can only be booked 60-90 days in advance. Schedules rarely change that much. These are the high-speed reserved-seat trains known as "Frecci" or "Red Arrow" trains of the Trenitalia rail company. Other trains are offered by Italo (https://www.italotreno.it/en), another rail operator. These also can only be booked 60-90 days in advance.

>>>TIP<<<
Italo vs. Trenitalia can be compared at "Omio www.omio.com.
>>><<<

Hotels—book anytime without a cash deposit (learn more in the hotel chapter). I use the word "hotel," but it can also mean hostel, BnB, Albergo (small hotel), guest house, etc.

Private driver – at Italy's airports, 3-4 weeks before arrival. It's the same with a private driver down the Amalfi coast.

ITALY NO TOUR NEEDED
You Can Do It Yourself

And one more final word, please do not accept this book as a complete tour guide of Italy. It is not, and will only give you the basics. If you want all those details (which you probably won't read anyway), purchase a five-pound book to lug around, which will give you all the details you need but won't tell you *how to visit* Italy. So here we go on to the basics. But, before that, I offer you the following:

DON'T BITE OFF TOO MUCH THAN YOU CAN CHEW
I am a member of several websites on visiting Italy, or "I Love Italy." I often review and critique itineraries for first-time visitors. I am amazed to read some itineraries for first-time travelers to Italy. I even get dizzy reading some of them. "We are flying into Rome, then going to Positano, then to the Cinque Terre, then to Venice, then to Lake Como, then Milan, then Taormina, and of course, flying home from Palermo. And, further, we are doing it all in two weeks." Yikes! Some people don't even know where these places are in Italy. They just heard or saw pictures of them and want to visit them.

Let's face it: Italy has more to see and do than any other country in Western Europe and perhaps the world. You cannot do it all in one fell swoop. Italy is a place, as they say, "You need to stop and smell the roses." How true. So bite off what you can chew in two weeks without feeling you need a "real" vacation when you get home. There will be plenty of time for that next trip to Perugia for the annual chocolate festival.

USE THIS BOOK AS A REFERENCE
You may use this also as a reference book. Since I don't know what you have read, I sometimes repeat various items. For example, you may find items about Pompeii under the day trip out of Rome and on a stopover on your way to the Amalfi area. It is probably best to read both chapters and sections that deal with Pompeii. There may be some overlap. Please excuse this.

CHAPTER 2

WHEN TO GO
PASSPORTS AND ETIAS

WHEN TO GO

Gee, everyone asks me the same question. When is the best time to go to Italy? Three variables will determine when you go. I am assuming you are flexible with your vacation (holiday) time. They are the time of year, usually dictated by the weather, the cost of hotels (and air), and "the crowds:"

SEASON/CLIMATE	MONTHS	COSTS	CROWDS
High - Hot	May to -mid- Sept	Highest	Lots
Shoulder - Mild	Mid- Sept to Mid Dec, Apr and May	Moderate	Some
Off Season – Chilly *	Mid Dec, Jan, Feb & Mar	Lowest	Very little

* Very mild in Sicily; they are growing tomatoes.

PASSPORT, ETIAS VISA, WORK VISAS

If you don't have a passport, you will need one. It's the full-blown one. Sometimes, it is called the Passport Book. You can't use a Passport Card or even a driver's license. For Americans, you need to consult https://travel.state.gov. The waiting time is 3-6 months. Obtaining a passport is one of the first things you ought to do if you intend to take a trip to Italy or leave the USA for any country requiring a US Passport for re-entry. The cost is $165 for a new (original) passport.

Secondly, if you have a passport, get it out and check the expiration date, not the date of issue. I don't know the reason for this. However, airlines and I believe cruise ship companies want an expiration date of a minimum of six (6) months forward. For example, if you are travelling to Italy on May, 12, and your expiration date is July of the same year, you must renew your

ITALY NO TOUR NEEDED
You Can Do It Yourself

passport now. You can renew your current passport (book) for $130. A renewal will give you an additional ten years.

Your passport will allow you to enter the USA and prove to Italian authorities that you are a US citizen.   Canadian's should check with their counterparts in Ottawa.

Once inside Italy, Italian law states that you must always have your passport (if it is not Italian) on you. Please do not leave it in your bags, room, or any other place. It must be physically on you. I always suggest you make a copy and keep the copy in your luggage, just in case you lose your passport. In this way, all you need to do is go to the American Embassy (there is only one in Rome) or consulate with the copy, and they will rush you a new one. Consulates are in major cities, e.g., Venice, Milan, etc.

In 2016, the European countries that are part of the Schengen group (named after a small village in Luxembourg) announced that anyone arriving outside of a Schengen country must have an ETIAS Visa in addition to their country passport. Italy is one of these countries. The ETIAS program has been pushed off until at least the Spring of 2025. It was originally supposed to start in January 2024; however, many counties in the group were not ready.

When ETIAS takes effect, you will only have to fill out a form online and pay about $7. You will also need to carry this visa document with you. More information will be coming shortly.

For now, you should not worry about this until you are advised by your airline or cruise company. Work Visas are another thing; consult the Italian Embassy. You should be aware that you cannot stay more than 90 days unless you have some type of Visa.

Enough of this paperwork... Now let's fly to Italy.

CHAPTER 3

GETTING TO ITALY

UNDERSTANDING TYPES OF AIRFARE
There are three types of air travel. Most of us are familiar with the "round-trip." However, suppose you plan on flying into one of the four major Italian airports, which offer nonstop flights to the USA, i.e., Rome, Milan, Naples, and Venice, and returning from a different airport either in Italy or elsewhere. In this case, you need to look at "multi-cities." Returning from a different airport is called an "open-jaw", or a multi-cities booking.

CLASSES OF FARES
Over the past five years, the airlines have restructured their categories from three classes to four: First Class, Business Class, Standard Coach, and Basic Economy. Standard Coach, called "Y" class for years, has been broken down into standard coach and economy. Several carriers, e.g., Delta, now have "Comfort Class," which gives you 6-8 more inches of extra legroom in coach. Your main concern when choosing a fare is to know the difference between the standard coach and economy fares.

In standard coach or "Y" class, you get all the amenities you always received in the past, i.e., one checked bag, seat assignment, etc. Many airlines still charge for your first and second bag, even in standard coach, unless you have a credit card or some other indicia keyed to their airline. On flights to Europe, in regular or standard coach ("Y" class), most airlines will allow you one bag (50lbs maximum) free and seat assignment. On economy or what I call "real budget," you must pay for your checked bag and seat assignment. If you don't pay online, you can pay at the airport. The first checked bag is usually $60. In addition, they will assign you a seat at the check-in counter. When checking airline fares, ensure you know what's included if it states "BASIC ECONOMY." The Basic Economy fee may not include baggage, carry-on, and seat selection. It varies by airline. And yes, you sit in the same cabin as everyone else, except the people up front who

14

ITALY NO TOUR NEEDED
You Can Do It Yourself

paid "mucho" dollars or used "mucho" frequent flyer points for the privilege of having a more comfy seat and enjoying a better meal than you did.

Now, here is an important fact. The person to the right of you, or left of you, or in front of you, did not pay the same price for that ticket to Rome which you paid. Yup, it's true. They call it dynamic pricing. The airlines use it to adjust fares according to their algorithms. Or better, the fares change according to the algorithms. I won't try to explain it. However, in simplicity, as available seats in a class are taken (i.e., used up), the price goes up. So, the person to your right may have paid $449 for a round-trip ticket, and the person to your left may have spent $689. This is why it is not a good idea to purchase tickets when the flights become available. Often, the price will drop. I won't go into all the details about when to buy your tickets, but suffice it to say it is usually 3-5 months before departure. And I can tell you to avoid buying your tickets within six weeks of flight time when airlines try to squeeze more revenue out of the remaining seats.

On the other hand, if you are using frequent flyer points, book your tickets as soon as possible and keep checking back to see if the required points have gone down. If they have, cancel your reservation and rebook with the lower points.

>>>TIP<<<
Take a look at the seats on the flight you want to book. See how they are filling up. Taking a look at the seats may indicate when to purchase your tickets. If you see a block of seats, perhaps 50 in the main cabin, all booked up about 9-10 months before departure, I can bet you, it is a group ticket. So, don't panic and feel, "We gotta buy tickets now; I can see the plane is filling up."
>>><<<

>>>TIP<<<
If you have 90 days or more before your outbound flight, try to obtain a credit card issued by a bank keyed to your airline. Delta is linked with American Express, American with Barclays and Citibank and, United are linked with Chase. You can usually

15

An Alternative to the Escorted Tour

obtain bonus points, and sometimes, they waive the annual fee, which will be far less than paying all those baggage fees.
>>><<<

>>>TIP<<<
If selecting seats, avoid the ones next to the toilets in the rear. There is always too much noise in this area. If you can choose those "bulk-head" seats (you may have to pay a little extra (Delta Comfort Class), you will have an additional two feet of legroom. However, depending on the aircraft type, you may not have a "drop-down" tray in front of you. On newer aircraft, all the trays are now in the armrest. If you want to go to sleep, I favor the window seat. Let's face it; nothing is outside except the dark Atlantic. If you select the left-hand window seat (the "A" seat), you will probably be facing land instead of water, as the approach to Rome (FCO-Runway 16) is in a southerly direction. The right-hand window views the "Med" for 15 minutes until landing.
>>><<<

If you can get by with a carry-on bag for the week, you will probably save $120-150 if you fly basic economy (not coach or main cabin). Remember, you are going to Italy and not on a safari. There are laundromats, pharmacies, and ATMs all over the place. However, if you have the resources to fly business or first class, there will usually be no baggage fees and a better meal, so go for it. Your body will thank you.

>>>TIP<<<
It would be best to compare the cost of that budget seat (basic economy) with the cost of a full coach ticket since they may be a few dollars apart. The best option would be to purchase the full coach ticket; you can sit right next to your traveling partner.
>>><<<

BEST ROUTES TO ITALY
Most Americans (and even Canadians) fly from American or Canadian domestic hubs to the four major cities: Rome, Milan, Naples, and Venice. You may want to compare the price, connections, and layover time. For example, a flight from Indianapolis to Rome may cost $750, involving a layover in

16

ITALY NO TOUR NEEDED
You Can Do It Yourself

Chicago or Newark and possibly another European connection. It would be better to drive (or take the bus) to Chicago (O'Hare) and fly non-stop to Rome for $450. If you are in Greenville, NC, consider driving to Atlanta, where there are lower fares. A one-way car rental will cost you about $100 ($200) roundtrip. However, you stand to save $500-$700 on the airfare. In addition, this may get you into Rome the next day at 7AM instead of 4PM with those connections. You will also get a day of sightseeing. The same applies to flights to Milan, Venice and Naples.

The major competitive hubs in the USA are JFK, EWR (Newark), Chicago, Los Angeles, San Francisco, Denver, Washington DC (Dulles), Boston, and Atlanta. You can view them all on "Major USA International Airline hubs." Canada has its own hubs, but competition to Air Canada comes from Montreal and Toronto.

>>>TIP<<<
Before purchasing airline tickets, plan your itinerary. You can always change the itinerary, "jockey" around dates, e.g., "Should we spend four nights in Rome or three." However, you won't be able to change flights (except by paying a fee most of the time). So best to block out your outbound and inbound dates and consider extra days. It costs $150-300 (for a double) per extra day in Italy.
>>><<<

USING FREQUENT FLYER (FFP) POINTS
Most airlines allow you to change your flights if you use frequent flyer miles as long as they are for the same city pairs, e.g., Chicago-Milan. Dates and times can be changed. However, remember that additional flyer miles (points) may be required. If you need more miles, consider moving points from other credit cards to frequent flyer points. For example, if you are short, 5,000 miles for a Delta flight, you may be able to move 5,000 AMEX points over to Delta. There is another benefit of using FFP's. You can cancel your itinerary completely, and rebook to another set of cities. For example, fly into Rome and return from Milan instead of your previously booked return flight from Venice.

An Alternative to the Escorted Tour

Also, avoid using Frequent Flyer points on any airline that connects at a London airport. The taxes are out of sight. It's best to connect in Lisbon, Madrid, Frankfort, or wherever. As they say, you should avoid London like the plague. Remember, this only applies to using your FFPs and arriving from North American airports i.e., USA and Canada.

THE 330-DAY RULE EXPLAINED
Airline tickets can usually be purchased only 330 days before the flight. If you are using frequent flyer miles, you must know that your best deals are to purchase those tickets as soon as the 330-day comes due. With respect to FFPs note you need to take a look at the return date. If you don't get these tickets on the 330 days or within a few weeks of your dates (if they are available), you may get what I call "crappy" flights. For example, you can easily book using frequent flyer miles a JFK flight on Delta to Rome with a return from Venice 330 days prior. However, try to use your miles 90 days before your departure date, and you might have to be routed from JFK to Salt Lake City or Atlanta and even give up an additional 30,000 miles for that flight to Rome.

Remember, you can change your tickets on frequent flyer awards or put them back for a slight fee or no fee. Consider monitoring the airline points "chart" every 30 days. If you bought the ticket for 80,000 points and it goes down to 65,000, you can usually put those miles/points back into your account and book the tickets again at the lower requirement. However, if you are purchasing tickets for cash, i.e., on a credit card, the best is to wait until 3-6 months before getting the best deal.

>>>TIP<<<
Use the OTAs (Online Travel Agents, e.g., Orbitz, etc.) to locate a few flights and remember the Multi-Cities option if you are flying into Rome and returning from Venice, Milan, or Naples. Then go to the airline's website, e.g., Delta.com, and purchase (or use your frequent flyer miles) tickets there. Why? It's simple. You will have more "rights" if flights are canceled, delayed, etc. I have never bought overseas tickets on any website other than the actual carrier, i.e., Delta.com, AA.com, etc.
>>><<<

ITALY NO TOUR NEEDED
You Can Do It Yourself

Many airlines do not list their schedules on ORBITZ or other OTAs (Online Travel Agents). Most of these airlines you probably have never heard of; here are some of them:

Turkish Airlines serves many cities in the USA.

Norse Atlantic- via JFK

Virgin

Airtransat (via Toronto)

Level

Icelandic

Basic

There are more.

>>>SMART TIP<<<

One more tip: You may consider flying into Nice, Zurich, or a nearby European city and taking the train to Milan and the Lakes or Venice. There are lots of ways to get to Italy.

>>><<<

GOING.COM   CHEAP FLIGHTS

If you want to travel dirt cheap and have the liberty to be flexible on travel dates, consider a yearly subscription to GOING.COM. This used to be called Scotts Cheap Flights. It is still what I would call a "bird-dog." For as little as $49 a year, GOING, will "push" ridiculously low fares, mistake or error fares. It's simple. Here is how it works. You sign up and fill out a profile, i.e., which airports you want to fly out of and where to, e.g., Europe, etc. When GOING sees a relatively low or an error fare, they notify you immediately. So, you may get an email, JFK to Rome, basic economy on Delta for $229 round trip, valid January 10 thru March 10. Huh? Once you get this notice, you have only a day or two (better, an hour or two) to get those tickets. The best is to book them immediately on the Delta.com website. You should note that GOING does not sell you the ticket. They only point you to the deal. Stated simply, "It's the early bird that gets the worm," or maybe "he who hesitates is lost." You should note that you need not pay $49 for this "push" service, but you won't get all the notices.

An Alternative to the Escorted Tour

If you want to use GOING.COM, it's best to make up an itinerary, and then when you are notified, "go for it." All you need do is know how many days you need, e.g., a block of 15-18 days. Also, note that many times you may have to return to your inbound airport. However, it's not a big deal to take a train back from Venice to Rome for about $50 the night before (do stay at the four-star Hotel Isola Sacre for $170 per night www.hotelisolasacra.) about two miles from FCO. There is more flexibility if you can return from the same airport you arrived at.

MOMONDO AND GOOGLE FLIGHTS

The easiest website to get a feel for when to travel is momondo.com. This website offers a top-notch, easy-to-use experience with dates and airlines on a one-page display. Google Flights should also be consulted.

Also, remember that if you are flexible, you will get the best airline fare. If you insist on flying to Rome on a Saturday, it may cost you $900. Go on a Tuesday, and it will cost you $600. Momondo and Google Flights give you a "spread" of days.

Avoid having coffee or any caffeinated drink by noon on your travel date. In addition to keeping you from sleeping on your overnight flight, it will make you use the toilet more often. It's best to drink water and plenty of it. If you can avoid alcohol, it's a plus unless you are in Business or First Class, then go for it and get that complimentary blanket out (if they still offer one).

Also, it is best to wear comfortable clothing. I recommend sweatpants and sneakers. And, yes a sweater to keep warm. It gets cold crossing the Atlantic; even colder next to the window.

If you are flying the day flights (as opposed to the overnight flights) on American or British Airways to Heathrow, you need to check if you can make the connection down to Rome that evening since the flights usually arrive about 9PM. Most of the time, you will have to overnight at Heathrow Airport. Also, be advised that if you fly in and out of London on frequent flyer miles, the taxes and surcharges may cost as much as $500 per person. If you want to see London for a few nights, the best would be to go directly to any

ITALY NO TOUR NEEDED
You Can Do It Yourself

European city, then fly up on a cheap fare instead of paying that out-of-sight tax surcharge.

My cousin thanked me for that tip and the free vacation in Paris! He flew to Paris (instead of London), spent three nights there, then took the train to London. What a brilliant idea. So, instead of paying the $500 surcharge per person using his frequent flyer miles, he used it to stay in Paris (airline tax was, I believe, about $34 per person) and take the high-speed (Eurostar) train for $75. These prices do fluctuate. However, I think you get the point.

Consider flying into nearby European cities and taking a train into Italy. It would be better if it were an inexpensive "local" flight. Perhaps fly into Madrid and get a local flight into Rome. Both are cheap! Now, on to those itineraries.

** SPACE BELOW FOR YOUR NOTES **

CHAPTER 4

SUGGESTED ITINERARIES & OVERVIEW

THE ITINERARIES

The variations of the itineraries discussed in this book are infinite. More than 30 years ago, when you could order a car from Ford or GM, they had a corporate saying that no two cars they built were alike. So true with visits to Italy. Folks return from Italy and tell me they visited Rome, Florence, and Venice. I asked them if they got to see "Moses" (a sculpture by Michelangelo) about four blocks from the Colosseum, and they said, "Gee, I didn't even know about it." In summary, everyone has a different experience, i.e., where they went, what they saw, what they ate, where they stayed, and more.

Taking this concept into consideration, I constructed the itineraries in this book for the first-time visitor to Italy and the second and third-time visitors. Since 1972, I have made over thirty trips to this beautiful country. Why? Because I love it so much. So, why am I telling you this? Simple. If you fall in love with Italy the way I have, you might want to venture off that road out of Rome and do a little exploring.

So, before I get into an overview of all these itineraries, you should understand why everyone just loves Italy. I will list them by importance:

1. The People. I have never met such warm and gracious people. On my first trip to Italy in 1972, I was on a bus in Rome and after five minutes noticed that we did not cross the Tiber River. So, I went up to the driver, showed him my map and he motioned to me that the river was the opposite way. He stopped at the next stop and allowed us to get off. Would you believe in about 3 minutes we were surrounded by several people offering to help two stranded Americans find their way around Rome?

22

ITALY NO TOUR NEEDED
You Can Do It Yourself

2. The Cuisine. Ask anyone in America or Canada what their favorite food is, and I will bet you they will say "Italian." There are probably no less than 1,000 recipe and cuisine books written on this subject. The cuisine varies throughout the country. Northern Italian cuisine is completely different from Southern Italian, which is rich in tomato-based sauces. And, no you will not find "Meatballs and Spaghetti" on the menu in any Italian restaurant! So, don't ask for it. Oh, I forgot pizza. Pizza has been around for about 1,000 years, but not the way we know it. Our type of pizza was invented in **Naples** in 1899, the tomato sauce, mozzarella, and basil leaves on top, now known as Margherita Pizza. It was named after the Dutchess of Savoy (Margherita of Savoy) by Raffaele Esposito, the Father of Pizza. We know Savoy as that Northwest section of Italy, which now incorporates Turin. He honored her with a pizza with the colors of the Italian flag. Pizza is Italy! There are numerous types, from thin crust to the bready deep dish Sicilian Pizza of Naples. I can tell you that I have never met anyone who did not love Italian food. I will make an exception with "Meatballs and Spaghetti" and call it Italian.

3. The Culture. Italy defines the words what is "laid back." It seems no one is in a rush. They take their time and enjoy the day. After lunch, the shops close and also most of the supermarkets. It's time for a siesta, a snooze, or whatever you want to call it. The people return about 4PM and work till about 9PM. They rarely watch TV. And if they do, you won't find murder mysteries and violence, except for a John Wayne re-run from 1955. The Italians like to watch soccer games and the shows that are the equivalent of "Dancing with the Stars" and "Wheel of Fortune." You don't hear every night of any mass shootings in towns or cities. It just doesn't exist. Maybe it's because the majority of Italy is Catholic. And, talk about the family. Did you know that "young" Italians don't leave the nest until about age 30? If you go to an Italian village, you will see old men smoking cigarellos and young couples taking their time chatting over a cappuccino or an espresso. It is truly a different lifestyle and a different world. Unlike Americans, who are always rushing around, Italians prefer to do "nada". It is just a much slower pace of life.

An Alternative to the Escorted Tour

4. and finally, the History. Italy is one living museum of Western civilization. You can't escape it. Everywhere you go, you are immersed in history. It runs the gamut from ancient ruins from about 3,000BC to the present day. Even if you stay in the Antiche Mura Hotel in Sorrento (highly recommended) you will note that the hotel lobby is built into the ruins of "The Valley of the Mills." It's not that old. But you can see ruins everywhere in Italy. One of my favorites is the ruins of the Temple of Apollo which dates to the 6th Century BC. And get this, it's right in the center of town, across from the gelato shop, the BnB Apollo, and the Ortigia Boutique Palace hotel, and open 24 hours a day for an after-dinner stroll or a sunrise photo op.

You won't find this type of history anywhere else in Western Europe or even anywhere else in the world. Italy has it all with almost 60 UNESCO World Heritage Sites.

Before the itineraries, it is best to read the basic city/town chapters. This will give you an idea of the over-the-road itineraries. I might note that place names (towns and cities) are in **bold**. It is just easier to spot. So here they are:

ARRIVAL AT ROME FCO AIRPORT- Chapter 5
How to rent a car, insurance restrictions, documents required. Included is also an overview of the Italian road system.

RAIL TRAVEL OUT OF ROME- Chapter 6
The hopoff concept explained and basics of rail travel in Italy.

ROME, ROME, ROME- Chapter 7
What to do and see. Number of days, etc. The walking tour of the Monuments: The Pantheon, Piazza Navona, Spanish Steps, Campo di Fiore and The Trevi Fountain. A day of Ancient Rome: The Colosseum, The Forum, The Wedding Cake, and a full day at Vatican City to see the ceiling of the Sistine Chapel painted by Michelangelo, and a visit to the Church of Churches, St. Peter's Basilica. If there is time at the end of the day, you may visit Castel Sant' Angelo, which is a very short walk from St. Peters and the Borgo Pio lunch area.

ITALY NO TOUR NEEDED
You Can Do It Yourself

ROME EXTRA DAYS- Chapter 8
Discusses the day trips that can be taken from the "Eternal City."
In addition to the overview and history of each site, the author
gives you all the details on how to get to the attraction either by
rental car or by rail. Day trips include The Amalfi Drive (yes, it's
a day trip), Baths of Caracalla, Villa Borghesi, The Catacombs, and
Appian Way, Orvieto, and Ostia Antica next to FCO airport.

Okay, okay, let's get to the over the road itineraries.

In the balance of this book, I describe most of the popular basic
itineraries in detail. For example, take a look at the **IT-ROME-TO-
FLORENCE Chapter 9.** However, to make it easier, especially if
you are a first-time visitor, I provide you with an overview. In this
way, you can pick and choose which itinerary(s) you would like to
follow. For example, many visitors arrive in Rome, spend only one
day, then go on to the Amalfi Coast, returning to the USA or
Canada after seven days. It's just their choice and there is nothing
wrong with this. I might note, that for each itinerary or city stay, I
suggest the minimum number of days you would need to spend to
cover most of the highlights. So here we go.

*** NORTHBOUND (FROM ROME) ITINERARIES ***

IT-ROME-TO-FLORENCE- Chapter 9
This itinerary starts in Rome (but does not include Rome, see
Chapter 7) and travels north to Florence, the City of the
Renaissance. For details about the City of Florence, consult
Chapter 10. There are two ways to arrive in Florence. You may
choose to go directly or make en-route stops for sightseeing,
lunch, or perhaps an overnight stay.

Rome to Florence - Direct no stops – 4 hours by car
 2 hours high-speed train
 Suggested stops: **Orvieto** 2 hours hilltop town
 Siena hilltop town 4 hours – or overnight
 San Gimignano- hilltop town, 2 hours,
 However, definitely an overnight stay.
I mention the 2-hour fast train if you will be doing a "hopoff."

An Alternative to the Escorted Tour

In other words, you get to Florence and then rent a car from there and do other itineraries.

FLORENCE- Chapter 10
Florence is known as the City of the Renaissance. Once in the City of Florence (or Montecatini) you will need a minimum of two full days. You can stay in the City of Florence, or Montecatini, a town located about 45 minutes away by car or 50 minutes by inexpensive rail. Trains run every 30 minutes.
What to see and do -   David and the Academy
Uffizi Gallery
Duomo Complex
Shopping – Ponte Vecchio Bridge
Nuovo Mercato

FLORENCE EXTRA DAYS- Chapter 11
Florence (or Montecatini) is an excellent jumping-off place for visiting other major attractions in Tuscany. Except for the Cinque Terre (the five towns on the hills), other sites can be reached in less than one hour by car or by rail. I detail them all in Chapter 11. They are:

Pisa
The Medieval city of **Lucca**
Montecatini Alto
Montecatini Terme (the baths)
The Cinque Terre

THE CINQUE TERRE Chapter 12
In the past 20 years, this area of Italy has gained prominence, almost on a par with the Amalfi area and towns like **Positano** and **Amalfi**. It is easily reached in about two hours from Florence. It is difficult to visit all the five towns in one day. At most, you can visit on a day trip only two. The best way to visit the other three towns or spend a few days hiking or on the beach is to overnight at one of the towns. Unless you are a "billygoat", visiting the five towns with a rental car is, to say the least, "challenging." I detail how to do it in this chapter.

ITALY NO TOUR NEEDED
You Can Do It Yourself

TUSCANY/UMBRIA HILLTOP TOWNS Chapter 13

This section of Tuscany and part of Umbria have more hilltop towns than any part of Italy or any part of Europe. And further, most of them are no more than 20 miles apart from each other. I discuss each town in detail. The best approach is to base yourself in one (or two) of the towns and make day trips to the others. You will need a minimum of five full days here. It would be best to make it seven days so you can "hang out" with the locals in your base town. Here is a quick summary:

Cortona is a medieval town where "*Under the Tuscan Sun*" was filmed. It has lots of old buildings, churches, restaurants, outdoor cafes, and plenty of shopping.

San Gimignano is very unique because it is the only hilltop town with fourteen remaining towers. We don't know the actual count but it is believed it was about 75. This is my first choice for a base to visit the other hilltop towns in the area. You can't beat the view from that La Cisterna Hotel. If you are on a honeymoon, this is the place.

Perugia, most of us know it as the chocolate capital of Italy and perhaps all of Europe. Few know that it is steeped in history. Perugia has a rather large labyrinth of Etruscan and Roman ruins below the city. **Perugia,** while a hilltop town is a large city with many suburbs. It is the capital of the province of Umbria. As a tourist, you may get lost here. However, in my detailed description of **Perugia,** I describe what to see and do on a day trip from your Tuscan or Umbrian base town.

Assisi, as we all know is famous or synonymous with Saint Francis, better known as St. Francis of **Assisi.** It is a great town for just walking. Assisi is actually in Umbria. Because of the layout of the town, you can walk from one end to the other and see everything. My second choice is only because of a great hotel I recommend with a fantastic view of the countryside.

Gubbio is another excellent town in Umbria, for viewing ancient Roman ruins. However, the ruins which are mainly the Roman

An Alternative to the Escorted Tour

Theatre are in a flat area at the base of the hill. The town itself is not medieval as it doesn't have a wall around it. However, several buildings from the medieval era are preserved. If you are interested in something special, **Gubbio** has a skyway, like a ski tow from the top of the hill to the bottom. It is worth a day trip.

Montepulciano is a medieval town. It overlooks the famous Val d'Orcia valley with all those rolling hills and vineyards. If you see a picture of it, you will know it is the Val d'Orcia. You can't get more medieval than this. But more important, it is the capital of red wines in the area. If you are into wines, this is the place to make your base. You can easily sample a different glass of wine every hour, no kidding. You can take a taxi from one winery to the other. I can personally vouch for this as I traveled the road from **Cortona** to **Montepulciano** (SP32 and SP10) across those beautiful hills. BTW the wine "Montepulciano" does not come from this area. It comes from Abruzzi.

There are many more medieval hilltop towns in Tuscany e.g. Pienza, Volterra, etc. However, I would have to devote an entire book just to this subject.

IT-FLORENCE-TO-VENICE Chapter 14
I always enjoy this itinerary. It's a nice leisurely day; there's no need to "beat your gums out" trying to rush up to Venice. Time to take it easy, as it is only one day of travel and a fast three-hour run. Have your choice of an option or two for the day:
Bologna is home to the oldest university in the world. If you are into meat, this is a must-stop for a pasta and a meat dish, i.e. Pasta Bolognese. Hopefully, you will be running late out of Florence and will make this a pranzo (lunch) stop at about 1PM, before heading on to wine tasting in the Euganean Hills at about 4PM. If stopping at Bologna, you can forget Padua, for the day at least, and make Padua a day trip, for you won't need a car.

Wine Tasting (Euganean Hills)
By now, if you haven't made it to Chianti or Montepulciano, wine tasting in the wineries of the Euganean Hills is a must. You need to plan the day accordingly. After leaving Florence at about 10AM head directly to one of the wineries in the Euganean Hills. Don't

worry about having a glass of wine on an empty stomach. Most wineries will give you pieces of crusty bread/and or bread sticks and salumi (yes, it's salami) to sop up that alcohol. Before, going on to Padua, if you have time, you can grab some pranzo at one of the nearby eateries. If you are short on time for **Padua**, continue to **Venice**.

Padua, since it is less than 30 minutes from Venice, is best visited on a full-day trip, unless you are running ahead of time from your departure from **Florence** and are not stopping for wine tasting. Then by all means make it a stop. Let's face it, if you arrive in Venice at noon or 1PM, your room probably will not be ready, so why rush? The Grand Canal won't be going anywhere. See more on Padua in chapter 16.

VENICE Chapter 15
In this chapter, I discuss what to do with your rental car, whether you should stay in Venice or Venice Mestre, and what to do after you visit Venice. I highlight all the attractions in Venice, when to visit, entry fees, etc. You will need in Venice a minimum of two full days. Three days would be better. The day trips out of Venice (Padua and Verona, Chapter 16) do not count in the two or three days in Venice itself. Included in Venice are the islands of Burano and Murano, in addition to the Lido. These locations within greater Venice can be visited in the afternoon.

Burano and Murano are nice islands in the Venice Lagoon worth visiting. You need to plan at least a whole day in Murano. It's free to visit because of the glass factories located there, and, of course, pranzo. I might note from Venice (San Marco), there is a courtesy boat to Murano and you do not need to purchase anything to return. What a deal.

The Venice Lido is best visited from May through mid-October. Bring your swimming attire (don't forget the SPF) and be prepared for a few hours in the sun. You can rent beach chairs and an umbrella for about 10Euros. If you are not into roasting in the sun, my recommendation is shopping and a long pranzo. If you are of

An Alternative to the Escorted Tour

the Jewish faith, you will also find an ancient Jewish cemetery only a block from the ferry terminal.

VENICE EXTRA DAYS- Chapter 16
Padua, if you have not visited Padua, no worries. It is available as a day trip from Venice. So, if you didn't get a chance driving up from Florence to drop in for a Cappuccino, you will get a second chance here. If you have turned in your rental car, you will find a local train every 30 minutes from Venice or Venice Mestre to Padua. You can also drive it in about 45 minutes. Taking the train will set you back about $10 per person, (round trip) and only takes about thirty minutes. The main draw to Padua is, of course, Saint Anthony's. There are other attractions within a few blocks of the St. Anthony complex and excellent places to enjoy lunch. See my discussion on the boat trip by canal from Venice to Padua in season.

MILAN AND THE LAKES- Chapter 17
I don't know what it is, but few of the masses that visit Italy, ever visit the northern part, known as the Piedmont and the Lombardy (Lombardia) region. What I like best about visiting the Lakes on day trips, is using Milan as a base. The beautiful lakes are all within one hour of Milan. In addition, there is so much to do and see in Milan.

Milan deserves a minimum of two full days. There is so much to do in this cosmopolitan city, which I might note, is also the leading fashion capital of Europe.

Lake Como, Varenna, Bellagio, Lake Maggiore, and Stresa, are all discussed as day trips from Milan. It is advisable to visit these lakes without your rental car as the rail alternative is far superior in terms of cost and convenience.

*** AMALFI AND SOUTHBOUND ITINERARIES ***

THE SOUTHBOUND (from Rome) itineraries are:
The Amalfi Coast and Naples Chapter 18
The Heel- Apulia (Puglia) and Salento Chapter 19
Sicily Chapter 20

ITALY NO TOUR NEEDED
You Can Do It Yourself

THE AMALFI COAST AND NAPLES Chapter 18. In this chapter, I include the highlights of the Naples area, and the Amalfi and Sorrentine Coasts. Since Paestum is about 90 minutes south of Naples I also include it:

The Amalfi Drive is by no question, the major draw to this area. The winding road, built by the Romans, which hugs the rugged coast for about 35 miles traverses all those villages with their colorful homes in Positano, Ravello, and the Amalfi area. Unlike other corniches carved into the sides of mountains, the drive is absolutely beautiful because of the meeting of the blue-green Mediterranean Sea and the magnificent coastal cliffs.

Pompei may not have existed had it not been for the eruption of Mount Vesuvius in 79AD. Unlike hundreds of other ruins, Pompei is very different. It is not a ruin or a "scavi" but an entire city covered in volcanic ash and lava which occurred over 24 hours. At almost the beginning of the Sorrentine Peninsular, it is probably the second largest draw to this area and a must-see.

Herculaneum also called **Ercolano** is about one-tenth the size of Pompei. Unlike Pompei, it was only covered in ash and not volcanic lava. The complex abuts a major outdoor shopping area in the Ercolano (southside) section of Naples.

The Island of Capri is located only three miles off the Sorrentine Peninsular. As they say, it is the playground of the very rich and famous. Three sites worth visiting (you will need to overnight here, if you want to see all three) are the Blue Grotto cave, the upper town of Anacapri, and the Roman ruins of Villa Jovis. You can figure a half day just for shopping.

Ravello is home to several estates, the most famous being Rufolo. This estate and its magnificent gardens are a must-see. The entire complex is perched high above the Mediterranean Sea which offers great views and photo ops. The Rufolo estate is located right off the main square of Ravello.

An Alternative to the Escorted Tour

Paestum is located about 90 minutes south of Pompei. I include it in this chapter only because I believe the complex is one of the best-preserved temple sites in all of Italy. Paestum the ancient city dates to about 600BC and is Greek, not Roman. In terms of a multi-temple site, I rank it second only to the Valley of the Temples in Agrigento, Sicily. If you have the time, drive the 90 minutes south from Pompei and overnight in the village of Agropoli and then visit Paestum before traveling on. Agropoli has excellent three-star hotels and wonderful in-expensive restaurants. Just pack your toothbrush and a change of clothing.

THE HEEL APULIA & SALENTO Chapter 19
There is a lot to see in this "not so touristy" region of Italy. The five main areas are Bari, Lecce, Taranto, Matera and Alberobello. If you base yourself in Lecce you will find day trips East to cities on the Aegean Sea and West to the Gulf of Taranto. All are reachable within one hour from Lecce.

SICILY Chapter 20
This is one place you need to take your time. Yes, you can see just the highlights of Palermo, Taormina, and Agrigento (the Valley of the Temples) in 3-4 days. However, to visit the entire Island you better figure 14-21 days. Sicily should be a vacation in itself. There is so much here to see and enjoy. In this chapter, I cover the three highlights stated above in addition to the medieval hilltop town of Erice with its sister Trapani (reachable by cable car). The temples of Segesta and Selenunte are included along with a visit to Syracuse and Cefalu. A detailed itinerary is provided. However, as usual, you can vary it. By the way, as I write this book, the Italian Government has finally approved a bridge over the Strait of Messina. Construction will start shortly on this auto/rail bridge which will link Reggio Calabria with Messina, Sicily. If you have any intention of visiting Sicily, I would suggest you visit it by 2030 before the crowds start to arrive.

HOTELS TELEPHONES INTERNET SECURITY DINING CUSTOMS ITALY EURAIL PASSES Chapter 21
This is one chapter you definitely must read. It details a technique for evaluating a hotel, what to do at check-in, and other pointers to make your hotel stay more enjoyable. Telephone and Internet

access are also presented, and security issues are also discussed along with dining and customs. There is no need for an Italy Eurail pass, and I explain why.

SUMMARY OF ITINERARIES
The itineraries I present are the most popular. They do not include visiting the Dolomites bordering Austria or the city of Turin since these are off the beaten path for tourists. However, feel free to mix, match, and extend the itineraries I have presented.

A WORD ABOUT SARDINIA
Since I have been writing books on Italy, many people have emailed me and asked, "How come I do not include Sardinia?" There are several reasons. First, I spent two weeks in Sardinia several years ago, when I circumvented the Island. While it does have some history, it does not have the ancient history of mainland Italy and Sicily.

If you are into sailing and want to rent a sailboat and sail around the Island in two weeks, you can. Just fly into the capital city of Cagliari, and away you go. I can only recommend the famous Costa Smeralda if you are interested in a resort area. If visiting the Costa Smeralda, you can fly into "Olbia" less than 10 miles from the hotel area.

What is interesting is the coastal road (on the Eastern side of the Island) from Cagliari to the Costa Smerada. It is best described as mountains and hills butting up to the ocean. The interior part of the Island is dotted with small villages. If you want something of a romantic "beachy" vacation, Costa Smeralda is the place.

WANT MORE HISTORY?
If you are looking for more history and other places to visit in Italy or Sicily, I recommend *"1000 Places To See Before You Die"* by Patricia Schultz by Workman Publishing.

CHAPTER 5

ARRIVAL AT ROME FCO AIRPORT RENT A CAR INSURANCE, ETC. TO: ROME, AMALFI, & FLORENCE

OVERVIEW
This chapter takes you from your arrival at Rome's FCO airport, not Rome's regional airport (Ciampino) to:

1. Your hotel in Rome, or
2. Your journey South to the Naples/Amalfi area, or
3. North to the Florence (Firenze) area of Tuscany.

Subjects discussed are rent-a-car, rail, or both. In addition, on arrival, you need not drive directly to the Amalfi area or Tuscany. I provide several alternatives to a long drive on arrival. Both drives are about two hours or less. If you are heading southbound to Amalfi, consider an overnight at Arpino. Likewise, if you are northbound, you may want to consider overnighting in Orvieto. Both of these towns allow you to "crash" and freshen up before reaching your hotels in the Amalfi or Tuscany area.

ARRIVAL AT ROME (FCO) AIRPORT
Most of you will be arriving on an overnight flight from the USA or Canada. You probably have had no sleep, and all you want to do is get into your hotel and crash. At this point, you have two options.

If you are visiting Rome first, you need to make your way to your hotel. If you are going to other points in Italy and will be renting a car, it is best to rent your car after visiting Rome. I will discuss this at length later.

If you are not visiting Rome and going directly to Naples or Florence, you need to rent a car. I have found that at most I can only drive two hours after picking up my rental. Don't try to beat your gums out to make it to Sorrento or Positano, etc. The same goes for northbound trips, i.e., to Florence and Tuscany

If you intend to bypass Rome, and not rent a car at Rome's FCO airport, you probably will be taking the train around Italy. Many people find it advantageous to take the train to their "hopoff" point and then rent a car. For example, if you are just visiting the hilltop towns of Tuscany, consider taking the train to Florence and then renting a car at the rail station. Likewise, if you are going to the Amalfi area, the best would be to pick up your rental car at the Naples train station (Naples Centrale).

>>>TIP<<< THE DAY ROOM
If you are going directly south to Amalfi/Naples or north to Tuscany/Florence and don't want to hassle renting a car immediately when you arrive, consider this: Did you know that you can request a DAY ROOM (at a substantial discount) from several of the hotels in the Rome airport area? You can usually check in immediately; however, you must be out by 4PM or 6PM. A day room will allow you to crash, take a shower, then go back to the airport and rent your car in a "refreshed" condition. I recommend the Hotel Isola Sacre. This hotel is about 3 miles from the airport. Also, consider a day room at the Hilton at the FCO airport. You will find it about three blocks past the rental car concession stands and the entrance to the Leonardo Express train to Rome's Termini station. It is ideal for a family of three or four. All you need do is walk over, check-in, drop your bags in the room, and crash! Also, do remember the daylight hours. You don't want to drive to Naples or Florence in the dark.
>>><<<

If you are hopping off the train, and renting your car either at Naples, for the Amalfi area, or Florence, for the Tuscany area you need to make your way over to the Termini rail station on the Leonardo Express (runs every 30 minutes) and then connect with your high-speed train. The trains to Naples and Florence run every hour or two depending on the time of day. You need to read the section below and then consult Chapter 6 (Rail travel out of Rome) for the details on the Termini Rail Station.

An Alternative to the Escorted Tour

HOW TO GET TO TERMINI RAIL STATION FROM FCO

If you don't have a lot of luggage to drag (one carry-on and one large roller bag per person) around, you should consider taking the Leonardo Express (it's a train) from FCO airport directly to Termini, Rome's main rail station. To locate the Leonardo Express station at FCO, you need to take the elevator to the parking garage (same route as the rental center) and follow the signs to the Leonardo Express (okay to follow the signs to the Hilton Hotel). The cost is about 15Euros per person, and it will get you to track number 23/24 at Termini in about 30 minutes. The trains run every 30 minutes. Tickets for Leonardo Express can be purchased with a credit card from the machine. Make sure you get it validated with that red/yellow machine on the platform.

TRANSFER TO YOUR ROME HOTEL VIA PRIVATE CAR

There are several ways to get to your hotel. If you are a party of four people, the best is to be picked up by a private car service. They will meet you outside those sliding doors at Terminal 3 after you pass through passport control and then customs. Just follow the green lights and arrows "Nothing to Declare." Once outside the controlled area, all you need to do is look for your name on a placard being held by your driver. Your driver will take your bags and escort you to your private car. The rates vary. However, I can tell you that a private car will cost you about 20 euros more than a taxi. However, they do include services i.e. carry your luggage.

I recommend only two private car services:

Transfersrome@gmail.com
Transfersrome.com
(transfers Rome Italy tours)
Attention- Massimiliano
Phone 39 393 076 0609

The other is:

Bob@romelimousines.com
Romelimosines.com
Rome Limousines Company
USA phone number- 330 942 3642
In Italy 39 342 125 0889
Bob has returned from Italy
and now lives in Ohio.

ITALY NO TOUR NEEDED
You Can Do It Yourself

I have found that most of the private car services are "brokers." In other words, you call them, and they hustle to find a driver. They will take a credit card deposit (their commission) and instruct you to pay the driver the balance. Many of these drivers are unreliable. Best that you read the comments.

You should note, that while you can reserve directly on the internet and guarantee with a credit card, you must pay the driver the full amount in Euros, in other words, NO DOLLARS and NO CREDIT CARDS.

TAKING A TAXI TO CENTRAL ROME
Another alternative to using a private car service or the Leonardo Express train to Rome's Termini train station is to take a taxi from the airport. A taxi will cost you about 50Euros. Also, if you are going to a hotel in Rome for a few nights, you might want to take a taxi instead of the Leonardo Express since you probably will have to take a taxi from Termini Station to your hotel, which may cost 20-30Euros. It would be better via a private car and driver.

>>>TIP<<<   OBTAINING EUROS IN A HURRY
If you don't have any Euros, just ask your driver if you get some Euros out of the "BANCAMAT" (it's also called an ATM or CASHPOINT). You will find it about 50 feet to the left of those sliding glass doors you just came through when you exited the secured area. You can only get 250Euros per day.
>>><<<

>>>TIP<<<   ADVISE YOUR HOTEL
It is best to send an email to your hotel and advise them that you would like to check in early, as you will have been flying all night from the USA or Canada. Also, I suggest that you would like a quiet (and dark) room, so you can sleep.
>>><<<

* DO NOT RENT A CAR IF YOU ARE STAYING IN ROME
ON LEAVING ROME, GO BACK TO FCO AND RENT THERE *

An Alternative to the Escorted Tour

INTERNATIONAL DRIVING PERMIT EXPLAINED

First, don't be fooled. Italy does have the lowest rates for rental, I think, in the entire world. Websites will state $5 per day. However, the total cost is $30 per day. Why? Simple, Italy has mandatory insurance, which is added. So, the actual cost is $35/day. There is absolutely no way to wave this charge.

Secondly, you need an International Driving Permit. You can obtain one at any AAA or CAA office in North America. There is usually no charge if you are a GOLD member. However, you may still have to pay for your photos. The International Permit must be shown to the agent at ROME FCO **WITH** your driver's license.

Thirdly, check with your credit card company if they include the $500 waiver of deductible for damage to the vehicle. If they do, you can waive that $500 deductible by using the credit card that offers it. **You also need to show the agent proof of insurance**, with **an insurance card or your policy.** In any case, they will want to know the name of your auto insurance company.

Fourth, take note of the rental agreement. Some rental agencies do not allow you to take the rental out of Italy, since they may not have a support system (in case your car breaks down) in say "Croatia." Many do not allow vehicles to be taken out and driven in former eastern bloc countries i.e. Hungary, Bulgaria, and The Chech Republic, even if they are being returned say to Milan or Rome. This is because of the high theft rate of the vehicles.

And Finally, remember to fill your car up with gas, before you turn it in. Remember, gas is about $6-7 per gallon (see section below: **gasoline, petrol, diesel**). So, it could cost you over $100 to bring the car back on the empty side. However, they won't charge you $7 a gallon, it will be $14 per gallon. Yikes. Also, don't be baited that it is better to prepay the gas now. Trust me on this one. You can never really bring it back empty. So, the rental agency gains the money. They charge you a very good rate. However, when you bring it back with half a tank, you have just paid double what you would have paid at an Autostrada fuel stop. Most airports have a gas station in the airport or just a few kilometers away. Just remember to fuel it up and get a receipt, and you don't want that full tank of gas!

38

ITALY NO TOUR NEEDED
You Can Do It Yourself

PICKING UP YOUR RENTAL CAR

To rent your car, take the elevator to the garage. Just follow the signs with the "logo, which looks like a key." It is a good 4-6 block walk. It is best to push one of those complimentary carts you can pick up at the baggage claim area.

After signing up for your rental car follow the signs to where you pick up the car in the garage. Unless they have changed things at the FCO airport garage, you will have to exit by placing your exit ticket in the machine. Hopefully, the gate will open. The ticket is usually attached to your rental contract or placed on the seat of your rental car. Don't lose it; you will need it to exit.

You ought to know something about the roads in Italy. However, before you get behind the wheel, read the sections below on the types of roads you will encounter in Italy.

THE AUTOSTRADA'S

Most of the time, you will be traveling on what is known as the Autostrada's; these are the Ax roads, i.e., A1, A4, A8, etc. Except for ring roads (GRAs around major cities) the Autostrada's are toll roads. Here is what you need to know:

Autostradas accept all charge cards. Just exit with your ticket (biglietto) and follow the blue signs marked "CARDs." Most exit lanes will also accept cash, up to a 20Euro note. When you place your entry ticket into the machine, it will tell you how much the charge will be. You can't leave the booth lane until that gate goes up. If you have a problem, you press the button on the machine, and an attendant will come and help you.

If you go into a CARD-only lane and you don't pay the charge within about 3 or so minutes, the gate will go up. However, you need to pull over to that little brick building next to the toll booths, park your car, go inside, pay the toll, and get a receipt.

Italy is big on catching speeders (doing more than 130KM or better than 80 miles per hour) on the Autostradas and also secondary roads. You need to watch those overhead signs that tell you there

39

An Alternative to the Escorted Tour

is a photo trap coming up. In addition, many secondary roads have cameras (known as Autovelox's) posted about one kilometer before the camera. They will take your picture from the back. If you were speeding, you will pay the rental car company 25Euros for tracking you down and giving the information to the authorities. You will then receive a notice to pay your speeding ticket. It can be as much as 200 Euros. You need to pay the fine online, immediately when you receive it. I might note this may be up to three months after you return.

>>>TIP<<<
If you fail to pay a toll for even as little as one Euro, your rental company will track you down when you get back to the USA or Canada. They will assess you a $25 fee for this effort (on the credit card you used to rent the car) and further advise you that you will receive a charge from the Autostrada people. This could also be very costly, the same as a speeding ticket. You need to clear this up immediately and pay your penalty, per the instructions online. Don't ignore it.
>>><<<

>>>TIP<<<   VERY COOL
Before you leave home, you might want to take a look at www.autostrada.it. It is packed with information i.e. rest stops, closures, etc. In addition, it shows about 100 plus real-time cameras on the system. I don't know if these are all speed trap cameras. However, the best is to just obey the speed limit and let the drivers in the left lane get pulled over for doing 140KM/hour!
>>><<<

If you want more information on the Autostrada, it is best to visit the URL www.autostrade.it.

NON AUTOSTRADA ROADs
These are roads that usually bear the name starting with an "N," "E," "SS," or "SP," i.e., SP21, E34, etc. Sometimes, they are referred to as the names of the two cities they connect, for example, "The Siena-Florence Road" or whatever. The most important fact you need to know is that what I call the glide-in lane is very short, unlike the USA's interstate system, which has long glide-in lanes. So, as you enter the glide-in lane, you will need to "floor it."

ITALY NO TOUR NEEDED
You Can Do It Yourself

The most important road outside of the "A" type road (Autostrada) is the SP or SR road (short for Strada Regional). The SS system is best compared to the USA's US road designations such as US-1, US-66, US-40, etc. They are marked by blue signs as opposed to the bright green signs of the Autostrada. And yes, they also have those speed trap cameras.

On many of the roads, there are arrows on the lanes pointing to an upcoming exit. Many newcomers traveling in Italy think that this lane is the exit lane. In other words, if you stay in that lane, it will take you off the main road, WRONG. That lane does not take you off the main road. It only tells you there is an upcoming exit. You should watch for the exit as you will have to depart that right-hand lane. I will discuss more of the road system, especially the scenic roads.

GASOLINE, PETRO, DIESEL

A word about fuel. Fuel is posted as Euros per Liter. Here is how it works. Multiply the price per liter by 4. So, 1.40 per liter is about 5.60 Euros per gallon. Since the Euro is about on par with the US dollar (the dollar being 10% less), you can figure 5.60 Euros at most would be about $6 per gallon. In my travels through Italy, I have found very little competition in the price of fuel from one gas station to another. For your information, most rental cars use unleaded (Sensa Piombo, or Benzine Verde). If you have a diesel, you fill up with Gasolio. It is best on your first fill-up to have the attendant "filler-up." You can motion with your hands to fill it up. You should observe how he opens the gas tank cap and selects all. Practically all stations will take your credit cards. Some stations are closed at night (except on the Autostradas); however, many allow you to put a 20Euro note in the dispensing machine. No change is usually given. So do make sure you can take at least 5 gallons, or 20 liters to play on the safe side. And, do remember to fill up before turning in that rental.

>>>TIP<<<   FLASH NOTICE

As of May 2024, the price on the Autostrada for gasoline is approaching two Euros per liter. That's about $8-$9 per gallon.

An Alternative to the Escorted Tour

Add on the tolls, and it might be better to take the train to Naples after your recovery and a four-day visit to Roma. It might be best to rent that car at the Naples Centrale rail station and do a hopoff. It will probably be the same price as driving down, and you won't have all that stress.

>>><<<

REST STOPS

Rest stops vary in Italy, from getting off the main road and having a café and a panini to stopping at a high-end full-service "Autogrill" (there are others, i.e., Sarni). Autostrada rest stops offer everything from a café to a full deluxe cafeteria-style hot meal, more than just a slice of pizza. You should keep in mind that prices in Autostrada rest stops are higher than you would expect to pay off the Autostrada. However, they are extremely reasonable. So consider purchasing your panini in a café, buy a case of bottled water at the Conad or Carrefour; keep it in the trunk, and stop at the rest stop for a picnic. It will save you a bundle. Also, fuel is much higher on the Autostrada, so the best is to fill up off the Strada. Now let's get on the road.

EXITING THE FCO AIRPORT IN YOUR RENTAL

There is only one main road (superhighway or Autostrada) that exits the FCO airport. The A91 goes only east; the Mediterranean Sea is about one kilometer due west. The A91 is also called the Roma-Fiumicino Road. You need to follow the signs from the FCO airport complex marked "Roma."

>>>TIP<<<   CAUTION

Do not accidentally leave the A91 and head on to the A12. It will take you to Rome's sea port on the Med, Civitavecchia which is about 40 miles Northwest of the airport.

>>><<<

>>>TIP<<<   DIRECT FLIGHTS NOW TO NAPLES

As of this writing, United Airlines now offers non-stop service from Newark (EWR) to Naples, Italy (NAP). You may want to consider this routing and then rent a car at Naples airport.

>>><<<

ITALY NO TOUR NEEDED
You Can Do It Yourself

>>>TIP<<< FLIGHTS TO OTHER ITALY CITIES

You need not start your visit to Italy in Rome, Milan, Venice, or Naples. Many smaller airports, such as Pisa, Florence, and Bari, have air service from major European hubs, such as Paris, Munich, and Amsterdam. However, in most cases, you will not find a nonstop flight from the USA to these smaller Italian cities.
>>><<<

GOING SOUTH- NAPLES/AMALFI AREA

About four kilometers after entering the A91: Exit the A91 onto the GRA (E90) toward (dir) A1/E45 "NAPOLI." Drive the A1/E45 about 238 km (149 miles), then follow my local directions. I recommend a fantastic hotel in Naples. And I mean fantastic! It is the four-star Villa Signorini. You will find it in a residential section of Naples, only 4 blocks from the ruins of Herculaneum, and a large shopping area filled with lots of restaurants. The "Villa Signorini" is a converted villa bordering on a palace (the owner of the palace made millions in the pasta sauce business, no joke) with beautiful gardens and free parking. An excellent breakfast is served. BTW, their dinner menu is extremely reasonable if you can wait till 8PM (20:00). Also, it is best to ask for a quiet room with a patio overlooking the gardens in the rear. And remember, you must book directly with the hotel for these requests (info@villasignorini.it). In other words, no booking engines (OTA) i.e. Booking.com, Expedia.com, etc.

Once leaving the airport, it will take you about 3 hours, including rest stops, to get to the Naples exits. If you are overnighting at the Villa Signorini, you can figure another 20 minutes after exiting the A1 since it is on the south side of the city.

You can figure about 4-5 hours to Sorrento from FCO airport. It is a slow road after exiting the A1 in Naples. You need to take the SORRENTINE PENINSULAR exit after passing through the Naples and Pompeii area. You can't miss this exit. The sign is humongous.

An Alternative to the Escorted Tour

>>>TIP<<<   90 MINUTES TO ARPINO
For years I have always favored the 90-minute drive to Arpino instead of going directly to Naples/Sorrento or elsewhere on the Amalfi coast. Let's face it: you had no sleep last night, you are "wrung out," and all you want is a bed to get some sleep. There is an easy way not to beat your "gums" out. Here it is:

If driving south on the Autostrada A1 in direction (dir) Naples, we drive to a quaint Italian town known as Arpino and stay at the Hotel il Cavalier d' Arpino. Google Maps says it's only 90 minutes from FCO airport and about 12 miles off the A1. The il Cavalier is a three-star hotel (should be a four-star) in a restored woolen mill just off the town center. Parking is complimentary on their beautiful grounds; rooms are large and they serve an excellent buffet breakfast. We usually walk about four blocks to the square in the center of the town. Arpino is the birthplace of Cicero known for his writing and philosophy. There is a monument in the square devoted to him.

What I like about Arpino is the street fair which is held on Sunday. For a real, authentic Italian dinner, you must visit the Trattoria del Corso, near the Piazza Municipio. You will find the menu on a blackboard with daily specials. Have "Sophia" or the desk clerk on duty at the Il Cavalier call the Trattoria del Corso, and ask what the special will be tonight and have him/her write it on a piece of paper and also the name of the restaurant. You can expect that they won't take plastic but will take your Euros. And, do remember that the tip (service) is always included. However, if the service is really good, it is best to leave an extra Euro or two on the table. BTW, Italians never "rush" a meal. All meals are slooooo. So take your time and enjoy another glass of wine. I would suggest you just walk over to the Trattoria del Corso; no need to take your chariot.
>>><<<

>>>TIP<<<   BONUS VISIT TO MONTE CASSINO
The next day, continue to the A1 South and Naples/Amalfi, and follow the road to Montecassino (it can be spelled either way) SR509 for about 52KM, or about one hour. You may want to make

a quick visit to the famous Benedictine Abbey of Montecassino. It's free and worth the visit.

The Abbey sits on a hill overlooking a valley and the town of Cassino. It is here, in WWII, that a battle ensued (for the liberation of Italy) between the Nazis and the Allied forces for control of the Latin Valley, in 1944. It is best to check the open times as the Benedictine Friars go to lunch, and the abbey is closed to visitors. There is a strict dress code, i.e., no shorts, and women must cover their shoulders. You can find more at https://abbaziamontecassino.it. The Abbey is open on Sundays.

After your Abbey visit, you can come down the hill and have lunch in the modern village of Cassino. If you are hungry, feel free to stop at many of the cafes in the town. From the town, it's only a mile to the A1 South toward Naples.
>>><<<

So much for driving South. Now, on to the North and Tuscany.

GOING NORTH– FIRENZE/TUSCANY/VENICE
If you are heading to points north i.e. Firenze (Florence and Tuscany, etc.) you need to exit the A91 to the GRA (ring road) Northbound. It is known as the A90/E35. There will be an Autogrill rest stop in about 4-5KM once you get on the GRA. It is best to stop here, and grab a cup of Americano coffee and a "bun." Follow the GRA ring road for about 20 minutes till you see the exit for Florence (A1–Firenze). This is exit 10. However, it's a combination exit i.e., Exits 8, 9 and 10. Keep on following those signs to A1- Firenze. This will put you on the A1/E35.

About 5KM after starting up the GRA, you will find an incredible Autogrill rest stop. This is a great place to enjoy breakfast or lunch before continuing to Florence or crashing in Orvieto. If you missed the Autogrill getting on the GRA about 15 minutes after leaving FCO, you have a second shot (a few KM after taking Exit 10 off the GRA) at one of them on the northbound A1. It's called Autogrill Roma Nord. You need to cross over the highway on that

45

An Alternative to the Escorted Tour

massive pedestrian-covered walkway. It's not a big deal. There is an elevator which will take you to the restaurant.

>>>TIP<<<   ABOUT 2 HRS TO ORVIETO
The medieval town of Orvieto is a little over two hours north by car. The town of Orvieto sits (it looks like a village, not my idea of a city) on a volcanic rock mesa. The city lies in the southwest corner of Umbria, touching the region known as Tuscany to the North and Lazio (Rome is in Lazio) to the South. Its actual elevation is about 1,100 feet above sea level. It is part of the metropolitan area of Terni. I discuss all the details of Orvieto under the   **IT-ROME-TO-FLORENCE** itinerary.   For now, I recommend this area as a good place to crash after that grueling overnight flight from North America. I like Orvieto because it is a hilltop town worth exploring after you take a snooze, wake up at about 6PM, take a shower, and then "walk the town." You will have dinner at about 8PM. So, there will be plenty of time to have that glass of wine or a cold beer at one of the many cafes.

If you are driving north, my favorite hotel in Orvieto is a few blocks from the main church, known as the Duomo. In fact, its right across the street. The hotel is called the Hotel Duomo. Gee, I would have never guessed!

If you are not driving South to Arpino or North to Orvieto and doing a "hopoff" you need to read on.

I define hopoff as a place you take a train to, and then rent a car from that location. You can then return the car back to Naples, Florence, Milan, etc. rail stations or return it anywhere in Italy, e.g. drive it back to Rome FCO at the end of the two weeks. I might note that return charges are very inexpensive in Italy. From the FCO airport, you will have to make your way first, to the main train station in Rome, known as Termini.

Once at Termini, you need to take one of the high-speed trains (Frecce's) of Trenitalia (Trenitalia.it.en) or its competitor Italo (italotreno.it).   See below for a detailed write-up of how to make reservations for these high-speed trains, prices, and classes. In

ITALY NO TOUR NEEDED
You Can Do It Yourself

addition, you will find details about Rome's Termini rail terminal in Chapter 6.   There are usually two trains every hour:
Here are the suggested hopoff points:
Naples/Amalfi area   - train to Naples Centrale, then hopoff
Tuscany/Umbria – train to Florence
Milan and the Lakes- train to Milano Centrale
Venice and north i.e., Austria Dolomites – Venice Mestre
Apulia and Solento – train to Bari or Brindisi

Most of the above are served by high-speed trains with no need to make any transfers to another train.

Naples (hopoff for the Amalfi area) and northbound to Florence (hopoff for the Tuscany/Umbria area):   You need to make a reservation, just like an airline, for your rail trip.   Many times, trains are sold out.   Tickets go on sale 60-90 days before your desired date of travel. If you don't make a reservation on a high-speed train, no worries. You can always take a local train with unreserved seats, oy, oy, oy. You can figure this will take several hours more to make the journey.

>>>TIP<<<   SCHEDULING YOUR RAIL JOURNEY
If your flight is delayed into FCO and you miss your high-speed train to Florence or Naples, it will be difficult to get a rail agent to make you a reservation on another train and re-issue you a new ticket. Here is what I recommend: If your flight arrives at 7AM, figure you need two hours to get through passport control and customs, claim your bags, head over to the Leonardo Express, and make your way over to Termini. Add to this one hour of "buffer time," and it brings you to 10AM, which is tight for an 11AM train. So, in this case, I would make a reservation for a Noon or, better, a 1PM (1300) train to Naples or Florence. In a worse case, if your flight is delayed into FCO, take a taxi to Termini, "rapido" (pronounced rappy-dough).

As an alternative, consider flying to Naples or Firenze. However, you still will have to clear passport control and customs, and you may have to claim your bags if you cannot check them through to Naples or Firenze from the USA or Canada. Also, don't expect to

An Alternative to the Escorted Tour

land at 7AM and get a connecting flight at 9AM. It also will be a tight or nearly impossible connection.

If you are visiting Rome for a few days or doing a hopoff itinerary, such as Naples, Florence, Milan, Bari, etc., you still must make your way to Rome's Termini station. Chapter 6 will also help you with day trips from Rome if you don't have a rental car. It explains Rome Termini station and things you will need to know whether you are taking day trips from Rome or using the hopoff approach. >>><<<

RESTATEMENT OF FUEL TYPES
To repeat, as of now (May 2024) Diesel (GASOLIO) is about $.20 per Liter less than gasoline (BENZINA). Most all service stations pump both products. Please remember to bring your rental back with a full tank. It is best to do this right before you enter the airport or the evening before.

>>>TIP<<<   FLASH NOTICE
Trenitalia is now running NON-STOP Frecci trains directly from FCO to Naples Centrale and Florence SMN stations. It appears to be an experiement. This eliminates going into Rome Termini and connecting with another train. Trains depart from the Leonardo Express station at FCO. You can check the times out, and make reservations on OMIO.COM. In a worse case consider having breakfast or lunch in FCO if you need to wait for the train. Else, connect in Termini.
>>><<<

** AND REMEMBER, NO DRIVING IN ROME.   HOWEVER, IT'S OKAY TO DRIVE AROUND THE CITY (the GRA) **

CHAPTER 6

RAIL TRAVEL OUT OF ROME

This chapter is about Termini, the main rail hub in Rome.

**GOING BY RAIL TO YOUR HOPOFF POINT
NAPLES/SORRENTO AMALFI, FLORENCE, ETC.**
If you didn't read the prior chapter, I define the word HOPOFF as a place you take a train to and then rent a car from there. You can then return the car to the rental location or anywhere in Italy. You can also return it to Rome FCO at the end of the two weeks.

If you are staying in Rome or venturing out in a few days, here are the ways to get to Rome centro. If you are connecting with a train in a few hours, you will have to make your way to the main train station in Rome, known as Termini. I also discussed this in the prior chapter, Arrival at Rome FCO. There are three ways:

1. You can take a taxi. It will cost about 50-60Euros. Just follow the signs to the taxi line outside the ground floor arrival area.

2. It is better to pay the extra 15-20Euros and have one of the private drivers and car lug your bags and take you to Termini. I discussed private cars and drivers in Chapter 5.

3. Take the Leonardo Express (a train) from FCO airport directly to Termini. This was discussed in the prior chapter. This is fine if you don't have a lot of luggage (one large roller bag and a carry-on per person) and only have one or two people in your party. You need to take the elevator to the parking garage (same route as the rental center) and follow the signs to the Leonardo Express (okay to follow the signs to the Hilton Hotel). The cost is about 15Euros per person, and it will get you to track number 23/24 at Termini in about 30 minutes. The trains run every 30 minutes. Tickets for Leonardo Express can be purchased with a credit card from the

machine. You need to validate it at the little red or yellow machine at the platform.

Once at Termini, you need to take one of the high-speed trains (Frecce's) of Trenitalia (Trenitalia.it.en) or its competitor Italo (trenitalo.it.en). See below for a detailed write-up of how to make reservations for these high-speed trains, prices, and classes. In addition, you will find details about Rome's Termini rail terminal. There is usually one train every hour to Naples and northbound to Florence. You need to make a reservation, just like an airline, for your rail trip. Many times, trains are sold out. Tickets go on sale 60-90 days before your desired date of travel. If you don't make a reservation on a high-speed train, no worries. You can always take a local train with unreserved seats, oy, oy, oy. You can figure this will take several hours more to make the journey as opposed to the high-speed train. Also, be advised that reserved seats "close out" usually one hour before departure. I made mention of this in the prior chapter.

ROME'S TERMINI STATION- BACKGROUND

As discussed, Rome's central train station is known as "Termini." For railroad buffs like me, it does not mean terminus or terminal. It comes from the Latin word "Terme." You see, in ancient times, this was the site of underground springs used for bathing. Very much like the baths of Caracalla. When the Italians built this massive rail station in 1863, they named it "Termini" after the abutting baths. The latest major renovation took place in 1950 and is what you see now.

Some quick facts: It is the second busiest rail station in Europe, second only to Paris's North Station (Nord). Termini has 33 tracks and handles 800 trains per day. Almost one-half million people visit it every day. Below the rail station is home to the Metro (subway) Lines A and B. The Metro station is marked TERMINI. Now here is what you need to know.

If you are a solo traveler or a couple "backpacking" consider taking the Rome Metro to Termini. Tickets are good for 75 minutes of travel and can be purchased via a credit card from the machines at all the stations.

ITALY NO TOUR NEEDED
You Can Do It Yourself

If you have your tickets already (hopefully reserved seats), you can proceed to the shopping area just behind the ticketing area and the information desks. Also, note that you need to do nothing if you have a paper ticket with a QR code or bar code. That piece of paper is the ticket. If you do not have a ticket, either use the red machines or wait in the ticket/information line and speak to a representative the agent will get you your seats.

Depending on the queues, you will need to take a number and be called. Obtain a number and watch the electronic board till your number is displayed. Many of the agents speak English, and it is so noted. Italo has its agents with red booths. They are easy to spot. If you are taking day trips from Termini, you can always use the automated machines. Just follow the instructions. Note, you cannot use these machines for the high-speed reserved seats trains (Trenitalia Frecce's). The machines will only provide tickets for local day trips, i.e., Orvieto, Ostia Antica, etc., where seat reservations are not required. And yes, they will take your credit card. Let's get something to eat or do "nada" (people-watching at the food court) till your train is called.

Walk into the area abutting the platform area where the trains are parked. Note that the tracks start at "1" on your left. About halfway down, walking toward track "25," you will see a flight of stairs. Look behind those stairs, and you will see two large elevators. These lifts will take you to what I would call the "food court." It is massive, running about four blocks in length. You should avoid those stairs; just too many people in a rush. After viewing all that really good stuff that will make your mouth water, you should have a cappuccino, a pastry, or perhaps some lunch. It is important to keep your eyes on the electronic train boards throughout the food court for your train posting.

Feel free to purchase as much food as you can as "take away" since all trains allow food to be consumed in your seat. You can buy drinks on the trains, however, it is best to bring your own water or soft drinks or even wine, as they are a lot less.

An Alternative to the Escorted Tour

Trains board about 20 minutes before actual departure time. Since you will have to clear security (have your ticket ready), you can figure that you must be down in the platform area about 30 minutes before departure. Security will not let you on the platform until the train is ready to board. Remember, this is Italy, and all the trains run on time (or they try to). If you arrive a minute after the posted departure time, your train will have left.

On early morning departures, about 8-10AM, you probably won't have enough time to visit the food court on the second floor. However, if you need to grab-and-go, you will find at least six places that sell coffee, pastries, and pre-made sandwiches. Oh yes, some sell pizza (pepperoni in the morning)?

Once your train number is posted, find your way to the platform (or bin number) have your ticket scanned, and proceed through security. Security is relatively light or what we would call "superficial." I think they are just checking for "suspicious" characters. Let's face it: everyone has backpacks and roller bags.

Look at the posting on the electronic sign on the platform and ensure you are boarding the proper train. I find it's best to walk the platform and locate your "carozza" (carriage or car).
If you are running late, board any car and walk the train till you get to the correct carozza.

If your bags are heavy (assuming you are not taking a day trip), train people or those most gracious Italians will help you with them. It's not a big deal for them. Also, on the "Frecci" (high-speed "Arrow") trains, there are ample places and luggage racks to stow your bags; likewise, for the Italo trains. By the way, Italo trains don't usually have cafes; instead, they have vending machines.

>>>TIP<<<   SELECTING SEATS ONLINE
It is best to always select seats in the direction of travel. This way, you don't have to twist your neck to see what you just missed. The train has ample clean toilets (same as the airlines). There is a café mid-train. Once seated, you should have your ticket ready for the ticket inspector. Always have someone watch your carry-on bags,

camera, etc., when leaving your seat. And remember, Italian law states that you must always have your passport on you if you are not an Italian citizen. So, do not pack it in your large luggage bag. >>><<<

If you are not on a reserved seat train in second or first class, you must validate your ticket in one of the platform's green or yellow machines. If going to Orvieto or Ostia Antica, you must do so. Also, if you missed that Frecci train to Florence and are taking a local train, you must validate your ticket at the platform.

TOILETS AT TERMINI
The toilets are modern and spotless. They all require one Euro to enter. If you don't have a Euro, all the facilities have a coin-changing machine at the entrance or an attendant. After all, someone has to keep them clean, fill the soap dispensers, break those twenty Euro notes, and all that other good stuff.

For a quick summary of Termini, I can only tell you it's a real "trip" or, better, a real experience. Maybe even on par with a trip to Pompei (lol). Secondly, allow extra time. You can always grab a bite or a café and do some people-watching. And finally, hang on to your personal belongings.

TAKING THE TRAIN TO YOUR HOPOFF POINT
If you have just arrived several hours ago at Rome FCO and are heading to your hopoff point, keep your eyes on the electronic board and watch for your train number and time of departure.

If you have just completed several days in Rome and are ready for your leisurely day trips read on.

EASY, AFFORDABLE DAY TRIPS FROM ROME
If you have an extra day to spare, there are five easily affordable day trips from Rome. They are all in the Naples area. These cost about $100 per person for the day (including rail fare). They are:

Ruins of Pompeii (train to Naples/Circumvesuviana)
Island of Capri (train to Naples/ferry to Capri)

An Alternative to the Escorted Tour

The Amalfi Drive (train to Naples, several alternatives)
Herculaneum (train to Naples/Circumvesuviana)
Ercolano Naples Shopping (same as above)

I include the ruins of Herculaneum since they require only an hour of your time. They are next to a section of Naples (Ercolano) with many outdoor markets and shops in a street market environment. I have included Herculaneum under the Amalfi area chapter. I might note that the ruins of Herculaneum also go by the name "Ercolano." You should target getting down to Ercolano at about 1PM, a perfect time for pranzo and shopping.

Two other excursions worth a day are:

Orvieto- a hilltop town a little over an hour from Rome and
Ostia Antica- Near the FCO airport, about 40 minutes away
Both of the above are easily accessible by train and will cost
no more than $20 per person.

You can read more details in Chapter 8, Rome Extra Days.

If you are planning a day trip or starting a hopoff experience, you can summarize Rome's main train station in one line: "A visit to Termini is quite an experience." It is not to be missed on your first visit to the Eternal City!

CHAPTER 7

ROME, ROME, ROME

If you have only a few days to spare and will only visit Rome, this itinerary is for you. If you are making Rome your first part of your visit or your last part, this itinerary is also for you.

ROME HOTELS

Rome has about 5,000 hotels, which does not take into consideration the BnBs, hostels, etc. Try to book hotels in the historic area. Hotels on the Vatican side of the Tiber River are far away from the historic center. You should avoid the Termini rail station area. It is too noisy and honky tonk. Do check out the Jewish Quarter.

ABSOLUTELY NO NEED FOR A CAR

Rome is a walking city. Except for Vatican City on the other side of the Tiber River, pretty much all of the historic sites can be found in about two square miles. Most of this area is called the Centro Historico, or the central historic district. Number two, Rome (at least the historic district) was not built for automobiles. Many streets are one-way, and it is difficult to navigate some of the seven hills of Rome (many of the hills now have tunnels).

Many streets are known as ZTL (Zone Traffic Limited) areas. This means the street, parking space, or whatever is off-limits to vehicles unless they display a "ZTL" sticker. Get caught in a ZTL, and it will probably cost you about 200Euros in addition to a fee from your rental car company. And don't worry. Your rental car company will track you down, and you can expect a bill in the mail about three months after you arrive back in the USA or Canada. And finally, there are very few traffic lights i.e. those red, yellow, and green things. This makes for one hell of a traffic mess. And trust me, it is. I don't know how many times I have sat in traffic in a taxi with the meter clicking away Euros. Many of those times, I

An Alternative to the Escorted Tour

have exited the taxi, paid what was the meter, and walked the balance of my journey.

WHAT IF I NEED A RENTAL CAR TO GO ON TO OTHER POINTS IN ITALY?
That's a simple one. You need to pack your bags, head back to the FCO airport, and rent your car there. Furthermore, don't try to rent your car at an in-town location unless you have taken a few valiums. And, one more item: don't count on your GPS to bail you out. It won't. If you are doing a hopoff all you need do is find your way over to Termini rail station and board that high-speed train to Naples, Florence, or wherever. Enough said.

BASIC FOUR FULL DAYS IN ROME ITINERARY
If you have just arrived at FCO airport and made your way to your hotel you are ready to start Day 2 "Recovery." Here is a short itinerary for those four full days:
Day 1- Overnight flight to Rome
Day 2- Check into your hotel and Recovery- Rome Orientation
Day 3- Walking tour of Monumental Rome- Pantheon, Piazza Navona
Trevi Fountain, Spanish Steps, shopping on Via Condotti
Day 4- The Colosseum area: The Wedding Cake, Colosseum, Roman
Forum, the Moses, and Trajan's Market
Day 5- Vatican City, Vatican Museum, Sistine Chapel, St.Peters, Castel
San Angelo, and lunch on the "Borgo Pio."

I might note that if you need to skip one day and are not interested in viewing the Sistine Chapel or visiting one of the largest churches in the world, feel free to eliminate the Vatican Day.

>>>TIP<<<   CRITICAL CLOSINGS
You may have to juggle the days around. The Colosseum and the Roman Forum are always closed on Monday. The Vatican Museum is usually closed on Sunday so don't plan on seeing the Sistine Chapel with its famous Michelangelo ceiling. It is best to check the Pope's schedule at www.papelaudience.org if he will be performing the papal blessing (The Angelos) on Sunday. Many times he is traveling or at his summer residence at Castel Gandolfo. If you want to attend the Wednesday Audience, it is best to consult with your Catholic Priest for tickets.
There is no substitute for planning!
>>><<<

ITALY NO TOUR NEEDED
You Can Do It Yourself

On Day 2, it is best to take a nap and a shower to freshen up. Don't worry about the shops closing at 5PM. Most of the shops (Gucci, Louis Vitton, etc.) on the Via Condotti are open till 7:30PM, and on Saturday, they even have late hours. If you are up to seeing the town, my suggestion is to go on the hop-on-hop-off bus. However, you won't have time to do any hop-offs and actual visits. You will pass the places you will not have time for in subsequent days, i.e., The Pyramid of Rome, Old City Walls, etc. Do not confuse my "hopoff" term with other "hops," i.e., the hop-on-hop-bus.

If you are not into a hop-on-hop-off bus, several operators offer 1.5 to 2-hour coach orientation tours of Rome. There usually are no visits. The coach just drives around and tells you about all the sites. It's best to check out the website, www.graylinerome.com. A single trip is only 17Euros, and a whole day is 25Euros. They have headsets broadcasting all languages. If it is inclement, you can sit down on the lower level.

It is best to have an early dinner (7PM or earlier; see your hotel front desk person) followed by a Sambuca or Galliano before retiring. By the way, most hotels have what they call a lobby bar. In this way, you can go right to your room once you have downed your nightcap.

Day 3 is also known as monumental Rome. It comprises a walking tour but excludes the Colosseum and the Forum. Please remember that the Colosseum and Forum are closed on Mondays. Also, it is best to avoid the weekends at these two sites since there are many weekend visitors from Paris, Amsterdam, and other European cities who just come to Rome for an escape weekend. I recommend several websites for the Colosseum and Forum tours. You need not purchase tickets for either site as they are included with an English-speaking guide, best is to consult their websites: Viator or Citywonders. There are others. It is best to get these tickets several weeks before your visit to Rome. Now, back to the walking tour.

An Alternative to the Escorted Tour

Just a note: You can also do the walking tour of monumental Rome after you arrive. If your room is ready, get those two hours of sleep, take a shower, and start that walking tour. The latest time you can actually do the monumental walk is 3PM. If you do the monumental walk after your arrival in Rome, you will free up a day for some good shopping or a day trip out of Rome.

Here is the walking tour for Day 3 (or Day 2 in the late afternoon) You can start anywhere. However, it is best to start at the Pantheon and work your way over to the Spanish Steps for a late lunch or an early dinner. There is an excellent restaurant just under the Spanish Steps. It's called "Alla Rampa." It is by far one of my favorites in Rome. It is best to start as close to your hotel and end at the Spanish Steps or your hotel.

** DAY 3   MONUMENTAL ROME

I call this the four monuments: Piazza Navona, The Pantheon, Trevi Fountain, and the Spanish Steps. There is now an entrance fee to the Pantheon of about 5Euros. It's worth it. Crowding in the peak summer months is causing a problem. This is another good reason for not visiting Rome in July or August.

Here is how you can visit all four sites with minimal walking and without backtracking. If you read on, I will tell you that you don't have to walk up the Spanish Steps, only down them, or better yet, don't negotiate them. By the way, they are all flat areas, so there are no hills to climb.

Let's face it. All day yesterday, you sat for ten hours in that uncomfortable airline seat. Now is the time to get some exercise. You can start anywhere. However, the best is to end up at the base of the Spanish Steps (Piazza di Spagna) or the Trevi Fountain since you probably will need a nourishment break. Feel free to start your walk at about 12Noon, but as stated no later than 3PM. No big rush.

My visit times include walking to or from the site. Here is a quick recap of the routing and the walking distances between sites:

ITALY NO TOUR NEEDED
You Can Do It Yourself

Start-
Piazza Navona
then to the Pantheon (about 300 feet from Piazza Navona)
then to Trevi (12 football fields from Pantheon)
then to Piazza di Spagna (10 football fields from Trevi)
Note- the Piazza is the square with the fountain at the base of the
Spanish Steps.

Alternate-
Piazza Navona
Pantheon (about 300 feet from Piazza Navona)
For Lunch (or dinner, about 5-6PM check open times) at the
    Spanish Steps, about 12 football fields then to
        to the Trevi Fountain – (about ten football fields)
        End with a Gelato at Trevi Fountain!

Start the walk at Piazza Navona. You will need 30-45 minutes here.
Perhaps enjoy a takeaway cappuccino in one of the cafes on the
side streets ("Two Sizes" is one of the best pastry shops in the
area) as you admire the statues and fountains—there are plenty of
places to sit on those stone benches.

There is no direct route to the Pantheon. So, you will have to
navigate alleyways and small streets. A short walk of about four
blocks will bring you to the ancient Pantheon.

The easiest way is to head for the Fontana (means fountain) del
Moro (the forward fountain closest to the Tiber River). About 50
yards past it, there is a small street. Via di Pasquino. Here are the
exact directions from Google Maps:

Head south on Piazza Navona (toward the Tiber River) toward
Via di Pasquino
Turn left to stay on Piazza Navona
Continue onto Via dei Canestrari
Continue onto Largo della Sapienza
Continue onto Via dei Sediari
Turn left onto Via del Teatro Valle

An Alternative to the Escorted Tour

Via del Teatro Valle turns right; becomes Piazza di S.Eustachio
Turn left onto Via di S. Eustachio
Slight right onto Salita de Crescenzi
Turn left onto Piazza della Rotonda
The Pantheon is on your right
Note all maneuvers are about 60 feet apart.
    If all else fails. follow the crowd or ask
        "Doe Vay ee il Pantheon?" Where is the
        Pantheon?

My preferred way to visit the four sites is to start at the Piazza Navona and end the day (after lunch, of course), at the Spanish Steps. If you would like to shop, you will find plenty of it on the abutting street to the Piazza Spagna, known as "Via Condotti."

After you are shopped out, walk over to the Trevi Fountain, take a lot of photos, and throw those three coins in the fountain. After this is all done, enjoy a gelato in one of the many gelato stands around the Trevi Plaza. Do be very street savvy in this area, and make sure you read my chapter on security.

Total walking distance is about 1.5-2 miles. You can figure 3-5 hours with stops. Here are the historical details on each site:

THE PIAZZA NAVONA- 30-45 MINUTES
The Piazza Navona is one of the most beautiful squares in Rome. It is a rectangle built in 86AD by Emperor Domitian. The square served as a stadium for athletic competitions. It measures two football fields in length and one football field across. At capacity, it held almost 20,000 spectators. It served its purpose as a stadium until the 17th century.

In about 1644, it was transformed by Pope Innocent X into a square of Baroque Roman art and architecture. His home, the Palazzo Pamphill, faces the plaza. Here is a brief description of those works of art:

The Obelisk in the center of the square was brought in from the Circus of Maxentius. Below it is the fountain of four rivers. The statue is the work of the Renaissance sculptor Bernini. The abutting church is the work of Rainaldi, Borromini, and others. There are two other fountains in the Piazza. At the southern end (towards the Tiber River) is the Fontana Del Morro. It is a basin of four tritons sculpted by Giacomo della Porta in 1575. In 1673 Bernini added a statue of a Moor wrestling with a dolphin.

At the northern end of the square is the Fountain of Neptune by Bitta. This was added in 1878 to balance the La Fontana del Morro on the other side of the square.

Numerous theatrical events were held in the square for almost 300 years, starting in 1652.

The farmer's market, which also occupied part of the square, was moved in 1869 to the present Campo de Fiore which is also worth a visit in the morning. The "Campo" is one large farmer's market. Please see more below.

THE PANTHEON- 30-45 MINUTES

Don't confuse this "pantheon" with the one in Paris. The Pantheon in Rome is a temple. and since 609AD, a Catholic church. On this site, there was an earlier temple. The present temple was rebuilt by Emperor Hadrian and dedicated about 126AD. The building is cylindrical. Interestingly, the height of the dome from the slab floor is identical to the width of the building. It is one of the most famous and best-preserved ancient Roman buildings. The earlier temple which stood here dates from Pagan times. The building is open at the top. And the floor gets wet when it rains. There is now a 5Euro entrance fee; buy tickets on the the internet to avoid waiting or get here before 10AM.

Emanuelle II and Umberto I and Umberto's queen Margherita (the pizza is named after her) are buried here. In addition, the famous Renaissance painter "Raphael," is also buried here with several other famous artists.

That obelisk (about 135 feet tall including its base) and the fountain you see in the piazza (Piazza della Rotunda) just in front of the Pantheon is known as the Fontana del Pantheon. The

61

An Alternative to the Escorted Tour

fountain was designed and built by Giacomo della Porta in 1575. The fountain, once again, like the Trevi Fountain is fed by an ancient underground aqueduct from several miles away.

The obelisk constructed by Pharaoh Ramses II for the Temple of Ra in Heliopolis was brought to Rome in ancient times (seems no one knows exactly). It was rediscovered in 1374 underneath the Basilica of Santa Maria Sopra Minerva. In the mid-15th Century, it was then moved to the Piazza San Macuto. The obelisk stood about several hundred meters to the southeast of the Pantheon. In 1711 it was moved to its current position in what is still called the "Piazza della Rotunda."

TREVI FOUNTAIN- ONE HOUR
Nicola Salvi designed it and Giuseppe Pannini (no, he did not invent the sandwich by the same name) and several others completed it. It is Baroque style, and was built from 1732 to 1762. The fountain has several statues. It lies at the junction of three ancient roads and aqueducts dating to 19BC. These aqueducts still supply the water to the fountain.

Since my first visit to Trevi and subsequent visits, I have never understood why the fountain is built into the side of an office building. This is Rome; would you not expect this gorgeous fountain to be located in a large piazza (a square)?

The Trevi Fountain you now see is the third Trevi. The first one was built in 19BC to supply water to the Romans. The name "Trevi" is derived from the fact that the Fountain lies at the junction of three ancient roads. Many modern-day sculptors believe the Trevi Fountain is the most beautiful fountain in the world. It is open twenty-four hours. It is also, best to view it at night when it is illuminated.

Of most importance is the fact the Trevi Fountain is used in the backdrop of many Hollywood movies. The water comes from 14 miles away through the ancient aqueduct, which is still in use today. The "Tritons" and horses are the main attraction in the Fountain. I describe more below on exactly how to throw the three coins into the Fountain and their significance:

ITALY NO TOUR NEEDED
You Can Do It Yourself

It's a myth! It started with the movie 1954 called *Three Coins in the Fountain* (20th Century Fox). The song, sung by Frank Sinatra, won the Oscar for best song of the year. Here is what it means: If you throw one coin, you shall return to Rome; with two coins, you will fall in love with an attractive Italian, and if you throw three coins, you will marry the person you met. Here is what you need to do: Hold the coins in your right hand and toss them over your left shoulder with your back to the Fountain. Oh, make sure someone takes a picture of you.

After this is all done, enjoy a gelato in one of the many gelato stands around the Trevi Plaza. The fountain yields about 3,000Euros each day, which is donated to charity. Do be very street savvy in this area, and read my chapter on security. Also, if you are caught removing any coins, there is a stiff fine. Many of those tourists are plainclothes police.

THE SPANISH STEPS- ONE HOUR OR MORE
The Spanish Steps were built with funds from the French diplomat to Rome and the Spanish Embassy. The 135 steps were built in 1723-1725. The steps go from the famous church Trinita dei Monti on Via Sistina to the base, Piazza di Spagna, with its beautiful Baroque fountain, "Fontana della Barcaccia." Of interest to note, on the right-hand side of the steps, you will find the home of poet John Keats. He died here in 1821. See my tip on visiting the Spanish Steps, where you do not have to climb the steps or the long slope on the Via Sistina. If you are going to have a coffee and a pastry, allow 90 minutes at one of the many cafes at the bottom of the steps in the Piazza. By the way, you can take great photos from the top of the Spanish Steps, and you need not climb them. Look at my tip below on elevator access. which you can use instead of climbing all those steps.

>>>TIP<<< CRITICAL READ
An ordinance passed in 2022 states that you are not allowed to eat or drink on the steps, sit, or lie on them. If you are cited, you will now be fined 400Euros. I always wondered why so much bubble gum was stuck on the steps.
>>><<<

An Alternative to the Escorted Tour

>>>TIP<<<   TAXI FROM THE SPANISH STEPS AREA
First the bad news. There is no taxi stand at the Piazza d Spagna. Now the good news. There is a taxi stand at the top of the Spanish steps just in front of the Hassler Medici hotel. You need to climb those steps or take the elevator. Please see my tip below.
>>><<<

>>>TIP<<<   THE ELEVATOR AT THE SPANISH STEPS
I always thought this was a top-secret, like that door at the Sistine Chapel (see Vatican section). If you look at the Spanish Steps from the Piazza d Spagna, with your back toward Via Condotti, you need to go around the steps to the left, not toward the AMEX office. In the corner, you will see the elevator. This elevator goes up to the Trinita dei Monti church above. It also goes down to the Metro station "Spanish Steps," and remember to keep your hands in your pockets!
>>><<<

>>>TIP<<<   TAXI FROM TREVI AREA
About two blocks from the Trevi Fountain on Via Marco Minghetti is an indoor shopping mall called Galleria Sciarra. Just ask any of the Italian's "Doe Vay et Galleria Sciarra"? You can usually find a taxi at the Galleria. You are not allowed to "hale" a taxi. Don't worry. If you do, they won't stop for you. Don't take it personally. It is best to go to a taxi stand or hotel.
>>><<<

>>>TIP<<<
Since I do not know the location of your hotel, I can't give you an exact route between the sites to visit. The best approach is to figure this out with a good map of Rome. You can get these maps online from Amazon. I recommend *"Streetwise Rome,"* by Michelin, Michael Brown, author. It's laminated and will allow you to use a water-based marker to highlight where you want to go. You can also ask the front desk or concierge for one of those free maps (they call them plans or Mappa).
>>><<<

ITALY NO TOUR NEEDED
You Can Do It Yourself

>>>TIP<<<
Sometimes these maps are difficult to read. I suggest you take an inexpensive plastic magnifier with you, in your day bag.
>>><<<

You are now ready to walk back to your hotel or get a taxi from one of the abutting hotels on the side streets or taxi stands. Rest up; tomorrow is Colosseum or Vatican City day.

So much for what I call "Monumental Rome. Now on to Day 4, the Wedding Cake, Colosseum, Forum, and more.

** DAY 4- WEDDING CAKE, COLOSSEUM AND FORUM

THE MONUMENT TO VITTORIO EMANUEL II A/K/A THE "WEDDING CAKE." 30-45 MINUTES

What is more commonly known as the "Wedding Cake" may be the last significant monument erected in Rome. Americans and Canadians see this building in many pictures of Rome but don't know what it is. But before I explain the Wedding Cake, here is some quick history. Before 1861 the land we now call Italy was made up of what they called "City-States." Even what we now call suburbs were included in the city-state. When the City States of Lazio (Rome), Firenze (Florence), Venezia (Venice) united to form what we know as modern-day Italy, they chose a king. That king was Victor Emmanuel II. He was the King of Sardinia and was brought over in March of 1861 to be the first king of the unified country known as Italy. The eternal light you see at the base of the Monument and the two soldiers guarding it is the tomb of the Italian Unknown Soldier. The Monument itself is built on Palatine Hill. It was constructed from 1895 to 1911 (finalized in 1935 with some additions) out of white marble from the area around Brescia (about one hour west of Lake Garda) in the northern Lakes Region of Italy. The unknown soldier was brought over and added in 1921, right after World War I. Victor Emmanuel II, who died in 1878, is buried in the Pantheon, not at the Wedding Cake. The Monument was built to honor King Victor Emmanuel II, the Father of the Fatherland, the new Unified Italy, and the Unknown Soldier of

An Alternative to the Escorted Tour

Italy. If you have time, you can visit the museum at the base of the Monument.

TRAJAN'S MARKET AND COLUMN- 45 MINUTES
Trajan's Market was one of the first attempts to establish a "shopping mall." The ruins you will notice are built in a multi-level structure. Emperor Trajan built the Market about 100-110AD. There are numerous stalls where merchants sold their goods, i.e., baked bread, grains, beans, meats, etc. You can visit the existing ruins from an entrance on Via Quattro Novembre (Italian) 94 and Piazza Madonna di Loreto. The complex is almost the size of a football field. The monument in front is Trajan's Column.

The column is about 125 feet tall and commemorates Trajan's victory in the Dacian Wars. A statue of Emperor Trajan disappeared in the middle ages (Medieval Era). That statue on top is a bronze figure of Saint Peter which was placed there in 1587. The column is composed of 20 round column pieces, each weighing 40 tons (giant "Lifesavers", white only). Inside that long column are 185 spiral steps leading to the square platform below the statue.

THE COLOSSEUM- 1-2 HOURS
What would a trip to Rome be without visiting the Colosseum? It's probably number one on everyone's bucket list.

The Colosseum is an oval theater in the city's center built in 80AD and still standing. It is the largest of all amphitheaters in the world. What you don't see is all the Travetine limestone facade. Over centuries it has been removed by peasants and others. It could hold about 50-80 thousand people for an event. The Colosseum was used for Gladiatorial contests, public spectacles, animal hunts, executions, and re-enactment and drama about Roman Mythology. It has a massive lower level where animals were stored and water for even depicting naval battles. Over the years, the Colosseum was sacked of all the beautiful Travertine facades, and the massive building fell into disrepair. It is listed as one of the New Seven Wonders of the World and is the iconic symbol of Rome. During the medieval period, the Colosseum was used as a hotel. The question always asked is, "what are those pockmarks or holes in the facade." From what I have been told, the holes were used to place tree branches in them and across to another hole. It was very similar to a shower curtain rod or pole. The peasants then laid over the branches of animal skins to form a lean-to. Peasants would live under these lean-tos.

The cross in the center of the Colosseum was placed there by Pope Paul II in 2000. It is dedicated to Christian martyrs.

THE ROMAN FORUM- One Hour

The Roman Forum, or simply the Forum, was the heart of Rome. It lies between the Palatine and Capitoline Hills. The Forum, at one time, was the site of triumphal processions of the Roman Legions. It housed criminal trials in its courts. It was the center of government. Today, it is an area of about two football fields in length and one in width containing fragments of an ancient civilization. There are still standing columns of various buildings, including the Temple of Vesta (7th century BC). Many of the buildings were rebuilt after the rise of imperial Rome. The Senate itself was housed in the Forum. The actual area dates to the Bronze Age, about 1200BC.

Discoveries over the years have unearthed prior Roman civilizations. An interesting fact, what you see is the final layer of the Forum. It was also here in 44BC that Marcus Junius Brutus assassinated Julius Caesar.

The Roman Forum is a great picture spot. The best pictures are the ones of people sitting on those ancient fallen Roman columns in the grassed areas.

SAN PIETRO IN VINCOLI- 30 MINUTES

The church where "The Moses" is located is also known in English as "Saint Peter in Chains." It is in a church on Oppian Hill, less than three blocks from the Colosseum. The church houses Michelangelo's statue of Moses. I have seen this several times, and I can tell you that next to the "Pieta" in St. Peter's Basilica, it is number two on my list of statues created by Michelangelo. It is easy to find. You need to walk up the Via Terme di Tito alongside the park on your right. You should note

An Alternative to the Escorted Tour

that there is a slight incline on "Tito." Take a hard left at the stand-up bar at the top of the street and follow the crowd. It's free and will only add about 20 minutes to your day. The church itself dates from 439AD. The "Moses" dates from 1515AD and is part of the tomb of Pope Julius II.

You are now ready to walk back to your hotel or take a taxi from one of the abutting hotels on the side streets or taxi stands. Rest up; tomorrow is Vatican Day.

THE WALKING TOUR OF THE WEDDING CAKE, COLOSSEUM, FORUM AND THE MOSES:
The times listed in the history section above include walking to and from (the next site). Also, some items and facts I already discussed in the above history section. I reiterate them here.

Now that you know a little about the history of the four venues, I will do my best to describe how you visit each one in an orderly way. I recommend doing about 1.0 to 1.5 miles on the first full day in Rome. Except for the slight incline to view "The Moses" at the Church of St. Peter in Chains, here is what you need to do:

Start your day off in the Piazza Venezia. You can either take a taxi if your hotel is too far or walk over. On arrival, note the balcony on the right-hand side of the square of that building.
This balcony is where Mussolini made all his speeches to his crowd of Italian Fascists in the days leading up to World War II.

Then view the **MONUMENT TO VITTORIO EMANUEL II A/K/A, THE "WEDDING CAKE ."** If you wish to go to the top of the monument, it will cost you 12Euros to use the elevator. However, you must first negotiate a flight of about 50 steps near the adjacent church and the cafe. Those 50 steps are wide and high. You will note it on the right-hand side of the monument as you face it. Then follow a passageway to the elevator. There are impressive views of the City. However, if you are in excellent condition, go for it. It is easy to spot that elevator, as the café is just outside.

ITALY NO TOUR NEEDED
You Can Do It Yourself

After taking photos of this massive white marble monument, go across the street. Then, go one block to "Via dei Forte Imperiali," and view Trajan's Market and Column. Supposedly this was the first shopping mall created. You can't buy anything here now. The place has been closed for more than one thousand years. There are lots of photos to take here. Do not attempt to climb the 184 steps to the top of Trajan's Column unless you are in excellent condition.

From Trajan's Market, continue walking down the Via dei Forte Imperiali. Note you will pass the Roman Forum on your right. The next stop is the Colosseum. Continue till you reach the Colosseum and locate the ticket "holders" line.

You should purchase your timed combination ticket (Colosseum and Forum online at www.coopculture.it/en/products/ticket-colosseum-roman-forum-palatine_24h/. Several weeks before your flight to Rome. The best is to figure a 1PM entrance. They will accommodate you if you arrive early or late in the off-season. It's not a big deal. Consider purchasing the combination ticket (instead of separate tickets), which will allow you to gain entrance to the Colosseum and the Forum across the street.

>>>TIP<<<
On arrival at the Colosseum, just next to the ticket booths, you will notice the bathrooms. It is best to take a break before your entry. By the way, always keep a Euro in your pocket. While it is free now, you never know when they will install those turnstiles.
>>><<<

After you have read up on the Colosseum, suggest you follow the signs to the elevator (ascensore in Italian). Do not attempt to climb the stairs to the various levels of the Colosseum. If you use the stairs (not advisable), beware of tour groups that may be going down the stairs like a herd of cattle and may be pushing some people out of the way to get back to their tour bus. It is perfectly acceptable to find your way back to the ascensore and go back to the ground level. Ground floors are marked as the zero floor, not the first floor. The ground floor is called zero (0). BTW, all hotels in Italy observe the same rule.

An Alternative to the Escorted Tour

After your visit to the Colosseum, you are ready to walk across the street (follow the crowd) to the Roman Forum. The Forum is ideal for taking great photos of yourself (and your partner) sitting on one of those ancient Roman columns lying in the grass.

>>>TIP<<<
Between your visit to the Colosseum and the Roman Forum, I recommend lunch and a time to take a biological break. The only places are directly behind and to the right and left of the Metro station at the Colosseum. They are Oppio Caffe (to the right), La Biga Ristoracaffe Wine Food, and Lauras Coffe (sic) Shop (all to the left, as viewed when you are entering the Metro station).
>>><<<

After you visit the Forum, it is best to walk about 3-5 blocks and view Michelangelo's "Moses." All you need do is go back to that Metro station and follow my directions from the above section on SAN PIETRO IN VINCOLI, "Saint Peter in Chains."

By now, about 5PM, you should be bushed. So taxi or hike back to your hotel, take a nap, shower, have a drink, and get ready for dinner. Remember, most restaurants do not open till 7:30PM or 8PM. Make sure you get lots of rest for tomorrow's VATICAN DAY. Also, it would be best to read my chapter at the rear of the book on dining in Italy.

THE CAPITOLINE HILL (IF TIME PERMITS)
This area of Rome never gets the attention of the Colosseum, the Roman Forum, and the other vestiges of ancient Rome. This hill was the center of the Roman Empire. There is evidence that there were inhabitants on the hill dating back to 1300BC. The hill housed many of the ruins of the ancient and most important temples of the Roman Empire. You won't find them here as they are buried below the new plaza. What you now see is a square designed by Michelangelo in the 16th Century. It is known as the "Piazza del Campidoglio."

The most important item to note is that the square faces toward the Vatican and not toward the Roman Forum. Michelangelo wanted to impress the populace that power and control now belonged to the Vatican and not to the old Roman Empire. If you go to the back of the Piazza, behind that large building, you can take some great photos of the Roman Forum.

By the way, that large building at the top of the stairs houses the present-day Rome City Council and a museum. There are several access points to the Campidoglio; just follow the crowds.

** DAY 5 - A VISIT TO THE VATICAN WITH LUNCH
TOTAL WALKING- ABOUT 1-2 MILES

>>>TIP<<<
If you do not want to be hassled by purchasing tickets online for the Colosseum and the Forum, the best way I have found is to book yourself on a half-day tour (prefer the morning) of the Colosseum and the Forum. Best is through Viator or any of the reputable tour operators. Note, these tours usually do not include lunch. If you are doing it yourself, please read on.
>>><<<

WHAT TO SEE AND DO IN THE VATICAN-
SEQUENCE OF YOUR VISIT- OVERVIEW OF THE DAY
The Vatican Museum requires a lot of walking. It is best visited when you have all your energy. It would be best if you arrived at the entrance to the Museum at about 10AM. Hopefully, you have purchased timed tickets between 10AM and 11AM. Then see the Museum and its Sistine Chapel. After exiting the Chapel, the facilities are next, and then the entrance to St. Peter's Basilica. If you read my tip, you will not return to the Museum's entrance area. You will go directly to the Basilica. After you visit the Basilica and take photos in St. Peter's Square, you will have lunch from about 1PM to 2PM in the Borgo Pio district abutting Vatican City. So here we go.

The Vatican City State (The Vatican) or sometimes called the Holy See, is an independent country. It is not part of Italy. The population is about 500, and it occupies almost 120 acres due west of the Tiber River. It has its police, own small army, own railroad station (not accessible), own post office, and its radio and TV stations. It was separated from Italy in February 1929 by the Lateran Treaty.

The Holy See is one of the smallest countries in the world. It is an island in the City of Rome and totally off limits to Italian Police, and other forms of security unless specifically invited. The Vatican is not a member of the UN, but is an observer.

Some quick facts about security at the Vatican. According to the Lateran Treaty of 1929, the Vatican police can call the Italian police (Polizia or the Carabinieri) to St. Peter's Square for crowd control if required. Other than that, the Vatican has its own security force. All visitors are screened before entry to the Basilica (St. Peter's church) by the Vatican authorities.

You won't need to show your passport to enter any Vatican City sites. However, Italian law dictates that a foreigner must always have their passport on them. That means you must carry it all the time, preferably in a secure pocket or in your day bag.

The Holy See ("See" means, in Latin, the "Chair or Office) is home to the Catholic Church and serves as its worldwide administrative headquarters or office. Of most importance, it is home to the Vatican Museums and St. Peter's Basilica.

You need to know two critical items if you will visit the Vatican. First, if visiting the Vatican Museum, you must purchase tickets online at www.museivaticani.va. If you attempt to go without tickets, you will wait in line for 1-2 hours, even off-season.

Secondly, if you want to join about 2,000 other parishioners for a Papal Audience, you need to contact your local priest or archdiocese. The papal audience, where the Pope appears on stage in the auditorium abutting St. Peters Basilica, takes place every Wednesday morning at about 10AM. Best to check with the Vatican online at http://www.papalaudience.org/schedule.

Proper dress is required and strictly enforced. I attended a Papal Audience in the summer of 1972, and I can tell you being in that

ITALY NO TOUR NEEDED
You Can Do It Yourself

fourth row with priests from all over the world was very moving. You usually will be escorted to your numbered seat by ushers wearing formal tails. If you are planning a Papal Audience, it will be challenging to adhere to either of my 14-day itineraries unless you allow an additional week in Rome at the beginning of your visit, or better, forget about the Angelus on Sunday morning and instead attend the Papal Audience on Wednesday morning.

Do not confuse the Papal Audience with the Sunday blessing in St. Peter's Square, known as the "Angelus." Except for the Sunday holidays, this usually takes place at 11AM and is over by 11:10AM. The Pope will bless all in attendance. I have attended three of these Angelus, and I can tell you, once again, it is very moving. Tickets are not required. It would be best if you arrived at least by 10:30. Groups are singing, and other festivities go on before the Pope's appearance from his Apartment. He appears once the Papal Flag is placed below his window.

The three main sites to see in Vatican City are The Sistine Chapel and its ceiling by Michelangelo (no, he did not paint this ceiling on his back as told in the movie *The Agony and the Ecstasy*), St. Peter's Square, and of course, St. Peter's Basilica with Michelangelo's statue of the "Pieta." You should note that I only provide a short overview of the Vatican. There are loads of books on the history of St. Peter's.

Here are the facts, just the facts and the details of your 3-4 hour visit to Vatican City.

THE VATICAN MUSEUM AND SISTINE CHAPEL
Most people who visit this monumental Museum are there for one reason, to see the Sistine Chapel and its ceiling. As stated before, you must purchase tickets at least 8-12 weeks before you visit Italy, or else you will need to wait in a long line. This line can sometimes be a half mile long and four deep.

Further, there are no "porta-potties" anywhere near that massive line. In addition, the next available bathrooms are past security after you enter the Museum. If you have not purchased tickets

An Alternative to the Escorted Tour

several months before, play it safe and get on one of those half-day tours of monumental Rome and the Vatican. You should note this is not the hop-on-hop-off bus tour. Another point of information, no backpacks or rucksacks are allowed. They can be checked, but you must exit and return to the check room. ALSO, YOU WILL NOT BE PERMITTED PAST THE SECURITY CHECKPOINT IF YOU HAVE A POCKET KNIFE. So men, it is best to leave it in your hotel room.

There is too much detail to describe the actual ceiling painted by Michelangelo. It was painted "Alfresco," i.e., into wet plaster. Part of the painting is called *"The Creation."* He painted it from 1508 to 1512 at the request of Pope Julius II. There are other paintings on the ceiling, including *"The Life of Moses"*, and *"The Life of Christ"* all painted by Michelangelo. Numerous tapestries adorn the Chapel, which I might note is used for several masses yearly. In addition, as we all know, the papal enclave meets here to choose a new pope when needed. The chimney of the Chapel is where the black smoke signals "no Pope yet," and the white smoke tells the world, "We now have a new Pope."

Here is how you negotiate the Vatican Museum and St. Peter's: First, with tickets, you must arrive at the Vatican Museum entrance *ticket holders line* and pass through security. The entrance has large glass doors and is flanked by Swiss Guards in their colorful red and yellow attire. You should note that the entrance to the Vatican Museum is about one-half mile from St. Peter's Basilica. If you are taking a taxi over, tell the driver that you want the Vatican Museum (Vaticano Museum). Don't even mention the words "St. Peter's." If you read this book in your planning stage, you should have purchased your Vatican Museum tickets online, printed them, or selected your option to pick them up at will-call.

Pass through those big glass doors and then enter the security line. After passing security, it's best to use the facilities. Then, you will need to make your way almost one-third of a mile down a hallway filled with the Vatican's most prized collection of sculptures, gifts, paintings, and tapestries. All you need to do is follow the crowd.

ITALY NO TOUR NEEDED
You Can Do It Yourself

You cannot get lost. You need to climb several flights of stairs at the end of that hallway or take the elevator.

Once at the Sistine Chapel level, you need to follow the crowd for another 2-3 blocks till you arrive at the Chapel. Once again, follow all those other tourists. They are going to the same place.

Once entering the Chapel via the one-way entrance, you will have about five minutes to take photos. Make sure you turn off your FLASH. If it does go off, you will be approached by one of the ushers. Also, there is no talking allowed, only whispering.
After viewing the ceiling of the Chapel, you will be directed to a door to your left. It's marked exit. Exiting this way will force you to view more of the Vatican Museum as you make your way back to the entrance, where you came through security about an hour ago. It is another grueling walk of about three football fields. If you have checked any bags in the cloakroom, you will have to exit this way and claim them near security.

If you want to have lunch, you have two options. You can enjoy lunch at the Vatican Museum cafeteria's or exit the Museum and find one of the many places across the street from that long waiting line to purchase tickets. In addition, the street named "Borgo Pio" has over fifteen excellent, inexpensive restaurants, one after another. See my tips below. After lunch, there are two options. Most folks will go over to either St. Peter's Basilica or the Castel Sant' Angelo.

It would be better to return to your hotel for a snooze and a drink before dinner if it's very late in the day.

>>>TIP<<<   CRITICAL
After you visit the Vatican Museum and its Sistine Chapel, your next stop is St. Peter's Basilica. You need to follow my directions, or else you will be routed back to the main entrance and the security point, a good three football fields and a lot of walking. You will then need to walk about one-half mile to your right against that long waiting line for tickets, pass those stunning Swiss Guards (don't worry, you can still take pictures with them later) until you

An Alternative to the Escorted Tour

make your way into Saint Peter's Square. You should note that to gain access to Saint Peter's Basilica, you will need to wait in line and clear security again. However, luck has it that there is a hidden secret door at the Sistine Chapel for tour groups and VIPs. Here is how you do it:

Take a look at the front of the chapel. There are two doors. One is on the left the other is on the right. There usually are ushers at both doors. If you go through the door on the left you will be forced to go back into the museum for that long walk to the main entrance where you entered, and hopefully, you did not check any bags. As described in the above paragraph you will then have to take that long one half mile walk to Saint Peter's, while hugging the Vatican walls. Here is the easiest way to eliminate that stressful walk. In addition, you will not need to go through security again. You also get to use immediately the bathrooms at Saint Peter's:

If you go through the door on the right (it is marked GRUPPO SOLO, groups only), you will go down an outside stairway. It is quite wide, but hold on to the black wrought iron railings. About four flights down, you will exit directly at Saint Peter's. You should make a rest stop here as the ladies' and gents' room is about thirty feet to your right. They are nice and clean, and yes, they do have toilet seats! There is no need to go through security again; you are in Saint Peter's. Or better, I should say the secured area. If you are on a day tour already, you are all set. Just follow the other people. Most of those guards at the two doors are looking for the headsets groups must wear. So, if you don't have a headset, you are a known "mark." So, it is best to bring an inexpensive headset.

If for some reason that usher comes over to you, just tell him "you were separated from your group and you saw them go through this door." He will open the door and say "okay, no problem", and thank him with a "Grazi."
>>><<<

The next stop is the Basilica itself. It is best to follow my directions below **"ST. PETER'S BASILICA."** You can take about one hour to walk about the Basilica and just marvel at its construction. You should figure another hour to participate in a Mass at one of the many alcoves if you are of the Catholic persuasion, see below.

ST. PETER'S BASILICA

Supposedly, St. Peter's Basilica is built over the remains of St. Peter, who was crucified in Rome. No one knows if this is true, as there was a belief that he was buried in one of the Catacombs of Rome. I don't see how St. Peter (Simon) ever traveled to Rome from Galilee (now in Israel), where he was a fisherman. Suffice it to say that in the 4th Century, on the present site, a church was constructed by Roman Emperor "Constantine the Great" called St. Peter's Basilica.

The Catholic church was based in Avignon, France, for almost seventy years. In January 1377, Pope Gregory moved the headquarters of the Catholic Church back to Rome. In April 1506, construction started on a new basilica. It was completed in 1626 (about 120 years, a long time, about six years after the Mayflower dropped anchor in Plymouth, Massachusetts).

The architects and artists of the Renaissance designed this massive Basilica. These were Bramante, Michelangelo, Maderno, and Bernini. It is the most renowned work of the Renaissance. It is not the mother church, which is a church in Rome called Saint John Lateran. St. Peter's still is regarded as the holiest of all Catholic shrines, i.e., right above Lourdes, Fatima, etc. However, it is considered the greatest of all churches in Christendom. In terms of size, it is the largest church in the world. Saint Peter's burial is directly below the high altar of the Basilica. Hundreds of popes and others are buried in crypts below the Basilica known as the Scavi, (hence where the word scavenger comes from, as in scavenger hunt).

You can book "Scavi" tours on certain days and times. You usually need to make reservations two months in advance.

There are stringent rules for dress in St. Peter's. Once again, like the Vatican Museum, bags are not allowed in the Basilica.

An Alternative to the Escorted Tour

If you entered directly from St. Peter's Square, you could check any bags after passing through security. There is a secured bag check to the right of the steps into the Basilica.

Also, women cannot enter wearing halter tops, short-shorts, or a "skimpy" t-shirt. There are places just outside St. Peter's on the main street (Via di Porta Angelica) where you can purchase a sizeable in-expensive scarf, which you can wrap around those exposed knees. However, if you are visiting in the colder off-season, you probably won't be wearing shorts; better to wear capris, pants, a dress, or a skirt that falls below the knees. Men must remove their hats in the Basilica.

Here is a quick overview of the structure:
The church is visible from all over Rome. It is massive. From the outside, those statues on top of the church, just below the dome, are the first-century apostles. You will note that there is no statue of Peter. The inside is a little more than two football fields in length and one-half in width. It is in the form of a cross with naves off both sides near the altar. The dome and the large columns supporting it are of utmost importance. The dome is about 450 feet from the floor and 140 feet wide at the top.

In addition to visiting the inside of the Basilica, you can visit the roof and the dome. Here is how you do it. The best is to take the elevator to the roof. It will cost you 12Euros and eliminate a climb of about 300 steps. From the roof (I have been there twice), you can view all of Rome and into the Basilica. There is now a bathroom and a gift shop also there. If you are in good shape, consider climbing about 250 steps to the top of the dome. However, be advised that those steps are very narrow.

>>>TIP<<<
If you wish to take a free tour of St. Peter's, you will find an information booth in St. Peter's square to the left of the Basilica, as you are facing the front. There are tours in English at about 2PM, and 3PM on weekdays and Saturdays. Best to check online as these tours do change times. Also, be advised that there is no entrance fee or tickets required to enter St. Peter's (unless you are an organized tour group). Check with the information booth about

ITALY NO TOUR NEEDED
You Can Do It Yourself

free audio tours. Also, you may find "roamers" in St. Peter's square offering you a narrated tour for 10 or 20Euros per person. This person may take your money and place you in the security line. Many of them will never see you again! Once again best on arrival is to go to the information booth.
>>><<<

If you are Catholic, you may consider attending an English Mass given several times a day, in one of the alcoves. You can check on www.vatican.va/content/vatican/en.html. Be sure to stop at Michelangelo's "Pieta," on you way out, it lies behind bulletproof glass. Just follow the crowd.

The Basilica is overwhelming. I have always started my groups off on the left-hand side (as you enter) and walked up and down the aisles, finally ending at the "Pieta ." If you pass some popes under plexiglass, you guessed it—most of them have been dead for a few hundred years. They are well preserved.

After you have completed your visit to the Basilica, your next stop should be the "Square." Remember to visit the checked bags area to claim items you may have given to the attendant.

ST. PETER'S SQUARE
First, I never knew it to be a "square." If you look at it, it is supposed to be two large hands embracing visitors to St. Peter's Basilica. Once again, one of my favorites, "Bernini," designed the square in about 1686. That Egyptian obelisk you see in the square was erected in 1586. It was originally erected in Heliopolis, Egypt. Emperor Augustus brought it to the Julian Forum in Alexandria, Egypt, and in 37AD, Caligula ordered the obelisk moved to Rome.

Bernini designed and built those embracing hands, four columns deep. He also designed that fountain in the square in about 1675. Of importance is that Bernini had to work around the constraint of the Papal apartments (where the Pope delivers the Angelus on Sunday mornings).

An Alternative to the Escorted Tour

Lunch follows, and I highly recommend the restaurants on the Borgo Pio. To locate the Borgo Pio, follow the Vatican wall till you reach a traffic light (at Via Sant' Anna, note the Swiss Guards). Opposite that gate to the Vatican is Borgo Pio. My favorite is the last one on the left, walking toward the Tiber River and the Castel Sant' Angelo. It's known as Borghiciana Pastificio Artigianale, and like Alla Rampa under the Spanish Steps, it is one of the best. You probably, like most Italians, will make this your main meal and have a very light dinner. You also get to steer at those incredible antipasto appetizers. There is always the inside if it's too cold for outdoor dining.

If you had a light lunch elsewhere in the "Borgo" you would hopefully have the energy to visit "Castel Sant' Angelo." I always look at this as a bonus. Or better, if you have another half or a full day in Rome. Since it is not part of the Vatican, I discuss it under optional sites to be visited. If you are up to it, it pays to see the "Castel" while you are less than a football field away. I discuss this first on the list of optional sites.

If you are now "stuffed" from that lunch (actually a dinner) at Borghiciana Pastificio Artigianale and it's about 3PM, ask the staff where you can get a taxi for your trip back to your hotel. I would suggest you don't walk it after that bountiful lunch. Arrive at your hotel about 4PM for a snooze (siesta), shower, and a light dinner. The next day we are off to Florence (Firenze). Please skip down to the Firenze chapter unless you take some of the day trips I mention in the next chapter or visit additional sites I describe below. So much for our Vatican day.

>>>TIP<<< SNEAKERS AND MORE SNEAKERS
There is a lot of walking between visiting the Vatican Museum and St. Peters. Wear comfortable walking shoes. Make sure you take appropriate sweaters or jackets. For ladies, do not carry a heavy handbag. The Museum, Cathedral, and Square will consume at least four hours. If you couple this with lunch at the Borgo Pio and a later visit to the Castel St. Angelo, it will probably consume the entire day.
>>><<<

ITALY NO TOUR NEEDED
You Can Do It Yourself

OPTIONAL SITES TO BE VISITED-
A FULL EXTRA DAY OR DAYS IN ROME –OR-
SKIP THE VATICAN

If you have an extra day to visit more sites in Rome, you should consider the following by order of importance:

Castel Sant' Angelo (If you have not already)
Baths of Caracalla
Catacombs (just one of them)
Circus Maximus
Villa Borghese and its Gardens

CASTEL SANT' ANGELO

If you are still in the Vatican area, and want to spend about one hour before you head back to your hotel, Castel Sant' Angelo is the place. It is also known as Mausoleum of Hadrian. This round circular structure has been around since 139AD. That's almost 1400 years before they started work up the street at Saint Peter's! Everyone that passes it on our tour buses always commented, "what is that?" Frankly, I don't know anywhere in the world, of a structure like this. Here are the facts:

Originally it was built by Emperor Hadrian to be mausoleum for him and his family. First, don't confuse this emperor with Emperor Trajan who built that massive outdoor mall and column near the Wedding Cake. The only thing in common is the last two letters of their last names.

In 139AD, Hadrian's ashes were placed in the "Treasury Room" of the mausoleum. The remains of emperors forward were also placed here. The last emperor to be interred (his ashes) here was Caracalla (Baths of Caracalla) in 217AD. In later years the Castel was used as a prison and as late as 1900 a theatre where Puccini's third act of Tosca was performed.

It is best you read up on these other sites, as they are beyond the scope of this book. For extra days out of Rome, see the next Chapter 8, Rome Extra Days.

CHAPTER 8

ROME EXTRA DAYS

AMALFI DRIVE, POMPEI
POSITANO
NAPLES & ISLAND OF CAPRI
RAVELLO, PAESTUM
ERCOLANO & SHOPPING

This chapter is about extra days you can spend while in Rome and as a side trip, out of Rome.

Let's face it. If you have been to Rome, and visited the Colosseum, Vatican City, Trevi Fountain and all that other good stuff, you probably should plan on a day or two to do something else. If you don't, I would certainly plan on one extra day and possibly two extra days. Here are my choices and the "funds" involved. Gee, where do I start?

By order of importance (my importance and interest):

The Amalfi Drive – rail to Naples & private car. Price varies.
Ruins of Pompeii- rail and entrance fee 120Euros per person.
Baths of Caracalla- 8Euros (just walk over or take a taxi).
Ostia Antica- 18Euros. Taxi or Metro 5Euros each way
Catacombs 10Euros, Appian Way and Quo Vadis free,
        Taxi both ways from your hotel or walk.
Orvieto rail – from Termini 30Euros round trip per person.
Villa Borghesi- Walk over or taxi, 13Euros
  There are lots more. I have only included a few.

NOTE- POMPEII IS ALSO INCLUDED UNDER THE AMALFI COAST & NAPLES- CHAPTER 18.
DAY TRIP ON THE AMALFI DRIVE

ITALY NO TOUR NEEDED
You Can Do It Yourself

Many people ask me, "Can I drive down the Amalfi Drive and visit Positano from Rome as a day trip?" The answer is absolutely, Yes. I will cut to the chase on this one. Here is how:

No, this is one place you do not want to rent a car in Sorrento (or any other location in Italy) and negotiate (not drive) the Amalfi drive. Notice I say "negotiate" and not drive. I have driven down the Amalfi Drive twice over the past 30 years. Two times was enough! In California, the Pacific Coast Highway from Monterey to San Simeon is a straight line compared to the Amalfi Drive from Sorrento to Amalfi (and on into Salerno).

On my last visit to the area, about three years ago, I emailed "Ugo" at Sorrentocars.com (Leonardo Travels) and asked him to send over a driver to my apartment rental in St. Agata (near Sorrento). The driver arrived promptly at 10AM and brought us back at about 5PM; no hassles. She parked the car, dropped us off for shopping in Positano, and took us to lunch (on our own) near Ravello. And, it was not a lot of money either—what a deal.

You can figure $250-$400 for the day with a private car and driver. You still need to make your way to the Naples rail station. Roundtrip prices are $30-50 per person (www.omio.com) and take about 90 minutes. The nice thing I like about a private car and driver is that you can choose when and where to make "facility," souvenir and photo-op stops.

Now, if you do not opt for a private car and driver (way to go), there is a way to do this on a budget. "Blue" SITA little vans depart the Sorrento Circumvesuviana rail station every 45 minutes. They are marked "Amalfi." The cost for the day is about $15 per person (total round trip.) You can get on and off at each town. Check with the ticket booth inside the Sorrento train station. However, unlike a private car and driver, you won't be able to stop at souvenir places selling artisan pottery, etc. In addition, if the next van coming into Positano is full and will not be dropping off passengers, you may have to wait 45 minutes for the next van to get a seat. Also, you can't ask the bus driver to stop for a facility break or a cappuccino while admiring the waves of the blue

An Alternative to the Escorted Tour

Tyrrhenian Sea. If you are basing yourself in Sorrento, taking the blue SITA bus may be a good cost-effective alternative for the entire day. Just make sure you wear your Right Guard, or better the person next to you is wearing it also, enough said.

Hiring a car and driver to navigate and narrate the Amalfi Drive will probably be one of the best life experiences in Italy you will have. Having your driver pick you up at Napoli Centrale if you are coming down from Rome is best. If you are visiting the Sorrentine Peninsular and staying at a hotel or apartment rental in Sorrento or Saint Agata, your driver will pick you up at Naples Centrale, drop your bags off at your hotel, and then take you down the Amalfi Drive. I am sure it will be extra, but it will be worth it. In summary, you get your transfers and the Amalfi Drive in one day. There is no need to hike over to the Circumvesuviana rail station at Naples Centrale with your baggage in tow. Let's face it; it's a drag! As they say, "no pun intended." Now, let's get back to the day trip.

>>>TIP<<<
Here is another creative tip. You can see the ruins of Pompeii and "do" the Amalfi Drive all in one day. Ask Sorrentocars.com or other private driver firm to pick you up at Napoli Centrale, take you to Pompei for 2 hours, and then do the Amalfi Drive. If you arrive in Napoli Centrale by 10-11AM, you can do it all with a panini for lunch somewhere on the Amalfi Drive. You probably will not have time for a two-hour lunch. No big deal; enjoy your panini or pizza. Remember that the Amalfi drive does not close. However, you don't want to come back in the dark. Also, see my tip (restrictions) on rental cars driving the Amalfi Coast on certain days.
>>><<<

STOPS ON THE AMALFI DRIVE
When booking your private driver, you need to inform the company that you want to make several stops for souvenirs and photo ops with a visit to Positano for picture taking. You want to end the drive and turn around in Ravello after visiting the Villa Rufolo estate and gardens (time permitting, this may cost extra).

ITALY NO TOUR NEEDED
You Can Do It Yourself

Depending on the time, lunch can be in either Positano, Amalfi, or Ravello Piazza.

>>>TIP<<<

You can check the ferry schedules (www.naplesbay ferries.com) as there are ferries from Amalfi and Positano back to the port of Naples. However, as stated in the off-season, they may not be running during your time frame. You will then release your driver in Amalfi or Positano. However, bear in mind that you will be still paying your driver for "deadheading" back to Sorrento or Naples where he/she picked you up. So nothing gained here.

>>><<<

RUINS OF POMPEII (A DAY TRIP)

Like the 57 other historical sites in Italy, Pompeii is also a UNESCO World Heritage Site. It is one of the top sites in Italy, attracting more than 2.5 million visitors per year.

The ancient city of Pompei (can also be spelled Pompeii) was destroyed in 79AD when the smoke, ash, lava, and pumice from Mount Vesuvius (about five miles away) covered the city to a depth of about twenty feet. Most importantly, it preserved an ancient Roman city dating to the 8th century BC when the "Oscans" built five villages there. You may see it as a "3-D" snapshot of history frozen in time for almost 2000 years. In 523BC, the Etruscans inhabited the area. The Romans came much later, taking control about 89BC. Essentially the eruption preserved the city until 1850, when it was discovered. Archeologists are still unearthing other areas of the ancient city.

In terms of making plans for the day, here are my suggestions:
It would be best if you planned on a high-speed "Frecci" or Italo train leaving Termini about 9-10AM. With lunch after exiting the Ruins of Pompeii, you should be able to get a return train to Rome from Naples Centrale at about 6PM (see my tip below). You can also book a later train and hang out at the station for an hour while doing some people-watching and having a cafe. This will not rush you. It may be a rush if you short the return trip to 5PM. You are in Italy; take it easy. And another point. I don't see any need for a

private car to just take you to and from the Naples Centrale train station. The best is to just take the Circumvisuviana Railway for about 20 minutes and exit at Pompeii Scavi. Things do change if you will be checking into your Sorrento hotel. In this case, have your private driver wait at Pompeii with your bags before going to your hotel in Sorrento.

>>>TIP<<<
If you are going for the day from central Rome, avoid renting a car. You will spend, round trip, on the Autostrada about six hours. And don't forget the cost of fuel (which isn't cheap), tolls, and parking. However, on a positive note, you do get the experience of driving with those crazy Italian drivers. Take the train and relax. However, if you are going South on the A1 Autostrada i.e. perhaps to Apulia, etc. consider a two-hour stop over at Pompeii.
<<<>>>

So here we go to Pompeii. On arrival at Napoli Centrale, follow the signs to the Circumvesuviana Railway via the underground passageway. There are escalators and elevators. Purchase a ticket (NA3) for about three Euros for the 30-minute ride to Pompeii. Note there are two outbound routes from Napoli Centrale. You need to take the train marked "Sorrento." The Circumvesuviana trains run about every 20 minutes. The exit station is marked as "Pompeii Scavi Villa Misteri or "Pompei." Loads of tourists will be getting off the train. Follow the crowd going across the street. They are all heading the same way toward the ticket booth. Note, elevators are available on both sides of the rail platform if you are physically challenged.

At Pompeii Scavi, there is considerable walking on well-defined asphalt and gravel paths. Depending on what you want to see, you will have to walk anywhere from 10-20 blocks in different directions to take in the breath of the entire complex. Having been to Pompeii three times, I can tell you this place is jaw-dropping and awesome!

There is no need to purchase tickets online or through other websites that are not the official website of the Scavi. As stated previously, ticket costs are usually marked up if you are not using the official website. In the off-season, you can buy tickets for about

ITALY NO TOUR NEEDED
You Can Do It Yourself

16Euros at the ticket booth. You need to check also for the entrance to the other adjoining ruins next to the main complex of Pompei. Some sections are closed on Tuesdays.

If you want to avoid walking back to the main entrance, you can exit near the bookstore, and this will save you from doubling back to the ticket booth. I quote from the official website: pompeiisites.org/en/visiting-info/timetables-and-tickets/.

If you have mobility difficulties, entering from the Piazza Anfiteatro entrance, you will be able to follow the "Pompeii for all" route, with the possibility of returning from the exit to Piazza Anfiteatro or possibly from Piazza Esedra using the lift of the Antiquarium." By the way, as in most sites in Italy, all of them now take VISA and Mastercard; many also accept AMEX. It is best to carry also a VISA or Mastercard with your AMEX.

Once again, consult the website mentioned above since the Antiquarium may be closed on the day you wish to visit. Also, try not to plan a visit to Pompei on Saturday or Sunday. There are just too many crowds. Also, the last Sunday of the month is free. However, the crowd is limited to 15,000. So best to avoid any weekend days if possible and also Fridays.

Also, remember to download the Pompei App on your smartphone and bring your headset. You should figure about three hours in the Scavi. A must-visit is the two amphitheaters, the house of "ill repute," the house of the two dummies, the temple, and more. The ticket booth also provides you with a map.

After your visit, about 2-3PM, enjoy lunch at many of the abutting restos. You will have to exit the Scavi complex. My favorite is Ristorante pizzeria Turistico. It's at the end of that paid parking area opposite the entrance to the Scavi; easy to find. And, yes, they serve a lot more than a pizza. Do ask a local for directions if you are lost. This is the place at about 3PM you want to make your main meal for the day. I suggest you watch the time and allow 90 minutes to get your train back to Rome. You should anticipate:

An Alternative to the Escorted Tour

Short walk to the Circumvesuviana rail station, about 10 minutes. Wait for the train for up to 20 minutes. Make sure the train is bound for Naples and not Sorrento. Also, make sure you validate your ticket. About a 30-minute ride to Naples Centrale. We are now at about 70 minutes (includes some buffer time).

On arrival back at the Napoli station of the Circumvisuviana, walk that underground passage (follow the signs to Napoli Centrale and make your way to the waiting room for the high-speed train (Frecci or Italo), which will deliver you to Rome Termini in about 90 minutes. Once again, note your train on the electronic boards. If it is not posted, don't worry; just have another café! They usually post times 20 minutes before departure. So much for your day trip to Pompeii.

So, a 90-minute allowance from Pompeii Scavi to Naples Centrale would be a little too tight since you need about 20 minutes to be there before the departure of your Frecci or your Italo train. It is best to book a return to Rome abou 6PM or later. You can always hang around for an hour and have a café and a cannoli.

You should note that it is very difficult to advance your train time i.e., get an earlier train. As discussed, trains "close out" about one hour before departure. Also, you cannot use an Italo ticket on a Frecce train and v/v and further you need a reserved seat on all Frecce and Italo trains.

>>> TIP<<<
I mentioned this tip before, however, here it is again. You have complete control of your time at the Scavi. However, I have always found that you can't control the time you spend at the restaurant. Even a request for the check and payment may take 30 minutes. Unless you are figuring a slice of pizza (instead of a sit-down lunch) on exiting the Scavi, add one hour to your planned departure on that high-speed train back to Rome. So if all the times suggest a 6PM train, take the 7PM train. A later train will eliminate all the stress. There is always time for a cold beer and a panini.
>>><<<

ITALY NO TOUR NEEDED
You Can Do It Yourself

THE BATHS OF CARACALLA

Everyone asks me (this may sound funny) "in ancient Roman times did they have toilet paper." The answer is no. When you needed to take care of business, you went to a communal latrine. There you were given a "Tersorium." This was a stick with a small sponge on the end of it which was dipped in warm water and vinegar or salt water. After doing your business, many then went to the baths. There were baths everywhere. Of all the baths, the most famous and still well-preserved are the Baths of Caracalla. They were the second-largest baths in Rome.

The Baths of Caracalla were built about 212AD, (yes, by Emperor Caracalla and Emperor Severus) and were not only baths but an entire spa complex. These baths covered over 60 acres. The Caracalla baths were about four football fields in length and a little over three football fields in width. There were 252 columns and some were as tall as 36 feet. Several million bricks were used to make the exterior and interior walls and rooms.

Water came to the baths via the Acqua Antoniniana aqueduct from the Acqua Marcia water supply. It still exists, and is located off the main road to the FCO airport, just before you get to the GRA ring road, about eight miles from the Baths of Caracalla.

The Baths had hot baths, cold baths and tepid baths, in addition to a swimming pool measuring fifty by twenty-two yards. It took ten tons of wood a day just to heat the water with cauldrons or "cisterns." There were even saunas. Works of art adorned the walls of all the rooms. There even was a library. On a typical day, these baths were visited by almost 8,000 bathers.
Underneath the baths, there were elaborate tunnels that distributed fresh water, removed the used water, and brought fresh air into the facility.

The baths were destroyed after the siege of Rome during the Gothic War, about 537AD and fell into ruin and dis-repair. The earthquake of 847AD, destroyed most of the complex remaining and left it in rubble.

An Alternative to the Escorted Tour

There have been numerous excavations of areas under the baths including a burial area, a gravel pit, and a subterranean worship area for the followers of Mithra, the Persian God.

Numerous buildings have been modeled after the Baths of Caracalla. They include the old Pennsylvania Station in New York City and Union Station in Chicago. I might note that Pennsylvania Station was reduced to rubble by 1967 and dumped in a landfill in New Jersey.

The Baths of Caracalla are certainly worth a visit if you have some extra time in Rome. I recommend after that nap on arrival, instead of the hop-on-hop-off orientation tour (no hop-offs), that you visit the Baths of Caracalla. The entrance fee is only ten Euros. I would strongly suggest that you hire a docent at the entrance and take a one-hour tour.

You should check current hours on the internet at www.coopculture.it/en/products/ticket-for-baths-of-caracalla, where you can also purchase your tickets.

DAY TRIP TO THE RUINS AT OSTIA ANTICA
If you landed at Rome's FCO airport, you were only a "stone's throw" (no pun intended) from the ancient city of Ostia Antica.

At one time, Ostia Antica was Rome's seaport. However, as time passed, the Tiber River silted up at its mouth, and the city of *ancient* Ostia moved closer inland. The site now lies two miles inland from the ocean. It is only 15 miles from Rome.

The site of Ostia Antica contains ancient buildings, frescoes, and mosaics. The oldest buildings you will find here date to the 4th century BC. In 68BC, the town was sacked by pirates. The port was destroyed. Later, Rome allowed Pompey the Great to raise an army to protect Ostia. The pirates were killed a year later. The town was rebuilt with protective walls. As of 2024, only one-third of Ostia Antica has been unearthed.

ITALY NO TOUR NEEDED
You Can Do It Yourself

Expect to see the ancient warehouses, villas, the House of Diana, The Forum, The Temple of Venus, the baths of Neptune, the old cemeteries, and the ancient synagogue.

The excavated site of Ostia Antica is open to the public. However, there is an entrance charge of 14Euros. There is a museum with many finds. Also onsite are dining and other facilities, as well as a theatre. If you care not to do this visit yourself, best to consult your concierge or front desk clerk. You should allow five hours, including the local train to and from Ostia Antica from Termini.

If you wish to do it yourself, you can find a boatload of information and pictures, etc., at the official website:
www.ostiaantica.beniculturali.it/en/opening-hours-tickets
And do ask the information desk if the restaurant will be open for il pranzo (lunch).

>>>TIP<<<
If you arrive at the Hotel Isola Sacra near Rome FCO airport the day before you are set to fly out, time permitting, you should consider a visit to the Ostia Antica Archeological Park. It is two miles away and about a seven Euro taxi ride. If you are driving, drop your bags at the hotel, and then spend two hours here. Then go over to FCO Airport and turn in the rental. Most hotels in the area do have their own shuttle vans.
>>><<<

>>>TIP<<<
In season, if you are checking into the Hotel Isola Sacra and it is a hot day, consider going to Rome's beach in Ostia (Ostia Lido). Grab some towels and either drive over or taxi over. Or better ask the front desk. This is the best way to cool off. In season, there is shopping and lots of places to enjoy lunch or dinner. Note, that parking is scarce. It may be better to take a taxi. Do ask the front desk clerk. You can bet it will be crowded on hot weekends. I might note that the Isola Sacra does have a beautiful swimming pool and also offers poolside cocktails. I don't think you will get that at the Ostia Lido.
>>><<<

An Alternative to the Escorted Tour

THE CATACOMBS, APPIAN WAY, PYRAMID, QUO VADIS

If you have some extra time, you might want to visit the Pyramid of Rome, the Appian Way, and The Church of Quo Vadis. They are all in the same area. It is about two miles from the Pyramid. Note: you may have to take a taxi down to the Church and have it wait for you as you visit for a few minutes.

In the New Testament, Peter is fleeing from the Romans down the Appian Way. Peter asks Jesus, "Quo Vadis." Peter replies, "I am going to Rome to be crucified again." Peter then gains the courage to turn around and return to Rome, where he is crucified. This encounter occurred at the Church of Domine Quo Vadis on the Appian Way.

If you want to walk the Appian Way (Appia Antica, no vehicular traffic on Sundays), you will find the Church about eight football fields beyond the Porta Sebastiano gate. The Church is of medieval architecture but was rebuilt in 1600. For those of the Catholic persuasion, Mass can be said daily. More information can be found on the Church's website: For information: http://www.dominequovadis.com/en/home-2/

THE CATACOMBS

I was first introduced to the Catacombs in 1987 when my 16-year-old son, Scott said "Dad, can we visit one of the Catacombs." To be honest I don't recall which one. However, I can tell you we did wait in the parking lot for them to open, at about 2PM.
So, after getting directions, (yes, even without a GPS), we went to one of them while en route to Florence. Remember, I don't drive in the City of Rome!

For most of you who are unfamiliar with the Catacombs, they are burial places; underground cemeteries. All of them are located just outside the old city walls of Rome. The two most famous are located on the old Appian Way. The San Sebastiano is located at Via Appia Antica 136 and the other is known as San Callisto at Via Appia Antica 126. Each one contains several miles of tunnels with burial chambers in the walls of the tunnels. You need not worry about sleeping tonight. Most of the skeletons in the Catacombs have been removed a long time ago.

First, there is a small admission fee for each site. Secondly, you can take a taxi to either one. However, getting a taxi back is a major problem. Taxis don't usually cruise the Appian Way. So, your best bet for the afternoon is to put yourself on a tour of the Catacombs. The tours include transportation to and from one of the above Catacombs, an entrance fee, and a knowledgeable tour guide. There are several. Best to check the web.

A DAY TRIP TO THE TOWN OF ORVIETO

You should not confuse this with a trip to the Naples area. Orvieto is located about two hours north, on the Rome-Florence rail line or the A1 Autostrada. The small city or town of Orvieto sits (it looks like a village, not my idea of a city) on a volcanic rock mesa about a short walk from the train station.

The city lies in the southwest corner of Umbria, touching the region known as Tuscany to the North and Lazio (Rome) to the South. Its actual elevation is about 1,100 feet above sea level. It is part of the metropolitan area of Terni.

Orvieto dates from the Etruscan era. In the 3rd Century BC, Orvieto was taken over by Rome. Because of its location on top of a volcanic rock mesa (or bluff), the town was impregnable to waring forces. It controlled the passage from Rome to Florence.
During the Middle Ages (medieval times), Orvieto became a cultural center of the region. Thomas Aquinas (later to be sainted) taught theology in Orvieto before being summoned to Rome in 1265 by Pope Gregory IX. Subsequently, he became the Regent master for the newly elected Pope Clement IV. When Rome fell, Orvieto was later controlled by the Popes.

Orvieto became a papal state until it was annexed to unified Italy in 1860. If you have about thirty minutes, I suggest you also slip into the archaeological museum (Museuo Claudio Faina e Museo), where you can view ancient remnants of the Etruscan civilization that inhabited the area several thousand years ago. You

An Alternative to the Escorted Tour

will find it opposite the Duomo. There is a charge of about five Euros. So much for the history of Orvieto.

Once arriving at the rail station (stazione), you need not worry. A Funicular will take you from the rail station to the central plaza in Orvieto. The Funicular (or Funiculari) runs every 10 minutes. The cost is about three Euros round trip. Make sure you buy a round-trip ticket. Walking down the switchbacks is rather tricky.

>>>TIP<<<
On arrival at Orvieto, look at the posted return train schedule and note the time. It would help if you figured from the time you finish your visit; you will need about 30 minutes. This allows time to get to the Funicular and desend the hill. Remember, the Funicular runs approximately every 10-15 minutes. This way, you will not have to wait long at the station for your return trip to Termini. So, if the next train to Rome is at 6PM, you must be at the upper funicular station by 5:30PM. No need to worry, the train station does have a café and toilets.
>>><<<

Very few cars are allowed in this medieval city's narrow streets, which date to about 1200AD unless you have a ZTL (Zone Traffic Limited) permit. However, a mini-bus will also take people from the rail station and the parking lot directly to the central square.

Once at the top of the mesa, you will find that most streets are flat and easy to walk. The numerous streets and churches are a must-visit. My favorite is the Duomo, located in the main piazza, known as Piazza Duomo or Piazza Cahen. Have someone take a picture of you and yours on those steps of the Duomo devouring a gelato. Here's the plan for your day:

If you are planning on lunch in Orvieto, the best would be to catch a local train 10-11AM. There is usually an 11AM and 1PM train, which makes the trip up to Orvieto in a little over one hour, and it's only nine Euros. Make sure you validate your rail ticket in Termini. On arrival at the Orvieto train station, you need to follow the crowd to the funicular, purchase your round-trip ticket, and head up to the historical district on the bluff.

ITALY NO TOUR NEEDED
You Can Do It Yourself

On arrival, plan on exploring the city and shops before lunch. If you enjoy shopping, this is the place. The main street is the "Corso Cavour ." I suggest you walk it from the funicular station to Via Duomo. It is only a few blocks away. You will find that on Via Duomo, there are also shops and eateries.

If you want to take excellent photos of the entire city, you want to visit the Torre del Moro. There is an entrance fee of five Euros to climb the 250 steps of this medieval tower or use the elevator. The lift will take you up about 160 steps. I believe at this level you will be able to take great photos. At the last stop of the lift, (at the 160-step level) you still have to climb about 100 steps to reach the top of the tower. By the way, that clock was recently added about 1850.

As a final thought, you might want to peek into some old churches, especially the Duomo. Also, don't forget to bring back that freshly baked artisan bread (best done on your arrival, else they sell out by the end of the day).

About 6-7PM, depart the city for your trip back to Termini. You should note that even though Orvieto is on the high-speed rail line, the "Frecci" high-speed trains usually do not stop.

THE VILLA BORGHESE GARDENS
If you have the time, this is another one of those must-see visits. It is extremely unique. This is the third largest park in Rome covering about 197 acres. In addition to the gardens, it contains the Galleria Borghese. The gardens as you see them now all date from the late 18th Century. This has nothing to do with the Roman Empire or Ancient Rome.

There are several villas in the gardens. The main villa is now called the Galleria Borghese. The building itself is magnificent. Other villas on the park complex include Villa Doria Pamphili and Villa Ada. The gardens, as you see them now, were created in the late 18th century. The Villa Borghese contains priceless paintings and sculptures spread over the upper two floors. There are many free days. However, there is a two Euro timed reservation fee. More can be found at: https://galeriaborghese.beniculturali.it. Note, that the website may be fire-walled. If you have any intention of seeing the Galleria, the best would be to just go over to the villa or check with your concierge or desk clerk. If you get to the Villa by 10AM you can spend three hours here, then walk over to Via Condotti (at the bottom of the Spanish Steps) for shopping and lunch. Good idea.

THE ISLE OF CAPRI

Here is a bonus. If you are interested in going to the Island of Capri for the day, you need to take the train to Naples Centrale and then take a taxi for less than 10Euros to the ferry terminal in the port area. You need to research the ferry schedules before you decide on this day trip. They can be found at www.capri.net. Please see Chapter 18 for more details.

There are many other day trips from Rome. However, describing them all would yield a five-pound book. So, best to consult the Internet. Oh, I forgot, how about "The Royal Palace at Caserta" it's a little bigger than Versailles (Paris) and only has 1,200 rooms and almost 1,800 windows to clean. It's only 20 miles North of Naples. The high-speed trains usually stop at Caserta, about 3 blocks from the Palace. Check with www.omio.com.

TIVOLI- ANOTHER DAY TRIP TO CONSIDER

Another afternoon can be spent at Tivoli. This is about 20 miles Northeast of Rome. There is lots of history here stemming from about 400BC through the Medieval era. Do not confuse this with Tivoli Gardens, which is an amusement park dating from 1843 in Copenhagen, Denmark. Tivoli (the town) is loaded with ancient villas, the most famous being Hadrian's Villa. Other villas worth visiting are Villa D' Este, and Gregoriana. What I never liked about Tivoli is that sections of the town are located in a somewhat run down area. On a positive note, all the villas are adorned with magnificent fountains, waterfalls, and sculptures. If you are spending 10-14 days in Rome, I would certainly put it on the list.

ITALY NO TOUR NEEDED
You Can Do It Yourself

CHAPTER 9

IT-ROME-TO-FLORENCE
ORVIETO & SIENA
SAN GIMIGNANO

The information in this chapter also applies to my chapter on day trips from Rome or Florence. Orvieto and Siena are reached via exits on the A1 Autostrada. All you need to do is follow the big green signs. So here we go....

If you have just arrived and are renting a car at FCO Airport and are going South to the Naples/Amalfi area, you need to consult Chapter 5, **GOING SOUTH—NAPLES/AMALFI AREA AND THE OPTION TO OVERNIGHT IN ARPINO.**

If you have just completed several days in Rome and are going to the Naples/Amalfi area, you need to go back to the FCO airport, rent a car, and follow my instructions in Chapter 5.

Driving North to Florence, etc., presents a different scenario since several "towns" line up before you arrive in Florence or the satellite town of Montecatini. Each one of these towns presents opportunities for overnighting and sightseeing. This is not the case with the drive to the Naples/Amalfi areas.

Driving north to Florence, Tuscany, Venice, etc., offers two classes of options depending on your itinerary. Either you have just arrived at FCO Airport and are ready to rent a car and head North, or you have just spent three or four days in Rome and will now be heading North.

OPTIONS MARKED "FCO" details your itinerary choices after arriving on an overnight flight from North America.

Here are the Northbound Options for Tuscany/Venice etc.:

An Alternative to the Escorted Tour

FCO OPTIONS- These are itinerary options after you have just arrived from an overnight flight to Rome. Your DAY 1 is your fly day:

FCO- DAY 2 ON ARRIVAL AT FCO
Choose one itinerary to follow from the four below:

FCO- Day 2 Option A-- Rent a car, then drive 4 hours to Florence/Montecatini. NOT RECOMMENDED. Overnight at Florence/Montecatini. You probably are exhausted. It is best to recover after a two-hour drive to Orvieto. Dinner and overnight at Orvieto.

-OR-

FCO- Day 2 Option B-- Rent a car, then drive two hours to Orvieto and overnight at Orvieto. Recover in Orvieto with sightseeing and dinner, best suggestion.

-OR-

FCO- Day 3 Option A-- Drive from Orvieto to San Gimignano with a stopover at Siena for Lunch. Overnight San Gimignano

-OR-

FCO- Day 3 Option B-- Drive from Orvieto to Florence (or Montecatini), stopping at Siena for lunch and San Gimignano late, about 3PM. Arrive Florence/Montecatini about 5-6PM.

****

ROM (ROME) OPTIONS- These are the itinerary options after you have completed a stay in Rome of 3-4 days or more, and are now ready to head to Florence/Tuscany. Choose one itinerary from below.

ROM-Day 5 Option A-- The "Florence Hopoff": Work your way to Termini rail station in Rome, and board a reserved-seat Frecci

ITALY NO TOUR NEEDED
You Can Do It Yourself

or Italo train for Firenze SMN Rail Station. Note that you must have tickets and reserved seats. Check into your hotel and spend two full days in Florence. See the next chapter. Then, go back to SMN Rail Station in Florence or Florence Airport and rent a car.

-OR-

ROM-Day 5 Option B-- Take the Leonard Express back to FCO airport, rent a car, and drive to San Gimignano, stopping in Siena for lunch. Continue to San Gimignano about 3PM. Overnight San Gimignano

-OR-

ROM-Day 5 Option C-- Take the Leonardo Express back to FCO airport, rent a car, and drive to Florence, stopping in Siena for lunch. Continue to San Gimignano about 3PM. Depart San Gimignano about 6PM for Florence/Montecatini. Arrive in Florence/Montecatini between 7 and 8PM. Note: You need to rent that car by 9AM. If renting later than 9AM, consider overnighting in San Gimignano.

-OR-

ROME—FLORENCE You are now in Florence/Montecatini or have just arrived from San Gimignano. After you arrive, use your rental for day trips around Florence (Pisa, Lucca, Montecatini, and Cinque Terre), Siena, and San Gimignano before continuing on to Bologna, Wine Tasting, Padua, and Venice. On arrival, turn the rental in at Venice or else keep the car if you are going on to Milan and the Lakes, Como, Maggiore, and Verona.

If you are renting a car out of Rome, use the same instructions when you arrived in Rome, i.e., back to Termini and catch the Leonardo Express to FCO Airport.
You will find the rental car counters about 300 feet from the exit of the Leonardo Express train terminal. Pick up your rental and exit the parking garage. Make sure you have your garage ticket.

An Alternative to the Escorted Tour

Continue with my instructions in the Arrival At Rome FCO Airport Chapter 5, the section marked **"GOING NORTH-FIRENZE/TUSCANY/VENICE"**

Here is a quick summary if you are DRIVING:
FROM FCO- (your flight just arrived from North America)
    Rent your car at the FCO Airport. Then drive to Orvieto.
    Overnight-   1st night suggested "Orvieto" 2 hours from FCO
    Sightseeing- Next day, Siena for Lunch en route stop
                    Overnight at Siena only if you can spare 2 nights
    Overnight-   2nd night San Gimignano 45 mins from Siena

FROM ROME-
    You need to go back to FCO Airport and rent a car there.
    Sightseeing- Then drive to Siena, overnight only if you can
                    spare 2 nights, else drive 45 minutes more to
                    the hilltop town of San Gimignano.
    Overnight   1 or 2 nights in San Gimignano

FURTHER DISCUSSION ON ARRIVAL AT FCO, WHERE TO OVERNIGHT – NORTHBOUND TO TUSCANY/VENICE/ ETC., ON ITINERARY OPTIONS

I don't know about you, but when I get off that plane at FCO, I am wasted! Further, in my present condition, there is no way I can drive more than two hours. Overnighting in Orvieto is the best approach. If you overnight in Orvieto, you will be able to see Siena for the day without overnighting there. Siena is a big place compared to overnighting in San Gimignano. My choice is always San Gimignano. If you overnight in San Gimignano you get to spend the next day sightseeing before driving the one or two hours to Florence or Montecatini. I always suggest leaving San Gimignano no later than 6PM.

You must decide on the one of the alternatives above in your planning stage since you will have to make hotel reservations for the proper dates. If you are not visiting Rome and heading north to Tuscany, my advice is to get out of the Rome area on arrival, drive those two hours to Orvieto, and overnight there.

ITALY NO TOUR NEEDED
You Can Do It Yourself

Another alternative is to stop in at Siena (do lunch, great pizza) at one of the many restaurants on the Campo. Then, drive 45 minutes to San Gimignano and overnight there. See my write-up on the Hotel La Cisterna below. Once again, that great view!

You will find the details of your visit to Florence in FLORENCE Chapter 10.

Here are the details you will need when visiting Orvieto, Siena and San Gimignano:

Orvieto- You need to check my chapter on Rome Arrivals. I highlight Orvieto if you are traveling North to Tuscany immediately upon arrival at Rome's FCO airport. See the paragraph **"ABOUT 2 HRS TO ORVIETO."**

Here is additional information on the hilltop town of Orvieto: Orvieto is located a little over two hours by car, North of Rome's FCO airport, on the Rome-Firenze (Florence) A1 Autostrada. The small town of Orvieto sits (it looks like a village, not my idea of a city) on a volcanic rock mesa about 200 feet above the road.

The town lies in the southwest corner of Umbria, touching the region known as Tuscany to the North and Lazio (that's where Rome is located) to the South. Its actual elevation is about 1,100 feet above sea level. It is part of the metropolitan area of Terni.

Orvieto dates from the Etruscan era. In the 3rd Century BC, Rome took over Orvieto. Because of its location on top of a volcanic rock mesa (or bluff), the town was impregnable to waring forces. It controlled the passage from Rome to Florence.
During the Middle Ages (medieval times), Orvieto became a cultural center of the region. Thomas Aquinas (later to be sainted) taught theology in Orvieto before being summoned to Rome in 1265 by Pope Gregory IX. Subsequently, he became the Regent master for the newly elected Pope Clement IV. When Rome fell, Orvieto was later controlled by the Popes.
Orvieto became a papal state until it was annexed to unified Italy in 1860. If you have about thirty minutes, I suggest you also slip

An Alternative to the Escorted Tour

into the archaeological museum (Museuo Claudio Faina e Museo), where you can view ancient remnants of the Etruscan civilization that inhabited the area several thousand years ago. You will find it opposite the Duomo. There is a charge of about five Euros. So much for the history of Orvieto.

You need to exit the A1 Autostrada at the Orvieto exit. Don't worry there is only one marked Orvieto. Follow the signs to Orvieto Centro and the Duomo. Looking to your right from the base of the steps in front of the Duomo you will find the Hotel Duomo. Do not confuse this with the BnB Duomo directly in front of the steps.

Very few cars are allowed in this medieval city's narrow streets, which date to about 1200AD unless you have a ZTL (Zone Traffic Limited) permit. Most hotels will allow you to unload and load your rental with no problem, even if you are in a ZTL area. Suggest you contact the hotel by email before entering a ZTL.

>>>TIP<<<
Do "scope out" your hotel location first. I suggest you park your car in the large muni lot at the rail station. Then take the shuttle bus to the top and have him/her drop you at the hotel. After you check-in the desk clerk will tell you how to bring your car up.
>>><<<

If you are overnighting in Orvieto and have arrived from Rome airport, check into your hotel, take a snooze, freshen up, and go out for a late lunch. You will find that on Via Duomo, there are also shops and eateries.

If you want to take excellent photos of the entire city, you want to visit the Torre del Moro. There is an entrance fee of five Euros to climb the 250 steps of this medieval tower or use the elevator. The lift will take you up about 160 steps. I believe at this level you will be able to take great photos. At the last stop of the lift, (at the 160-step level) you still have to climb about 100 steps to reach the top of the tower. By the way, that clock was recently added about 1850.

As a final thought, you might want to peek into some old churches, especially the Duomo. Also, don't forget to bring back that freshly baked artisan bread. Time permitting, you may want to explore the underground caves in Orvieto. There are about 1,200 of them. You will need about one hour to visit the main caves, which are over 2500 years old. It is best to visit the website info@orvietounderground.it. The tour is only 45 minutes and costs about eight Euros. You will not be able to see all 1,200 of them. However, 2-5 should be enough.

OVERVIEW   SIENA AND SAN GIMIGNANO
Siena and San Gimignano can be visited on the same day. However, seeing both towns will be difficult if you are returning to the airport to get your rental car and then going on to Siena. So best is to consider Siena a "way stop" en route to overnighting in San Gimignano. enjoy the day, then about 4PM head over to San Gimignano and overnight there before heading on the next day late in the afternoon to Firenze/Montecatini.

SIENA   BACKGROUND AND HISTORY
Siena is a hilltop town built in the medieval ages. Like many historical sites in Italy, it is also a UNESCO World Heritage Site. In addition to the historical significance, Siena is best known for the twice-annual horse race and exhibition known as the "Palio di Siena" held in the "Campo." The term "burnt sienna" comes from the fact that the buildings in the Palazzo are all that burnt red/yellow color known now as "burnt sienna." Note: it's not a mistake. The color has two "n" s.

You can exit the A1 Autostrada on any Siena exit. The best is Siena Ouest (SS715). Just follow the signs to Siena Centro and the historic district. You will pass the bus check-in point and off-site parking. However, follow the winding round around to the upper level where the historic district is located. The road will wind around, just keep looking for that red brick wall to the right of you against the old City walls where you will find lots of gates and car parking. Just follow the road around the walls, and you will see lots of parking "Parcheggio." Remember to purchase a ticket from the machine, or else you will have a costly souvenir on your windshield when you return.

An Alternative to the Escorted Tour

>>>TIP<<<   MAKE A NOTE WHERE YOU ARE PARKED
You should note well where you have parked, and further which gate and street you entered. Siena all looks the same (at least for tourists), and you can get lost trying to find your car and getting out of the historic district.
>>><<<

Note, that you cannot drive into the old city (historic district) unless you are in a taxi or making a delivery. If you don't heed these instructions, you will get a stiff fine from the Policia!

There is no fee to walk into the City. Here are your instructions for seeing this lovely Tuscan town (I think it's a city).

On arrival at the top of the hill, you must make a strategic decision. Do you head for the Piazza del Campo (the main square) first or see some of those gorgeous churches? The problem with Siena, it is just one giant maze, and I mean an absolute labyrinth! My suggestion is to make your way to the Piazza del Campo and locate a place for lunch. There are no less than 15 places on the piazza, and they all serve great inexpensive pizza, most of them made in wood-burning ovens. If the crust is too burnt, send it back. It's not a big deal. The staff will eat it.

Then, after lunch, you can explore some of the churches. My first choice is, without a doubt, the Basilica Cateriniana San Domenico followed by the Duomo di Siena. The first runner-up is the Basilica of San Francisco. All of them contain exquisite Renaissance works.

Once you make your way into the "Campo," you may be tempted to climb the Torre del Mangia, which is that big tower (about the same height as a football field) in front of you. There are 200 steps and no elevator, and there is an admission charge of ten Euros per person. You can figure a half-hour for the up and down. That building to the right is known as the Palazzo Pubblico or, better, the city hall. It is now a museum.

If you are of the Jewish faith, you may want to spend a few minutes after lunch visiting the Synagogue of Siena (at least the medieval one). It's easy to find because it lies on the street directly behind that large tower (the campanile)—the one you don't want to climb with those 200 steps. Just follow the signs to the "Sinagoga," or ask any one of the locals.

A SHORT HISTORY OF SIENA- JUST THE FACTS

From what we know, Siena was founded at the beginning of the 4th Century BC as a Roman Colony during the reign of the Roman Emperor Augustus. However, it is believed that about 900 BC, it was inhabited by a small group of Etruscans who called it Saina. The Roman colony was called Saena Lulia. It did not flourish under Roman rule because it was "off the beaten path," i.e., no significant roads and ports existed.

For about 600 years, control of Siena bounced around between various archdioceses, namely Arezzo. It was not until the beginning of the 10th Century AD that Siena became an important trade route between Rome and Florence. In the 12th Century, Siena went to war against Florence.

Siena was a major Italian banking center until the 14th Century. The oldest bank in the world still in existence is the Monte dei Paschi Bank of Italy. The bank has been operating since 1472.

During the Renaissance, the arts made their mark on the churches of Siena.

The Campo was a marketplace just before the 13th Century. It was built on a sloping site and paved over in red bricks with a herringbone design.

Shopping abounds on all the "spoke-like" streets emanating from the Campo. Here you will find native food products (salami, wine, cheese) and lots of handmade Italian products. Nothing in these shops is commercial.

Here are some questions you probably want to ponder as you eat that great pizza in the Piazza del Campo, or better, wait for it to be delivered to your table:

An Alternative to the Escorted Tour

Q: Why is the Piazza divided into nine pie-shaped sections? Does this represent a pizza?

A: No, each wedge represents one of the nine politicians (the committee of 9) who laid out the Piazza of Siena a/k/a "The Campo" during the 12th Century.

Q: What's with all those flags?

A: Each one represents one of the neighborhoods of Siena.

Q: And finally, what's with that fountain in the middle of the square? Or shall I say, at the top of the square?

A: That fountain is known as the "Fonte Gaia" or Joyous Fountain. It was built in 1419 by that committee of nine. The fountain serves as the watering hole for the area as it was the end point of several conduits. It is still in use today. However, the water from this fountain is not potable, so don't drink it.

Now onto San Gimignano, my favorite Tuscan town. I say this only because of the hotel (see below) and yes the gelato.

It's only a 45-minute drive on the Firenze-Siena road to San Gimignano. You need to take the Poggibonsi exit. It should be also marked San Gimignano. Don't worry. Follow the signs around the rotary in Poggibonsi. The road SP1 will take you right into the main parking lot of San Gimignano.

SAN GIMIGNANO- THE TOWN OF TOWERS

No other town or city in the world compares to this place. This is not New York or Chicago. These towers go back 800 years, not eighty. I love it!

It is a walled hilltop medieval town in the province of Siena, Tuscany. And, yes, it is also a UNESCO World Heritage Site. It is best known for its medieval architecture and a dozen towers remaining. Those towers you see are houses. The town dates from about the 3rd Century BC when it was an Etruscan village. Two brothers, Muzio and Silvio, fled the Roman Republic for a hilltop village called Valdelsa. The brothers built two castles atop that hill and called it Silvia. The name was changed in 450AD by Bishop

106

ITALY NO TOUR NEEDED
You Can Do It Yourself

Geminianus. The Bishop was able to spare the destruction of the two castles from Atilla the Hun.

In the 6th and 7th Centuries, the wall was built around the town. From about 900AD forward, the village was controlled by Volterra's bishops, another medieval hilltop town a few miles away. The small town was called the "Castle of San Gimignano."

During the Middle Ages and the Renaissance, San Gimignano was a stop-over on the Via Francigena road, stretching from England across Europe and through the Apennine Peninsula, now known as Italy. This stop-over point hosted pilgrimages en route to Rome and further to the Holy Land through ports on the Apennine Peninsula.

In 1199AD, the fledging town became independent of Volterra. Public buildings and churches were built. However, this peace did not last long. For the next 200 years, there were conflicts between the Guelphs and the Ghibellines, and to further add more conflict, the wealthy families of San Gimignano began to fight each other; and enter the towers.

The competing families of San Gimignano started to build tower houses to house their families. At the end of the medieval period, there were 72 tower houses. Today 14 remain standing. As each tower was erected, the next tower to be built had to be taller. This competition was like "keeping up with the Jones."

This competition continued until the town council said no tower could be taller than the campanile tower abutting the Palazzo Comunale, which is 230 feet tall. The city continued to grow until the Black Plague hit most of Europe in 1348 when about half of the population of San Gimignano died. Florence later governed the town. You will note throughout the Town Gothic houses built in the Florentine style. Many of the towers had to be leveled to the height of the abutting buildings. This lasted until the 19th Century when San Gimignano became a tourist attraction. The present-day towers can be seen for miles.

An Alternative to the Escorted Tour

Oh, one more item. People always ask, "What happened to all the other towers"? Simple, they were lost to wars, neglect, and finally, urban renewal.

Here is a little geography of the town. First, only three sides of the old wall still exist. The fourth wall was torn down during the 16th Century. There are now only eight entrances from the road which encircles the town. If you have a car, it's a nice "drive-around," and will take you no more than ten minutes to circumnavigate the town. It is best to locate the central parking area where all the buses park. This parking area abuts the "Coop" market. Also, around that ring road, you will find several hundred metered parking spaces.

I have visited San Gimignano about a dozen times. There are two main piazzas. The first is the Piazza della Cisterna. It looks like a triangle. You can't miss it. It is the one with the water well in the middle (i.e. cistern). The well dates from 1346AD. Across from one end is the Hotel Cisterna, and on the other side is the Hotel Leon Bianco. On the other side of this triangle, you will find the Gelateria Dondoli, supposedly the best gelato in Italy.

The second piazza is the Piazza Duomo. It's just off the Piazza della Cisterna next to the Dondoli Gelato shop. With your back to the well, go toward the right passing the side of the Hotel Leon Bianco. In about 200 feet, you will come to the Piazza Duomo. The first building on the left is the Palazzo Comunale. It is essentially the town hall. You can't miss it as it has a campanile (Torre Grossa) on the right side of it. Continuing to your right is the Collegiate Church. If you continue past the Collegiate Church several blocks, you will come upon a small square with a street to the right and one to the left. The Piazza Agostino is named for the Church of Sant' Agostino on that square. All three churches are worth a short visit to view the beautiful artwork on the walls and ceilings.

NAVIGATING AROUND SAN GIMIGNANO
San Gimignano is one town that is not a maze and one town where you want to do some serious shopping. There are two main streets,

and they are wide. The first one (Via San Giovanni) starts from that small park, "Piazzale Montemaggio" at Viale Roma and works its way uphill at about a 5-7% incline. It starts at the beginning, where you come up from the parking lot and pass the "Coop" supermarket. It would help if you watched those stairs or take the ramp.

San Giovanni is lined with all types of shops and eateries. In about six blocks, it takes a bend to the right and goes under a house (yes, a house) before coming out at the Piazza Cisterna; note the line on the left in front of the Dondoli Gelato shop (Gelateria Dondoli). As you pass the city hall with that big tower and the Collegiate Church, bear to your right down the Via San Matteo until you get to Via Cellolese, then go right for about two blocks. Here you will find the Piazza St. Agostino with the church by the same name located on it. If you don't make the right-hand turn on Via Celloese, you will wind up going out the Porta Matteo gate onto the ring road. You must turn around, walk back a block, and take a hard left.

There are ample public facilities in the town, or better, swing into a stand-up bar or a sandwich shop and ask to use the toilet. I find it best to order an Americano Coffee and THEN head for the toilet (WC). It's not a requirement but a nice gesture.

>>>TIP<<<   SOMETHING SPECIAL
HOTEL LA CISTERNA – SAN GIMIGNANO
One of the most romantic hotels I have ever stayed in is the "Hotel La Cisterna" just right off the square in San Gimignano.   You must ask for a room on one of the upper floors which looks over the Tuscan countryside and not overlooking the square. These rooms are truly "A room with a view."   BTW… You should view the movie *"Tea with Mussolini"* since it was filmed at the Hotel La Cisterna. You can drop your bags in front of the hotel, but you still have to park overnight at public parking. The bellman will direct you where to park.   Also, you need to book this one immediately so you can get one of those rooms overlooking the Tuscan countryside!! Please book directly.
>>><<<

An Alternative to the Escorted Tour

After you have visited Siena and San Gimignano and you are all shopped out, it's time to head through the wine country of Chianti to Florence, the city of the Renaissance, about 60KM away.

After leaving San Gimignano, the question is: "Are you in a rush?" or "Would you like to take the slower scenic route through the vineyards?" Without any stops, the scenic vineyard route will take you about one hour longer (you can figure two hours) than the high-speed Firenze-Siena road.

If taking the "high speed road" you need to follow the signs back to Poggibonsi and take the Firenze-Siena road, toward Firenze.

On the other hand, if you want a magnificent scenic drive through the Chianti wine country, you need to follow the signs to SR222 and head for Grieve in Chianti along what is known as the - Strada del Vino. The road is officially the "Chiantigiana."

This road will take you through some of the most scenic hillside towns of the Tuscan vineyard areas and passes through the towns of Grieve, Panzano, Castellina, Vopaia, and more. After leaving San Gimignano go back to that rotary in Poggibonsi and look for SR222. The signs usually say Castellina in Chianti.

Most of the towns on the Chiantigiana have lots of shopping, outdoor cafes, and yes, wine tasting. If you are serious about wine tasting feel free to watch for those roadside signs for the tasting rooms at many of the vineyards. Remember to have a designated driver, or else you will be forced to overnight in the Chianti area if you are both "sloshed." A better idea would be to plan on overnighting somewhere in Chianti instead of Florence.

>>>TIP<<<   THE CHIANTIGIANA
If you are into wines, the best idea is to check out of the Hotel Sisterna in San Gimignano about Noon and make your way over to SR222. This allows you to traverse the Chiantigiana during the daylight hours. I would still overnight in one of the towns along the road. Most of them are called Albergos, since they are small hotels. You will also find lots of country inns and Agriturismos.

110

ITALY NO TOUR NEEDED
You Can Do It Yourself

These are working farms that have guest rooms and offer dinner, in addition to your breakfast. You will find more on Agriturismo.it.

The SR222 or the SR2 will take you to the Florence Ring road in South Florence better known as Firenze Sud. From the Florence GRA, you will need to find your Florence hotel or go to Montecatini. If you are going to a hotel in Florence itself, after passing through the Florenc Sud toll plaza, it is best to follow your GPS instructions to your hotel.

On the other hand, if you are staying in Montecatini Terme (I just refer to it as Montecatini), after passing through the Firenze Sud toll plaza you need to follow the signs to the A1 North. In about 14KM you then need to exit the A1 and take the A11 (it only goes one way) toward the Mediterranean.
>>><<<

MONTECATINI EXPLAINED
Would you believe there is a town west of Florence that has over 400 (yes, you read right, 400) hotels and sleeping establishments? The town is called Montecatini Terme. Most of the time it's just referred to as Montecatini. However, do not confuse this town with the other Montecatini located next to Modena, Italy. You can reach Florence with your rental car within 50 minutes. However, like Rome, Bologna, and Florence it is another place you don't want to drive in.

Montecatini is the "Baden-Baden" of Italy. It has natural springs and mineral waters under the town, which feed the public baths within the town. Besides the baths (the Terme), Montecatini is an excellent place to use as a base for exploring the area in and around Florence: Florence, Pisa, Lucca, and San Gimignano are less than one hour away. In addition, the Cinque Terre is about two hours away. Siena and Assisi, are also about 90 minutes away by car.
What I like best about Montecatini is that the cost of a four-star hotel room is about half what you would pay in Florence. Further, you won't have to pay to park your car each day or get one of those ZTL fines when you return home. See more below on Montecatini.

111

An Alternative to the Escorted Tour

THE TRAIN TO FLORENCE FROM MONTECATINI

Trains depart for Florence Santa Maria Novella (SMN) station every hour, and in peak hours of the day there are two trains per hour. The fare runs about $10 round trip. Trains make the two stops in Montecatini which are known as Montecatini Centro and Montecatini Terme. If you are planning on visiting the City of Florence for two or three days, this is the way to go. So it is best to leave that rental at your Montecatini hotel and walk over to one of the two stations, purchase your round-trip ticket, and hop on the train. There are no reserved seats. Tickets are purchased through those big red machines with a credit card and are valid any time. Make sure you validate your ticket with the yellow or red small machine on the platform.

Hotels in Montecatini are no more than a 10-minute walk to either station in town. Did I mention that Montecatini is also a beautiful modern Tuscan town? In addition to the main shopping area, there are beautiful tree-lined residential streets and a wonderful park with fountains, etc. You will also find excellent restaurants. You should plan an afternoon to visit Montecatini Alto.

Montecatini Alto is a section of the city that is reached by a funicular. It is not a lot of money, usually will run about 8Euros round trip. The funivia runs every 30 minutes. Several restaurants as well as gelato stands are available for a sunset snack before dinner. You may even want to consider dinner at the Alto. On a note, do not attempt to walk up or down the "Alto" on the auto road as it is too narrow and dangerous.

If you are staying in Montecatini, trust me on this one; not only will you save money on the hotels, but you will also take the stress out of driving in Firenze. Montecatini is always my choice for hotels, restaurants, convenience and being with the locals in this beautiful town. Here are my hotel suggestions:
Hotel Puccini- One of the best. Book direct with "Pasquale."
Hotel Columbia, Hotel Minerva Palace, Albergo Terme and the Ercoline & Savi right in the heart of town (large rooms). The Croce di Malta is also a good bet in a beautiful residential section of town, however it is a longer walk to the rail station than the others.

112

CHAPTER 10

FLORENCE
CITY OF THE RENAISSANCE
DAVID AND THE ACADEMY
THE UFFIZI GALLERY
THE DUOMO COMPLEX
PONTE VECCHIO BRIDGE
NUOVO MERCATO

INTRODUCTION

No city in Western Europe has given more to humanity than the City of Florence. Think of it? From the time Rome fell in 470AD, till about 1300AD, Europe lay dormant. This was the medieval period, sometimes called the Dark Ages. It consisted of castles, feudal lords, and just existence.

It wasn't till about the 14th Century that the arts and sciences began to flourish. It all started in Florence. It was a rebirth of Art, Architecture, and the Sciences. Most of us associate this time in history with names like Michelangelo, Da Vinci, Galileo, Copernicus, and more. The vestiges of the Italian Renaissance remain here in Florence. If you visit Florence, you will have the opportunity to view some of the most famous pieces of art and architecture in the world. You need a minimum of two days to absorb all this.

FLORENCE IS A WALKING CITY

Below are the major attractions of Florence. The nicest thing about them is that they are all no more than a 15-minute walk from each other. In addition, the train station known as Santa Maria Novella (SMN) is also in the heart of the town. SMN is minutes from all of the attractions. If you drive your rental car into Florence, you can keep it parked, (if you can find a spot outside of the historic district) for the next two days. The whole area is one

An Alternative to the Escorted Tour

big massive ZTL zone. And yes, the taxis do have their privileges. Here are the major attractions:

1. Academy (Accademie and its David)
2. Duomo complex
3. Uffizi Gallery – Right off the Piazza della Signoria
4. Nuovo Mercato- Great inexpensive shopping
5. Ponte Vecchio Bridge – expensive jewelry shopping

To get from one location to another just follow the crowd or ask any local Italian "Por Fay Vorray or Scoozie…." Or "Doe Vay…..Uffizi, etc." Hopefully, he/she will also point you in the proper direction with their hands.

PLANNING IS MANDATORY

In addition to the Duomo and Ponte Vecchio bridge, there are major attractions—or should I say "draws"—to Firenze. The first is "David," the hand-chiseled statue of David from the Old Testament. Michelangelo sculptured this 6-ton piece of marble between 1501 and 1504. It is now in the Academy, a/k/a "The Academie."

The second major attraction is the Uffizi Gallery. This is a museum that houses the priceless paintings and sculptures of the Renaissance.

Both of these attractions are several blocks apart and can be easily visited on the same day. However, you do have to purchase your tickets at least 90 days before arrival in Italy. If you can't get the reservations on the same day, hopefully, you can stagger them over two days. If you don't have tickets to see "David" you will wait 2-4 hours in line to purchase them. You need about 30 minutes to marvel at this magnificent work of art.

The Uffizi presents a different problem. Because of its popularity, entire days will be listed as sold out at the ticket booths in front of the entrance. So, if you expect to purchase tickets after seeing the "David," you can expect to see those electronic signs stating "next opening is in 3 or 4 days."

ITALY NO TOUR NEEDED
You Can Do It Yourself

The Duomo (basilica or church) and the Duomo complex do not present any problem, as it is free to enter. In addition, there is no charge to visit the "scavi" (ancient ruins) below the church.

Here is the information you will need to make your reservations and purchase your tickets.

THE ACCADEMIA AND THE UFFIZI
Whether you are staying in Montecatini, coming into Florence by train, or arriving in your rental car from Rome, make your reservations:
https://www.galleriaaccademiafirenze.it/en/tickets.

It would be best to book your timed reservation for two hours past your arrival time in Florence, either by train or car. You can figure about 30 minutes to view David. However, the ticket holders line, security, etc., will bring you to a full hour.

The next day, it is best to visit The Uffizi Gallery around 11AM if you can not get tickets for the afternoon following the Academy and the David. You will also need timed tickets to the Uffizi. You can figure one to two hours. These reservations will allow you to have lunch at about 2PM. Even though it can be done, it is difficult and stressful to do both David and the Uffizi in one day, especially if you are coming up from Rome by car or train from Montecatini. Both museums are booked months in advance.

You won't have to do a lot of walking to view the "David." You pass through security, and "walla," there's David in all his glory. "David," because of its sheer weight, stands a few feet off the entrance on the ground floor. Michelangelo chiseled out one massive block of marble over a four-year period that ended in 1504. On the other hand, the Uffizi requires lots of walking—so much for preparation for Florence. There are no cafés or eating establishments in either the Academy or the Uffizi. Both, however, do have excellent bookstores.

If you are driving up from Rome and staying in Florence (instead of Montecatini, see later in this chapter), after you have checked

An Alternative to the Escorted Tour

into your hotel or checked your bags with the bellman, you are off to see the town. I would suggest an arrival in Florence at about noon. The first stop is the Galleria dell Accademia (Academy) to visit "David." You can figure a timed entrance at about 2PM. The best is to pick up one of those free maps from the front desk or the concierge. It's only a few blocks to the Accademia. And, because Florence is on the border of being called a "maze," I suggest you keep asking "Doe Vay et Accademia Gallery," or better, just follow the crowd.

If you are staying in Montecatini you can easily see both the David and the Uffizi in one day. Take the train in and see David at 12Noon, and the Uffizi 2-5PM. This will give you time for lunch in the Piazza della Signoria.

SHORT HISTORY OF MICHELANGELO'S DAVID
Michelangelo's David is the symbol of Florence and the Renaissance. You cannot visit Florence without seeing David. David "is" Florence.

Here are the facts: It stands almost 17 feet tall and weighs six tons. It was chiseled by a 26 old Italian artist, Michelangelo 1501-1504. It's the David we all know from the Old Testament, complete with that slingshot on his left shoulder, which he used to take down Goliath. His right arm appears larger than his left (it is). He also seems to be cross-eyed.

David also symbolizes Florence's defense of civil liberties embodied in the Republic of Florence, an independent city-state. The independent republic was threatened on all sides by more powerful states. Florence, like David, would not be bullied.

There were two attempts to chisel David for placement on the roof of the Cathedral of Florence (The Duomo). The two chosen artists gave up (one quit after ten years of work), and the unfinished work lay in a yard in Florence for 26 years before Michelangelo re-started the work effort. The final work was erected in the Palazzo Signoria (Palazzo Vecchio), where a copy of it now stands. In 1873 it was moved to the Galleria dell' Accademia, where it stands today. If

116

you go to lunch in the Palazzo della Signoria, you can't miss that copy of David.

The David was originally intended to be placed on top of the Duomo. However, weighing six tons, it was too heavy to lift onto the roof of the Duomo. In addition, the roof probably would not support this weight.

The original marble block came from Carrara, which is near Massa. If you are taking a day trip to the Cinque Terre, you will pass Massa on the right-hand side of the road. You can't miss it with all those white blocks of marble in the yards.

In 1527, when David debuted, anti-Medici protesters pelted David's left arm with stones, breaking it into three pieces.

Of significant interest is the fact that David is not circumcised. Since David was Jewish, he would have been circumcised. However, this is consistent with Renaissance art, as most biblical males are shown not circumcised. Many argue that he is circumcised, but just a little, lol.

Security is tight at the Gallery of the Academy of Florence. There have been several attempts on David. The most recent occurred in 1991 when a deranged person snuck a hammer into the hall and started destroying David's left toe.

The only thing now that can harm David is an earthquake. In addition, archeologists are worried about the vibration's of viewers footsteps harming the statue.

>>>TIP<<<
It is best to plan a leisurely two-day trip to Florence. On one day, you can schedule a visit to the Academy and David in the morning and the Uffizi on the second day. In the afternoons, you can visit the Duomo, shop at the Ponte Vecchio Bridge, and the Nuovo Mercato as you enjoy a gelato after your panini.
>>><<<

An Alternative to the Escorted Tour

It's a short walk over to the Duomo then onto Piazza della Signoria and the Uffizi Gallery.

THE DUOMO

The Duomo is right up there with the David as a symbol of Florence as a must-see, and it's free. The appearance of the Cathedral and the other buildings in the complex are striking. It was originally called the Cathedral of Saint Mary of the Flower (Fiore in Italian). The massive basilica is officially the Cathedral of Florence, now called in Italian "The Duomo of Firenze." It appears in practically every photo of the City. You can't miss those red bricks which cover the dome.

The Duomo was begun in 1296 in a Gothic style of a design by Arnolfo di Cambio and was structurally completed by 1326. The dome was engineered by Filippo Brunelleschi, the famous architect, engineer, and sculptor of the Renaissance. It is the largest brick dome ever constructed. The exterior is made up of two colors of green and pink marble, which has a white border. It is a 19th Century Gothic Revival façade designed by Emilio De Fabris. In round numbers, the Cathedral is 500 feet long and has a height of 380 feet. It is one of the world's largest and the largest medieval building in Europe.

You can visit the inside of the Duomo. Of most importance are the Roman ruins (scavi) below the floor of the church. They can be viewed via the stairs next to the bookshop.

Also, the painting in the dome itself represents the *Last Judgement*, not the *"Last Supper,"* which is in Milan.

>>>TIP<<<
While you can visit the top of the dome of the Duomo you should note that there is no elevator, and further, you need to walk up 463 steps. Down should not be a problem. For pictures and photo ops of the City, after you cross the Ponte Vecchio bridge, consider a six-block walk to the Pitti Palace or the Boboli Gardens, which abuts the Palace.
>>><<<

ITALY NO TOUR NEEDED
You Can Do It Yourself

>>>TIP<<<
You can purchase a three-day combination ticket to the Uffizi Gallery, the Pitti Palace, and Boboli Gardens for 50% off the price of single tickets. More information can be found at www.visitflorence.com. Note, that it does not include admission to the Academy to see "David."
>>><<<

MORE DETAILS OF THE DUOMO COMPLEX
There are two other buildings in the Piazza del Duomo. They are the Baptistery and Giotto's Campanile. The Campanile is that tall tower. Including the Cathedral, the three buildings are part of the UNESCO World Heritage Site. Those two other buildings are decorated in the same style as the Cathedral.

The tower is known as Giotto's Bell Tower. You guessed it, designed by "Giotto." It was started in 1334 and completed in 1359. The Campanile stands 400 feet and is about 45 feet on each side. If you are fit enough, you can climb the 414 steps. There is no elevator. In addition to Giotto's design, Pisano and Talenti also worked on the tower. Those many hexagon pieces of inlaid artwork depict scenes from the Old and New Testaments.

There are now seven bells in the tower. The first was installed in 1705, and the last five in 1956. The Baptistery (or Baptistry) building was built 1059-1128. It is of Florentine Romanesque design. There is also one more building you may want to visit on a separate ticket or one of the combination tickets. It is called the Museum dell' Opera del Duomo. It's right in front of the Cathedral and is committed to conserving the Duomo and other artworks. Here you will see the works of Michelangelo, Donatello, Raphael, Davinci, and more of Italy's Renaissance artists.
It should be time for lunch when you have completed your visit to the Duomo complex. So head to the Piazza della Signoria. It's only a few blocks away.

LUNCH ON THE PIAZZA DELLA SIGNORIA
The Piazza della Signoria is sometimes called the Palazzo Vecchio. It is the equivalent of a city hall plaza in most major

An Alternative to the Escorted Tour

American cities. It is the meeting place of the Florentines and is located just a few blocks from the Piazza del Duomo and one block from the Uffizi Gallery.

That big building you see in the Piazza is the town hall. You can't miss it with that crenelated fortress-type roof. The tower, or campanile with its crenelated top, is a part of the main building. It overlooks the copy of Michelangelo's David. Remember, when the original was moved to the Academy, they needed another one to replace it. So what you are looking at, is the replacement.

The name "Signoria" comes from the name of the ruling body of the Republic of Florence.

The square had several names. It wasn't until the Medici duke's residence was relocated across the Arno River to the Pitti Palace that they renamed the square "Signoria."

That building to the right of the Palazzo Vecchio (as you face the city hall) is known as the Loggia dei Lanzi. It backs the Uffizi Gallery. It is an open-air sculpture museum.

Around the Piazza, you will find numerous restaurants, stand-up bars, pastry, and gelato shops. Oh, I forgot to mention the excellent sandwiches (paninis) at several shops.

THE UFFIZI GALLERY
In terms of Renaissance art, the Uffizi Gallery is second only to the Academy and its David. The name "Uffizi" comes from the building that houses all these priceless paintings that used to be the offices of the official Florentine magistrates or judges. Hence, the name Uffizi means official. The building was started in 1560 and completed in 1581. The Uffizi is right up there with the Louver and the Prado. It was built for Cosimo I de' Medici. The top floor was made into a gallery for the Medici family to house their collection of Roman sculptures.

You can purchase your Uffizi tickets online at
https://www.uffizi.it/en/tickets

ITALY NO TOUR NEEDED
You Can Do It Yourself

Unless you are into sculpture, I recommend you start your visit at the Uffizi on the floor right below the last sculpture floor. The sculptures are located on the upper floors. You will need two hours to work your way down from floor to floor, viewing all the great paintings of the Renaissance. These paintings are priceless.

THE NUOVO MERCATO
After you visit the Uffizi, your next stop should be the Nuovo Mercato, originally called the Mercato del Porcellino. This mercato is where you want to do your inexpensive shopping, and I don't mean bottle openers or snowglobes that say Florence, which are made in China. They have everything from silk ties to leather jackets and beautiful handmade ladies' handbags and wallets, all made in Italy.

At the Mercato, if you purchase a boatload of items, expect to haggle on the price. You can conserve your cash as they take most credit cards. However, you will get a better price if you pay in Euros, as in CASH. I might note that there are also numerous stand-up bars around the Mercato. In this area be very street savvy, and watch your wallet and handbags. Here is how to get to the Mercato:

The Nuovo Mercato is easy to find:
1. Exit the Piazza della Signoria by locating the Il Bargello restaurant. Ask any of the locals or one of the Polizia or Carabinieri where the Il Bargello is, or better just ask "Doe Vay et. Nuovo Mercato?"
2. Go past the Bargello restaurant about one block.
3. Take a hard right on Via Calimala, and you will see the market about one block up.

THE PONTE VECCHIO BRIDGE
If you are finished at the Nuovo Mercato and still have some energy, and better some Euros left over; you might want to turn around and walk about four blocks to the Ponte Vecchio bridge for some high-end shopping, and a gelato (on the other side of the bridge).

An Alternative to the Escorted Tour

I can't say enough about this beautiful bridge turned into a high-end extravaganza of jewelry shops selling everything from fine watches to gold chains and everything you can think of.

As for the bridge itself, it was declared so beautiful that the Nazis in WW2 were ordered not to bomb it. However, buildings abutting the bridge were bombed and destroyed making the bridge impassable. The first bridge over the narrowest part of the Arno River was built in Ancient Roman times and was ordered by Roman Emperor Hadrian in 123AD.

Several bridges from 123AD forward were built at this point over the River. In medieval times and up to about 1700AD, vendors (and butchers) on the Bridge sold everything. The smell from the butchers was so intense that the City of Florence magistrates mandated only jewelry could be sold. In addition, the bridge would be closed to all vehicular traffic. And, that's the way you see it today. Over the years the Bridge suffered severe damage mostly due to floods on the Arno River. On November 4th, 1966 the Arno River flooded after several days of very hard rain. The river overflowed its banks and reached a high water mark of 13 feet (above the street) in the historic district. Several places were even flooded to a height of 22 feet. Fearing the Valdarno dam upriver would burst, and even flood more of the City, the authorities released the water from the dam into the river below. It rose so fast that there was not enough time to remove all the priceless paintings at the Uffizi Gallery. Many of the first and second-floor paintings were covered with water mud, and oil (which had seeped into the river). It took several years to patiently restore these priceless paintings.

When you walk around the historic district, you will notice markings on many of the buildings indicating "High Water Mark of the November 4, 1966 Flood." So much for the 1966 flood, and an overview of Florence, what to see and do.

Hopefully, I will have wet your appetite and got you "psyched" on your visit to Florence.

ITALY NO TOUR NEEDED
You Can Do It Yourself

ARRIVAL IN FLORENCE AND HOTELS

When your train arrives at the end of the line at Florence's Santa Maria Novella (SMN) station, you will find three exits after clearing the platform area. The main entrance is in front of you.

As you exit the station, if you look directly in front, you will notice the Santa Maria Novella church. Just a few words on the church: The Dominican Order built a new church in 1221 to replace the older 9th Century church. Construction started about 1276 and lasted 80 years. The Romanesque-Gothic bell tower and sacristy were finally completed. In 1360, Gothic arcades were added to the façade. The church was consecrated in 1420.

The basilica and the cloister house contain art treasures and funerary monuments. There are frescoes by masters of Gothic and early Renaissance. Unlike many other treasures in Florence, which the church financed, these were funded by the most important and wealthy Florentine families. By doing so, they ensured themselves a burial place on consecrated ground. This church is worth a minimum of a one-hour visit to admire these magnificent frescoes. Now back to your arrival at the Santa Maria Novella Stazione.

You should spot your hotel in relation to the train station. It is best if you exit the station on the right-hand side since there are several hotels in this area. It is best to spot your hotel on Google Maps or booking.com. If it is on the left-hand side of the station as you look at the map, then exit on the right-hand side as you leave the train. The boulevard is marked Via Luigi Alamanni. If your hotel is not on the left-hand side, proceed through the main or front entrance, where most of the hotels are located. They involve walking 1-4 blocks. Just watch the traffic. If you are going to Venice or Milan, choose a hotel close to the station instead of taking a taxi. If you want to stay at several upscale four and five-star hotels, you will find them abutting the Arno River. The walk over to the Arno River is too far. So follow the signs at SMN station to the taxi line. It should cost you no more than 10Euros for the trip over to your hotel on the Arno River.

An Alternative to the Escorted Tour

If you are using Florence as a hopoff point, you will find that you can rent a car at the SMN rail station or the airport just a few miles from SMN. You will have to take a taxi to the airport.

>>>TIP<<<   PALAZZO MAGNANI FERONI
If you want an authentic experience staying at a 16th Century palace, this opulent, all-suite hotel is a 13-minute walk from the Duomo di Firenze. It is called Palazzo Magnani Feroni. The palace sits one block back from the other side (Oltrarno) of the Arno River. I have stayed at the "Palazzo," and can personally tell you it's a "10" and a real experience. If you are driving, they have parking in an old carriage house. Also, bear in mind that parking is extremely limited in most of the hotels in the historic district. Check with your hotel about their parking policy.
>>><<<

Just a note, it's best to stay at any hotel within that four-block radius of the SMN rail station. However, you should note that you will still have to walk over to the historic district, where you will find the Uffizi Gallery, the Piazza Signoria, the Ponte Vecchio Bridge, and the Duomo complex, in addition to all the other interesting sites. I should note that for some reason, as you get closer to the Arno River, the hotel prices seem to go up.

If you book a hotel on the other side of the Arno River (Oltrarno area), you will have to take a taxi or drag your bags over one of the bridges. You should avoid, if possible, the crowds at the Ponte Vecchio bridge. Once again, it is best to stay at the hotels which are around the SMN rail station. Or, a better idea would be to stay in Montecatini. If you did not take the train into Florence, it would be best to check for parking before you enter the City.

MORE ON MONTECATINI- STAYING WITH THE LOCALS
I discussed this subject at the end of the Rome to Florence Chapter 9. However, if you are coming in from Venice or somewhere else, you need to read this.

The Village of Montecatini Terme (note you need the Terme) is about 50 minutes from Firenze. It's also 40 minutes from Pisa and Lucca and a little over two hours from the Cinque Terre.

124

ITALY NO TOUR NEEDED
You Can Do It Yourself

Montecatini makes an ideal base for exploring the area. In addition, hotels are almost half what you would expect to pay in the historic district of Florence. There is also an abundance of restaurants. Known for its natural underground thermal springs, Montecatini is one of eleven UNESCO World Heritage Spa sites in Western Europe. I might note the best thing about Montecatini is that it is not "touristy." Expect to pay normal prices for dining and other items. And, no there will not be any shops selling T-shirts and magnets for the refrigerator. So before committing to a hotel in Florence, consider the relaxed town of Montecatini. So much for the hotels and where to stay.

>>>TIP<<< WILD BOAR ANYONE?
Whether you are staying in Florence or Montecatini, do check out the Osteria Cinghiale Bianco. It's a short walk on the other side of the Arno (Oltrarno, Pitti Palace side) from the Ponte Vecchio bridge. In case you don't know, your Italian, "Cinghiale" is wild boar, which is excellent with wide noodle Pappadelli pasta. The Osteria Cinghiale is easy to find. Take a hard right at the far side of the Arno River after crossing the Ponte Vecchio bridge. Then go up about 2 blocks, and you will see the Cinghiale on the left-hand side. It's about a fifteen-minute walk from the train station, and you can gauge it from your hotel. If you are too bushed, take a taxi for about ten Euros.
On the return, if you are too tired to walk back, they will call a taxi for you; not a lot of Euros here. Also, do check their opening times. I believe the trains run to Montecatini every hour till at least 11PM. So, you can dine and head back to Montecatini after that, Sambucca or Amaretto di Sarono.
>>><<<

Once you check in or at least drop your bags, you are ready to explore the City of the Renaissance: The David, the Uffizi, the Duomo, the Piazza Signoria, Ponte Vecchio, and, of course, the Nuovo Mercato are all waiting for you.

If you are taking the Three Capitals Tour, your next destination is Venice. However, we have some decisions to make first:

An Alternative to the Escorted Tour

DECISIONS, DECISIONS, AND MORE DECISIONS
1. Do I go to Venice IT-FLORENCE TO VENICE Chapter 14
   -or-
2. Do I continue to stay in Florence or Montecatini and
   do those days trips: FLORENCE EXTRA DAYS Chapter 11:
   Pisa/Lucca
   Cinque Terre
   Siena
   San Gimignano
   -or-
3. Perhaps explore the hilltop towns of Tuscany and Umbria
TUSCANY/UMBRIA HILLTOP TOWNS, Chapter 13.

While all the above day trips or perhaps weeklong stays can be accomplished by train, it is best visited by car.

One exception, if you are going to Venice and staying in the Lagoon (Venice Chapter 15) or even in Venice Mestre, consider turning in that rental at the SMN rail station in Florence or the airport (FLR). You should compare the cost of the rental for several days, fuel, tolls, and parking against the rail tickets to Venice. It may be less of a hassle and even save money.

>>>TIP<<< TIMING YOUR RETURN RENTAL IN FLORENCE
It may be better to do those Florence Extra Days i.e. Pisa/Lucca and Cinque Terre at the beginning of your Florence visit, then turn in your rental when you don't need it for the next three days in Florence, and then go on to Venice via train.
>>><<<

If you have flown in directly to Florence from major European hubs, or have taken the train up from Rome or the Amalfi area, it is best, as stated above to rent that car after you visit Florence for those two full days. You should consider your hopoff rental as either returning it to your Florence location or driving it back to your flyout airport. You need to weigh the cost of a different return location with what it would cost to take the train e.g. drop the rental in Milan airport and fly home from Milan.

CHAPTER 11

FLORENCE EXTRA DAYS PISA/LUCCA SIENA & SANGIMIGNANO MONTECATINE TERME CINQUE TERRE

Did you know places like Pisa and Medieval Lucca are less than one hour from Florence? These are excellent places to see if you have an additional day or two. If you want to spend another hour on the road, you can visit one or two of the towns in the Cinque Terre. I also provide details on how to reach Siena and San Gimignano. So, it is best that you read on.

OVERVIEW- THE THREE FLORENCE DAY TRIPS

If you have two or three extra days in Florence, a/k/a, the capital of Tuscany, you should plan on enough time to fit in all these four locations. Some of them can be done on the same day. Pisa and Lucca are easy to do in one day. Siena and San Gimignano are a little more complex. If you plan your day accordingly, it is relatively easy to visit San Gimignano at the end of the day after leaving Siena at about 2PM.

If you can spare a whole day, you can also pay a visit to the Cinque Terre or, should I say, one (possibly two) of the five towns. You pick it. But my favorite is Manarola. Not too much history in the five towns, just beautiful villages with gorgeous houses painted with those pastel colors strung against the mountainside, often confused with a picture of Positano.

HEADING WEST- PISA AND LUCCA

There is ample public parking at both Lucca and Pisa. You should note that in Pisa, all cars must park in the large municipal lot about one-half mile away from the Tower complex. However, a courtesy

127

An Alternative to the Escorted Tour

tram every 10 minutes will take you to and from the Tower. The best way, without any hassles, is to take the train. Trains run about two per hour between SMN and Pisa Centrale. The trip takes about one hour. You can drive it also in one hour. Your credit card will work with the tolls no problems.

First, here is a quick overview of Pisa and Lucca:

Both Lucca and Pisa lie due west of Florence toward the Tyrrhenian Sea. They are only 27 minutes away by a connecting train. So you can take the train to either and hop that "shuttle" train to the other. You can return to Florence from either Lucca or Pisa. If you are staying in Montecatini, you can only return from Lucca since Pisa to Montecatini will require a change of trains.

PISA
If you don't know the name or what's in Pisa, you should probably be planning a visit to New York City, not Italy. Yes, everyone knows the Leaning Tower of Pisa. It's a must to visit. You will need 2-3 hours here.

HISTORY OF PISA
The name "Pisa" means in Etruscan "mouth." the town of Pisa dates to about 200BC. In ancient times, about the 5th Century BC, it was inhabited by the Etruscans. It lies at the mouth of the Arno River. It's the same Arno River you see in Florence. At one time, the actual city of Pisa was closer to the Ligurian Sea. However, over time it has receded from 2.5 miles to about six miles from the coast. This river recession made Pisa an excellent port on the Mediterranean (actually the part of the "Med" known as the Ligurian Sea), the next port being Genova to the north and Ostia (Rome's old port) to the south. If you are driving up the coast road, you can see that marshy area where the sea was about 2,000 years ago. Before the river receded, ships could navigate up the Arno into the city of Pisa.

In the 1980s and 1990s, archaeological remains were discovered dating to the 5th Century BC. Of considerable importance was the discovery of a tomb of an Etruscan prince. At about 180BC, Pisa

ITALY NO TOUR NEEDED
You Can Do It Yourself

became a Roman colony. The Romans used the port as a war base against the Gauls and Ligurians.

During the final days of the Roman Empire (about 476AD), Pisa became a leading trading partner of destinations that could easily be reached from its strategic port. These were the islands of Sardinia and Corsica and the port cities of France and Spain.

Over the years, the Pisans were naval warriors and fought against dozens of invading navies. Most of the time, they were successful. In about 1290, the Pisans lost a major sea battle with the Genoese fleet (from Genoa). From here, it was all downhill for the Pisans. The maritime strength of Pisa would never be again. Pisa continued to be just a trading port.

THE LEANING TOWER OF PISA

First, few travelers realize that the Leaning Tower is in a complex called the Piazza dei Miracoli or the Plaza of Miracles. The complex is also a UNESCO World Heritage Site. It contains the Pisa Cathedral, the Pisa Baptistry, and the Tower, also known as the Campanile. The complex is about two blocks wide and five blocks long and is enclosed by a wall. There is also a small cemetery, but it is known as a "Camposanto" or the holy fields, which dates from 1464. It's that large, long building on the far left, which abuts the perimeter wall as you enter the complex. You will notice it if you look on the other side of the Baptistery and the Basilica. The Camposanto is home to 84 Roman sarcophagi and numerous works of art.

There is no charge for entering the Plaza of Miracles. However, there is a charge for climbing the Tower of Pisa.

To climb the Tower, you must purchase a timed admission ticket and then wait in a long line. There is no elevator, and you must negotiate 296 steps against opposing tourists coming down. I do not recommend climbing the Tower for the view or standing outside the top of the Tower for a photo op. You will see many tourists taking that picture of their partner or a friend pushing up the Tower from the grassy area in front.

An Alternative to the Escorted Tour

The website is https://www.towerofpisa.org/tickets/.

Here are the technical facts about the Tower:
It is 183 feet from the ground to the top; you can figure out about ten stories. After a "heave-ho," with lead weights and a pushup of the Tower with a new concrete base, the corrected lean is slightly less than 4%. Taking into account the foundation, the Tower is almost 200 feet tall. The outer diameter is about 50 feet, and the inner diameter is 25 feet. Before the correction, the lean was 6%, and it appeared that it would fall eventually. The weight of the Tower is 16,200 tons; there are seven bells in the belfry.

Here is a quick recap of the construction:
It took a little over 200 years to ultimately build the Tower. The foundation was a gift of Donna Berta di Bernardo in 1172AD. In 1173, the primary stones which still form the foundation were laid. In 1178 the Tower began to sink during the second-floor construction. This sinking occurred because of the extremely weak subsoil. Construction was halted for almost 100 years as Pisa went to war with Genova, Florence, and Lucca. In about 1264, it was observed that the soil under the Tower was becoming unstable since the existing structure was compressing the underlying soil. In that year, they noticed that the Tower was beginning to tilt. So, in 1272, work restarted with cut marble from mountain pits near Pisa. Construction proceeded by making one side of the Tower floors taller than the other. They felt that this would correct the leaning.

Work stopped again in 1284 when Genova defeated the Pisans at the Battle of Meloria. Work continued several years later until the 7th floor was completed in 1319. The belfry was added in 1372. There are seven bells, each representing a note from the major scale. The completion of the belfry was achieved in 1655. The Tower continued to lean, oy, oy, oy.
In 1990, the Tower was at a tilt of almost 6%, not too good. If nothing were done, the Tower would ultimately fall. Over the years before 1990, numerous efforts were made to restore the Tower to an upright position. However, some even worsened the tilt. The Tower was closed in 1990 and re-opened in 2001 after a significant stabilization effort. The effort involved pushing the Tower back

ITALY NO TOUR NEEDED
You Can Do It Yourself

with lead weights, removing the bells in the belfry, removing soil, and replacing the foundation under the base of the Tower. Here is how they did it:

Finally, in 1993, the Italian Government devised a plan to tilt the Tower back to at least 3-4%. It was decided not to eliminate the lean since the "Leaning" Tower was a key tourism draw. Let's face it: who would come to see the Tower of Pisa if it were not leaning? The British proposed, and the Italian Government took them up on the offer. The plan worked with the lead weights used to bring it back temporarily as it fell back in a 3-4% tilt into a hole created by 43 screw augers removing the earth. The lead weights were then removed, and the Tower re-opened. It should last now for almost 300 years. The Tower tilt, since 2001, has been measured. In 2008, the Tower was completely stabilized, and there was no more progression in the tilt.

Four earthquakes have occurred throughout the tower's life. For some reason, the soft earth below is believed to have cushioned the quake's shock, thus allowing no damage to the Tower. So much for the tower's history.

If you have the time, I suggest you visit the Basilica and the Baptistery near the Tower.

Of interest, aside from the lean of the Tower, is that Galileo (the astronomer) who lived in Pisa is said to have dropped two cannonballs of different masses to demonstrate that their speed of descent was independent of their mass, thus reinforcing the law of free fall. Regarding Galileo, Fibonacci, the famous mathematician (The Fibonacci sequence), was also from Pisa and lived about 400 years before Galileo.

Abutting and entering the complex are fast food, gelato stands, and souvenir shops. There is lots of shopping at those stalls. You can negotiate the price. Depending on the day of the week, you will also find those "Senegal or Dakar Merchants" selling everything on blankets, from fake Rolex watches to copies of Gucci handbags on the walkway leading up to the Tower. Best to

131

An Alternative to the Escorted Tour

buy them before the local police raid them, which usually takes place every 3-4 hours. And yes, you can negotiate the price.

No visit to the Tower complex is complete without a visit to the Cathedral of Pisa. The Cathedral is the large church in the Plaza of Miracles. Here are the basic facts: Its style is medieval Roman, also known as Romanesque architecture. It is dedicated to the Assumption of the Virgin Mary. It is the oldest of the three structures, consecrated in 1118AD. Construction began in 1063 and was completed in 1092. Enlargements were made in the 12th century, and a new façade was built. The cathedral's roof had to be replaced after a fire in 1595. The inside is worth a visit. Of interest are the coffered matrix ceiling and the Renaissance paintings. The dome underwent restoration from 2015 to 2018.

That smaller round building, which I might add is also tilting, is the Baptistery, which replaced an older baptistery. It is officially called the Pisa Baptistery of St. John. Construction started in 1152 and was completed in 1363. Yes, 1363! It was the second building to be built on the Plaza of Miracles. It was a "slow build," taking 211 years. Because of the soft soil below, it, like the Tower of Pisa, also began to tilt. It now tilts .6 degrees (a little more than one-half of a degree).

Leaving the Plaza of Miracles is quite simple. It will cost you about three Euros more than two people taking a bus back to the central rail station. So best to take a taxi back to the railway station. Note Pisa has two rail stations. You want Pisa Centrale. You can easily walk it. The distance is about one mile, and it's flat. However, after doing all that walking, you may be bushed. It is best as stated above, to just take a taxi for about 6Euros.

On exiting the complex, go straight past those food stalls to that main boulevard (Via Bananno Pisano), and you will see several taxi stands there. If you are parked in that massive parking lot, the best is to spot that tram for your return trip. I believe it departs from the same place as the drop-off point.

>>>TIP<<<   LEANING TOWER PROBLEM
After the recent "fix" on the tower, it is now set to last for a minimum of 200 years. No worries here. However, if there is a

major earthquake, the tower will definitely fall. Soooo, it is best to visit it on your first trip, else you may visit a pile of rubble.
>>><<<

LUCCA

Lucca is one of the walled cities of the medieval ages, which is not on top of a hill. However, most of the wall and the old gates remain. Lucca is flat and home to Giacomo Puccini (1858-1924), the famous operatic composer (Madam Butterfly, La Boheme). Lots of restaurants and just a delightful place to stroll and visit all the churches and squares. You will also need three hours here; if you figure lunch, anticipate four hours. There is no charge to enter the town. Also, along with the easy walking, the city's main gate is directly across from the rail station. If you are taking the train, it is best to note the return times to Florence and Montecatini. Driving is easy as the A11 affords two exits for Lucca (east and west). Either one will bring you into town. On the A11 the tolls accept all credit cards. Parking is plentiful in Lucca. However, make sure you feed those meters.

There are several ways to plan your visit to Lucca:
1. The classic half day from Pisa in the morning i.e., you visit Pisa in the morning, then arrive in Lucca for lunch about 1-2PM,
2. A full day in Lucca
3. A half day in the morning and then onto the Cinque Terre for an overnighter, you are only an hour away.

Like many towns in this area, the Town of Lucca was inhabited by the ancient Etruscans. The City's name appears to come from the Ligurians (Ligurian Sea), who settled this area after the Etruscans. It means "marsh" and dates from about the 3rd century. In about 180BC, the Romans took over and created a town hall in 89BC. The wall around the town is actually from the medieval era and not from Rome or ancient Roman times.

The Roman's created the rectangular street plan. The outline of the original Roman amphitheater can still be seen in the Piazza dell' Anfiteatro. What is left of the theater sits about nine feet

An Alternative to the Escorted Tour

below the center of the large oval piazza. It was built during the 2nd century and could hold 10,000 spectators.

Lucca was an important city and medieval fortress in the 6th century. In 553AD, Narses took over the city. From 576 to 797, the Lombards came down from Lombardy, took it over, and made it the capital of the duchy, which also included a large part of Tuscany and the province of Viterbo (part of the same province of Rome, "Lazio"). Lucca minted its coins.

There was a significant presence of Jews in 859AD, led by the Kalonymos family. The City was one of the leading destinations of the Via Francigena, which was one of the major pilgrimage routes to Rome from the north.

The main products of Lucca during the 11th Century were silk fabric woven with gold or silver threads. Production of silk and woven silk products continued for the next 200 years. In 1160, after Matilda of Tuscany passed away, the City became an independent commune with a charter. For almost 500 years, Lucca remained an independent republic. About 1273 and again in 1277, and as far into 1789, the French Revolution, Lucca was controlled by numerous foreign entities. From then on, Lucca would be the second largest Italian city-state after Venice, with a republican constitution.

Lucca lost its independence in 1860 when it became part of the Kingdom of Sardinia under the control of the Grand Duchy of Tuscany. It became part of the Italian state in 1861.

Okay, so much for a short history. Now, what do we do in Lucca? Here is a list:
If you have a full two hours, consider walking on top of the wall around the city. It is about 2.5 miles. You can stop for a café and a gelato at the halfway point or when you are pooped. There are numerous places where ramps have been installed that you may exit onto the local streets of the town.

Look around for the Guinigi Tower. It is built between two mansions that date from the 14th and 15th Centuries. You can

ITALY NO TOUR NEEDED
You Can Do It Yourself

climb the tower. However, there are an awful lot of stairs in this 135-foot-tall tower. Note, it's the one where trees are growing on the top. There is a taller tower (campanile) next to the Cathedral of Lucca. This one has a crenel top and is about 210 feet tall. Work on that church started in 1063 and was redone in the Gothic style in the 14th century. It is worth a visit.

If you want lunch, stop at one of the many eateries at the Piazza dell Anfiteatro (Plaza of the Amphitheater). There are numerous churches and squares to visit in Lucca. Shopping is also excellent as there are souvenirs of the operas by Puccini.

I saved the best place to visit as the last in line. However, you might want to make it your first stop. It's the Puccini Museum. If you are an opera fan, this is the place. You would need an hour or two here. It is located at Corte San Lorenzo, Number 8.

DAY TRIPS TO SIENA AND SAN GIMIGNANO
BELOW IS ADDITIONAL INFORMATION:
Siena and San Gimignano have also been covered under the Northbound itinerary IT-ROME-TO-FLORENCE, Chapter 9. Some information has been repeated since I do not know if you stopped at these historic cities/towns before Florence. Siena and San Gimignano are easily reachable by train or car from the Florence SMN train station:

DESTINATION	BY CAR	BY TRAIN/bus
San Gimignano	1.25 hrs	1.45 hrs
Siena	1.75 hrs	2.25 hrs

If traveling from Montecatini, add one more hour.

Both San Gimignano and Siena have ample parking. The best is to visit both towns by rental car since San Gimignano requires a transfer for a 20-minute bus ride from Poggibonsi to the town muni parking lot. In addition, if coming from Montecatini you will have to change trains at Florence SMN. You should note that San Gimignano is on the same rail line as Siena.

An Alternative to the Escorted Tour

SAN GIMIGNANO AND SIENA OVERVIEW

As stated before, these medieval Tuscan cities can be visited on the same day. Just a little planning is needed. First, you must visit Siena in the morning and have lunch there. Once you are on top of the hill, there is flat walking throughout the historic center. If you depart the "Campo," the main square, at about 1-2PM you will have enough time to visit San Gimignano, the Medieval town of towers. If you see the town the way I suggest, San "Gimi" becomes all downhill. Using my suggestions allows a stroll and final shopping before you leave the area.

To visit both towns on the same day, you must depart a local train from Florence's Santa Maria Novella 9-10AM. At this time, don't purchase any additional rail tickets. You may be too bushed to visit San Gimignano or wish to stay in Siena all day.

>>>TIP<<<

If you are planning on visiting San Gimignano in the afternoon, I usually don't suggest purchasing any "heavy," e.g., salami, a bottle of wine, or souvenirs in Siena. You will be forced to carry them around San Gimignano. You can buy most of the stuff that you see in Siena also in San Gimignano. The best souvenirs in San Gimignano are the area's products, wine, salumi, olives, etc.

>>><<<

SIENA

Siena is a hilltop town (it's really a city) built in the medieval ages. Like many historical sites in Italy, it is also a UNESCO World Heritage Site. In addition to the historical significance, Siena is best known for the twice-annual horse race and exhibition known as the "Palio di Siena" held in the "Campo." The term "burnt sienna" comes from the fact that the buildings in the Palazzo are all that burnt red/yellow color known now as "burnt sienna." Note it's not a mistake. The color has two "n"s.

In the past 20 years, the City has built escalators and people movers. There are now three escalator complexes. I think the one from the rail station may be the longest escalator in the world outside of the ones you see at airports. It stretches almost three football fields. That's about 1000 feet. It will lift you to the top of the historic district in about 10 minutes.

>>>TIP<<<
Before you leave the rail station, find out when the trains depart for San Gimignano (going north). The fare is less than $4, and the journey is less than 45 minutes. The best is to check with the ticket agent. Make a note for trains around 2-4PM which will allow you about two hours to visit San Gimignano. You don't want to arrive at the Siena rail station only to wait 40 minutes or so for the next train to "San Gimi." Note, the stop is called Poggibonsi-San Gimignano.

If you are driving, you can figure about 45 minutes. The main road to San Gimignano is a national road. You can't miss it. All you need do is follow the signs to Firenze and exit at Poggibonsi-San Gimignano. There are no tolls.
>>><<<

If you are arriving by train, follow the signs to the escalator, which will take you to Porto Camollia. If you are arriving by car, there are plenty of public parking lots.

I usually recommend parking directly against the City walls. Just follow the road around the walls, and you will see lots of parking "Parcheggio." Remember to purchase a ticket from the machine, or else you will have a costly souvenir on your windshield when you return.

On arrival at the top of the hill, you must make a strategic decision. Do you head for the Piazza del Campo first or see some of those gorgeous churches? The problem with Siena, it is just one giant maze, and I mean an absolute labyrinth! My suggestion is to make your way to the Piazza del Campo and locate a place for lunch. Then, after lunch, you can explore some of the churches. My first choice is, without a doubt, the Basilica Cateriniana San Domenico, followed by the Duomo di Siena. The first runner-up is the Basilica of San Francisco. All of them contain exquisite Renaissance works.

An Alternative to the Escorted Tour

Once you make your way into the "Campo," you may be tempted to climb the Torre del Mangia (the Campanile), which is that big tower (about the same height as a football field) in front of you. There are 200 steps and no elevator. There is an admission charge of ten Euros per person. You can figure a half-hour for the up and down, great for photo-ops. It is best to climb the "Torre" before lunch. That building to the right is known as the Palazzo Pubblico or, better, the city hall. It is now a museum.

If you are of the Jewish faith, you may want to spend a few minutes after lunch visiting the Synagogue of Siena (at least the medieval one). It's easy to find because it lies on the street directly behind that large tower (the campanile)- the one you don't want to climb unless you had your Wheaties for breakfast. Just follow the signs to the "sinagoga," or ask any local.

A SHORT HISTORY OF SIENA- JUST THE FACTS
From what we know, Siena was founded at the beginning of the 4th Century BC as a Roman Colony during the reign of the Roman Emperor Augustus. However, it is believed that about 900 BC, it was inhabited by a small group of Etruscans who called it Saina. The Roman colony was called Saena Lulia. It did not flourish under Roman rule because it was "off the beaten path," i.e., no significant roads and ports existed.

For about 600 years, control of Siena bounced around between various archdioceses, namely Arezzo. It was not until the beginning of the 10th Century AD that Siena became an important trade route between Rome and Florence. In the 12th Century, Siena went to war against Florence.

Siena was a major Italian banking center until the 14th Century. The oldest bank in the world still in existence is the Monte dei Paschi Bank of Italy. The bank has been operating since 1472.

During the Renaissance, the arts made their mark on the churches of Siena.

ITALY NO TOUR NEEDED
You Can Do It Yourself

The Campo was a marketplace just before the 13th Century. It was built on a sloping site and paved with red bricks in a herringbone design.

Here are some questions you probably want to ponder as you eat that great pizza in the Piazza del Campo, or better, wait for it to be delivered to your table: You will find all the answers to these questions in Chapter 9.

Q: Why is the Piazza divided into nine pie-shaped sections? Does this represent a pizza?

Q: What's with all those flags?
Q: And finally, what's with that fountain in the middle of the square? Or shall I say, at the top of the square?

If you are ready to leave Siena and go to San Gimignano, you need to walk back to Porto Camollia or take a taxi to the train station. If you care not to walk back to the train station, there is a major taxi stand at the Piazza Independenza. The taxi stand is no more than one block from the Piazza del Campo. In terms of proximity, it is about one block behind that gorgeous fountain known as Fonte Gaia. If you are lost, ask one of the locals, "Doe Vay et Piazza Independenaz- Taxi." The fare back to the stazione usually runs about ten Euros. If you know where you parked your car, the taxi will also take you back there. You can figure about twelve Euros.

Now onto San Gimignano. If you have driven, follow the signs to Firenze. If you are going by rail, board the train bound for Firenze and exit at Poggibonsi-San Gimignano station. By the way, a bus will be waiting for you, which will take you to the main parking lot at San Gimignano, where you will find facilities, a café, and a moderate-size super mercato.

SAN GIMIGNANO- THE TOWN OF TOWERS
No other town or city in the world compares to this place. This is not New York or Chicago. These towers go back 800 years, not eighty. About ten years ago, I walked into a real estate office and asked about buying a home here. That's how much I love this

town, not to mention it has the best gelato shop in all of Italy, or maybe in the world! Let's face it, how many times have you downed a gelato of cream with saffron and pine nuts?

>>>TIP<<<
If you are arriving by train from Florence or Siena at the Poggibonsi-San Gimignano rail station, you need to note the times for the return trains to Florence. You can ask that shuttle bus driver. If you are staying in Montecatini Terme, you still need to change trains in Florence.

If you are going on to Montecatini Terme, one ticket will do it all. On that big red machine, just type in Montecatini. On arrival at Firenze SMN, you won't have to buy another ticket from SMN to Montecatini. However, it would help if you still gauged your time back to the station. My suggestion would be to allow 30 minutes in total. The taxi ride back to the station is only 10 minutes. However, you must find a taxi (in the main parking lot next to the "Coop" market) and buy that return ticket at the station. You may consider the shuttle bus back to the station, however, it takes about twenty minutes and it may not be worth it even if you are on a tight budget, as a taxi will cost you 12-15Euros. The bus departs from the main parking lot and will cost you no more than two Euros. Now on to the history of San Gimignano. Many of the facts are covered in Chapter 9.
>>><<<

San Gimignano is a walled hilltop medieval town in the province of Siena, Tuscany. And, yes, it is also a UNESCO World Heritage Site. It is best known for its medieval architecture and a dozen towers remaining. Those towers you see are houses. The town dates from about the 3rd Century BC when it was an Etruscan village. Two brothers, Muzio and Silvio, fled the Roman Republic for a hilltop village called Valdelsa. The brothers built two castles atop that hill and called it Silvia. The name was changed in 450AD by Bishop Geminianus. The Bishop was able to spare the destruction of the two castles from Atilla the Hun.

In the 6th and 7th Centuries, the wall was built around the town. From about 900AD forward, the village was controlled by

ITALY NO TOUR NEEDED
You Can Do It Yourself

Volterra's bishops, another medieval hilltop town a few miles away. The small town was called the "Castle of San Gimignano."

During the Middle Ages and the Renaissance, San Gimignano was a stop-over on the Via Francigena road, stretching from England across Europe and through the Apennine Peninsula, now known as Italy. This stop-over point hosted pilgrimages en route to Rome and further to the Holy Land through ports on the Apennine Peninsula.

In 1199AD, the fledging town became independent of Volterra. Public buildings and churches were built. However, this peace did not last long. For the next 200 years, there were conflicts between the Guelphs and the Ghibellines, and to further add more conflict, the wealthy families of San Gimignano began to fight each other; enter the towers.

The competing families of San Gimignano started to build tower houses to house their families. At the end of the medieval period, there were 72 tower houses. Today 14 remain standing. As each tower was erected, the next tower to be built had to be taller. This competition was like "keeping up with the Jones."

This competition continued until the town council said no tower could be taller than the campanile tower abutting the Palazzo Comunale, which is 230 feet tall. The city continued to grow until the Black Plague hit most of Europe in 1348 when about half of the population of San Gimignano died. Florence later governed the town. You will note throughout the Town, Gothic houses built in the Florentine style. Many of the towers had to be leveled to the height of the abutting buildings. This lasted until the 19th Century when San Gimignano became a tourist attraction. The present-day towers can be seen for miles.

Oh, one more item. People always ask, "What happened to all the other towers"? Simple, they were lost to wars, neglect, and finally, urban renewal.

An Alternative to the Escorted Tour

Here is a little geography of the town. First, only three sides of the old wall still exist. The fourth wall was torn down during the 16th Century. There are now only eight entrances from the road which encircles the town. If you have a car, it's a nice "drive- around," and will take you no more than ten minutes to circumnavigate the town.

I have visited San Gimignano about a dozen times. There are two main piazzas. The first is the Piazza della Cisterna. It looks like a triangle. You can't miss it. It is the one with the water well in the middle. The well dates from 1346AD. Across from one end is the Hotel Cisterna, and on the other side is the Hotel Leon Bianco. On the other side of this triangle, you will find the famous Gelateria Dondoli, supposedly the best gelato in Italy.

The second piazza is the Piazza Duomo. It's just off the Piazza della Cisterna next to the Dondoli Gelato shop. With your back to the well, go toward the right passing the side of the Hotel Leon Bianco. In about 200 feet, you will come to the Piazza Duomo. The first building on the left is the Palazzo Comunale. It is essentially the town hall. You can't miss it as it has a campanile (Torre Grossa) on the right side of it. Continuing to your right is the Collegiate Church. If you continue past the Collegiate Church several blocks, you will come upon a small square with a street to the right and one to the left. The Piazza Agostino is named for the Church of Sant' Agostino on that square. All three churches are worth a short visit to view the beautiful artwork on the walls and ceilings.

NAVIGATING AROUND SAN GIMIGNANO

San Gimignano is one town that is not a maze and one town where you want to do some serious shopping. There are two main streets, and they are wide. The first one (Via San Giovanni) starts from that small park, "Piazzale Montemaggio" at Viale Roma and works its way uphill at about a 5-7% incline. It starts at the beginning, where you come up from the parking lot and pass the "Coop" supermarket.

San Giovanni is lined with all types of shops and eateries. In about six blocks, it takes a bend to the right and goes under a house (yes, a house) before coming out at the Piazza Cisterna; note the queue on the left in front of the Dondoli Gelato shop (Gelateria Dondoli). As you pass the city hall with that big tower and the Collegiate Church, bear to your right down the Via San Matteo until you get to Via Cellolese, then go right for about two blocks. Here you will find the Piazza St. Agostino with the church by the same name located on it. If you don't make the right-hand turn on Via Celloese, you will wind up going out the Porta Matteo gate onto the ring road. You must turn around, walk back a block, and take a hard left.

There are ample public facilities in the town, or better, swing into a stand-up bar or a sandwich shop and ask to use the toilet. I find it best to order an Americano Coffee and THEN head for the toilet (WC). It's not a requirement but a nice gesture.

HOW TO VISIT SAN GIMIGNANO
If you have decided to drive here, you will find a municipal parking lot about three blocks from the Piazzale Montemaggio Park at the beginning of the Viale Roma and San Giovanni. A medium-sized supermarket (The Coop) and café abutting the parking lot. You cannot miss it. Follow the ramp and steps to the right, bringing you up to the Viale Roma at the park's far end. If you are driving, you can follow that ring road until you get a parking spot. Remember to feed that meter or else a ticket. Because San Gimignano is a hilltop town, what goes up must come down. So either way, you will huff and puff.

Return by train or your rental car to Florence or Montecatini. You should be at your hotel about 7PM, just in time for a snooze, a shower, and dinner at 8PM.

MONTECATINI (TERME)   A DAY TRIP
If you will not be staying in Florence and instead will be staying in Montecatini (wise idea) there are several very interesting sites in this historic town. The Town is also excellent for a day trip from Florence. For one thing, no visit to Montecatini is complete without a trip up to Montecatini Alto. The "Alto" is perched on a hilltop overlooking the town and the surrounding countryside. Yes, you can take a taxi up to the top. However, the Montecatini

143

An Alternative to the Escorted Tour

Funicular is only a 15-minute walk from the Montecatini Centro rail station, where all trains stop. The fee is 7.5Euros for a round trip ticket. On top of the hill, you will find several excellent restaurants which are great for lunch. There is some shopping and of course a few gelato shops. You should allow at least two hours for your visit to the "Alto" and a minimum of three hours to walk the main street and visit the parks in the Town itself.

After you are all shopped out, do visit the Pasticceria Giovannini for a piece of that great Italian pastry, or better take it back to your hotel room and devour it there. Remember to ask for those plastic forks.

If you are interested in visiting the "Baden-Baden" of Italy, you have found it. Just pack your swimming attire and head to one of the thermal baths. More information can be had at www.visitmontecatine.com

THE CINQUE TERRE IS A DAY TRIP FROM FLORENCE AND IS COMPLETELY COVERED UNDER ITS OWN IN CHAPTER 12, THE CINQUE TERRE.

CHAPTER 12

THE CINQUE TERRE

THE CINQUE TERRE- AN OVERVIEW

First of all, let's get it right. The Cinque Terre pronounced, "CHINK-QUAY-TER-RAY." The Five Lands (five towns) is a coastal area against the Ligurian Sea (part of the Mediterranean) about 75 miles south of Genova and 60 miles north of Pisa. It is part of the province known as Liguria. The five towns that are UNESCO World Heritage sites are (starting from the north) Monterosso al Mare, Vernazza, Corniglia, Manarola, and Riomaggiore. They are one of the National Parks of Italy. Due to the beauty of the colorful houses perched on the cliffs, the five towns have been one of the most photographed areas of Italy.

Several towns, namely Manarola, are often confused with Positano in the Amalfi area south of Naples. The Cinque Terre has become Italy's "hot" tourist spot in the past thirty years. In peak season, the towns are flooded with day trippers from all over Italy. Rail, small roads, and boats connect the five villages. Footpaths and hiking trails also connect the towns. A fee is charged and maps provided if you want to hike from one town to the others.

The towns were accessed only by boat until 1874 when the Italian State Railway (FS) decided to connect La Spezia in the south with Genoa in the north. Tunnels were bored in the rock mountains abutting the sea until all the towns were connected. For most of the journey via rail, the trains will pass through 51 tunnels connecting the five villages. It was a significant engineering feat considering it was done in 1874 when the tools (tunnel boring machines) used today were unavailable. Some tunnels are so short that the trains need to stop in them to access the stations. In addition, the train tracks are laid about four feet from the ocean and are perched on the rocky incline.

145

An Alternative to the Escorted Tour

You can visit at least one of the five towns if you have a whole day. I have found that it is doable to see two of the towns but difficult. So here are my recommendations:

First, you need to read this paragraph two or three times. Do NOT attempt to visit any of the five towns by car. Second, if you have rented a standard transmission car, you will probably burn out the clutch, the brakes, or both. Secondly, you risk an accident if you are backing up (especially in a downhill location) in any parking areas, which may also be difficult to find. If driving, you will probably only make it to the first town, Riomaggiore.

TWO APPROACHES TO VISITING THE CINQUE TERRE
There are only two ways to see the Cinque Terre. First, you can go for the day or take it easy and overnight there. Many folks prefer to overnight in one of the abutting towns.

>>>TIP<<<
If you insist on driving from Florence or Montecatini, your best bet is to drive to the La Spezia Centrale rail station and find a parking space. You may have to walk about eight blocks—no big deal into the abutting area, where you will find a parking space on the street. At La Spezia Centrale, you will join the herds of people and those tour buses full of tourists waiting for the train (about every 20 minutes) to go up to the five towns. It's about twelve minutes to the first town, Riomaggiore, and another five minutes to Manarola. So once again, don't drive! Watch your personal possessions on the train and the snack bar.
>>><<<

QUICK HISTORY OF THE FIVE TOWNS
Like the other 57 other UNESCO World Heritage Sites, the Cinque Terre is also one. The Cinque Terre is also the smallest National Park of Italy. As far as I know, there are no historic Roman sites to visit. As far as we know, the Cinque Terre towns go back to the 11th Century. At that time, the inhabitants began to terrace the hills and grow olives and grapes. Farming continued until the 19th Century and into the 20th Century when the houses you see began to flourish. It wasn't until the 1900's that the Cinque Terre towns became a tourist attraction.

ITALY NO TOUR NEEDED
You Can Do It Yourself

The environment continues to do a number on the five towns. Over the last twenty years, torrential storms have caused many landslides. In addition, the Cinque Terre is in a low Earthquake zone. In January 2023, there were tremors of 1.0, and in 2022, the area was hit with five quakes of more than 4.0. So if you are there and the ground rumbles, it's no big deal.

HOW TO VISIT THE CINQUE TERRE
I describe a day trip to Manarola either from Florence or Montecatini Terme. It is best to depart between 8 and 9AM by rail or car. If you figure the train from La Spezia (best approach) you should be at Manarola about 12-1PM. This is perfect for lunch. If you want to do the Walk of the Lovers (via della Amore) you need to get off the train in Riomaggiore which is the first stop after boarding the train at La Spezia.

It would be best if you took a train to Riomaggorie (see below) or Manarola. There is no other way around it unless you take a day trip on tour (best to check with your hotel). That bus tour is a good idea. However, they still will take you to La Spezia rail station for that 12-minute ride to Rio Maggiore. There may even be enough time at the end of the day to visit Pisa. However, it will probably be a long day with a departure at about 8AM from Florence. If it's a van tour, expect it to be about $150 or more per person. Best to do it on your own: It's simple and cheap.

After almost ten years of closure, the "Via dell Amore" (walk of the lovers) re-opened. It was closed because of horrific landslides, which destroyed a section of the walk. You need to purchase a rail ticket in Montecatini or Florence for the first town which is Riomaggiore. There usually is a connection at La Spezia. Otherwise, after you park your car in La Spezia just purchase a ticket to Riomaggiore at the rail station (stazione). The stop in Riomaggiore is weird. The train will stop half-way in a tunnel. Here you must exit the train and follow the crowd. There is plenty of room on the sidewalk in the tunnel for the tourists to walk and the train to pull out.

An Alternative to the Escorted Tour

Upon exiting the rail station in Riomaggorie, follow the crowds to the Via della Amore. BTW, there are no restroom facilities on the Via della Amore. So best you take care of your needs before paying that entrance fee. I would suggest the Riomaggorie rail station or one of the cafes in the town.

It will take you about 30 minutes to do the walk. You will have to pay an entrance fee of about 7Euros and then go down a flight of stairs. It is a nice walk on the side of those cliffs abutting the Ligurian Sea. Once you reach Manarola you will have to climb up a flight of stairs leading to the street level. Before climbing those stairs, you may want to make a rest stop at the very clean facilities at Manarola rail station. At Manarola, you will have to climb another flight of stairs or take the elevator to the street level. Once at the street level, follow the crowd down that long graffiti-lined tunnel.

If you bear to the left you will come upon the main street through the town that will take you down to the sea. See if you can hold your appetite till you get down to one of my favorite restaurants on the right-hand side. Here you will find "Alla Marina" (I believe it may have been called "Marina Piccola"). You can't beat the seafood; those clams and mussels were caught this morning, and the pasta is always "al dente." After lunch, walk out of the restaurant and take a sharp right. Turn around and snap a photo of all those beautiful pastel-painted houses on the hillside. Hopefully, it will be good enough to frame.

If you care not to have a sit down lunch, you will find lots of shops selling fried calamari in paper cones along with Sicilian deep-dish pizza slices. Frankly, I don't how they got to sell Sicilian pizza. The only thing I can think of is that by the time you reach the Cinque Terre, you have had your fill of trational Italian pizza that you would want something different. So much for food. I'm getting hungry.

If you are not hungy, take a sharp right out of that graffiti lined tunnel. It will let you into a small shopping area, the post office, and an ATM. In this area you will find lots of bed and breakfasts. It is a quiet area in the evening when all the day tourists have left.

ITALY NO TOUR NEEDED
You Can Do It Yourself

If you are planning an overnight trip to the Cinque Terre to see the other towns, this chapter provides a description and what to see in Corniglia, Vernazza, and Monterosso al Mare. If you are visiting several towns, staying overnight in one of the inns or BnBs is best. My first choice for an overnighter is Vernazza, followed by Manarola. It would help if you packed a carry-on with your toothbrush and a change of clothing. Also, don't expect to find major hotels in the Cinque Terre.

OVERNIGHTING JUST OUTSIDE THE CINQUE TERRE
If you want to visit several towns, staying in La Spezia for the evening is best. Here you will find many inexpensive, friendly hotels; all you need to do is walk a few blocks to the La Spezia Centrale rail station. Note, make sure you go to Centrale, as La Spezia has two stations. Trenitalia runs more trains from March through November, stopping at all the Cinque Terre towns. The train is known as the Cinque Terre Express and starts in La Spezia on the south and resort of Sestri Levante on the north.

If you want to stay at some upscale hotels in the area, I recommend the four-star hotels in Sestri Levante. It's only a 40-minute fast run to the Cinque Terre towns. In season you can expect the Cinque Terre Express trains to make the journey in about 25 minutes as they do not stop at many of the local stations before they get to Monterosso al Mar.

If you plan to spend a minimum of five days at the Cinque Terre, consider the most northern town, Monterosso de Mar. Unlike the other four villages, the town is a resort town with lovely beaches. However, this will not help you in the off-season, when most of the "luxury" hotels are closed for the winter season.
Here is a quick overview of the other towns. The fare from one town to the other is about one Euro. You can also purchase a day rail pass. If you are serious about hiking the Cinque Terre check at the information booth at the rail station. Once again, driving through the five towns is not advisable. The best is to stay outside, or take the train to one of the towns and find a BnB to use as your base for several days. Now on to the other towns:

An Alternative to the Escorted Tour

CORNIGLIA

Corniglia is the middle village of the Cinque Terre towns. At last checked, the population was around 200. It sits like Manarola, on a bluff about a football field back from the Ligurian Sea. Very few tourists visit Corniglia.

First, while it has a rail station (after Manarola and just before Vernazza), it has no streets. So access by automobile is impossible. It has what I would call "sought of access" to Manarola. It defines the saying, "You can't get there from here;" if you are driving, best to plan on bypassing Corniglia. Since there is no direct road to Manarola from Corniglia, you need to go to the outskirts of Vernazza on Via Stazione, where you pick up the SP51 road going south toward Manarola. Once again, not adviseable and best to take the train.

Here is the real scoop on Corniglia: To get to the heart of the town from the rail station, you need to climb the "Lardarina." The Lardarina comprises 33 flights of stairs and about 380 steps. Get this; all of them are switchbacks. Oy! There are lots of rest stops. From the top of the Lardarina, there are sweeping views to the left and right of the other towns.

Once at the top of the Lardarina, you will find a short main drag known as Via Fieschi. Here you will find little streets with BnBs and small restaurants. However, you won't find any authentic multi-room hotels. If you are the type of person who works out at the gym every day and is in great shape with no cardiac issues, you will find the beginning of the Lardarina at the northern end of the train station just as it goes into the tunnel. Better to go down the Lardarina instead of climbing it.

>>>TIP<<<
There is a mini-bus that meets the arriving trains. This mini-bus will take you to the top of the hill and drop you right in the heart of Corniglia. There is a charge of about one Euro. You may need to purchase a ticket at the rail station. As usual, you should note the train return times.
>>><<<

ITALY NO TOUR NEEDED
You Can Do It Yourself

VERNAZZA

Vernazza, better known as town number four, lies just below Monterosso al Mare. I love this town. If you are overnighting from Florence or Montecatini, this is one of the best places in addition to Manarola to stay. First, it's the only one of the Five Lands with a harbor. It's got a lovely sandy beach. It has plenty of BnBs and excellent restaurants and is predominantly flat walking. However, be advised that many of the BnBs require access via a staircase or ramp. You should check with your innkeeper, and remember the ground floor is the "zero floor," not the first floor. So best to ask, "Is the room on the ground floor or the first floor" (piano terra, or primo piano)?

Also, if the room is on the first floor, you probably will have to negotiate some stairs since most of these places do not have lifts (elevators). If walking up stairs creates a problem, better to check in at Monterosso al Mare or Riomaggiore for accommodations with elevators.

Vernazza is off-limits to all cars. There is, however, a small parking lot located about a quarter mile from the town. Once again, because of the walk and the difficulty driving in the Cinque Terre, a car is definitely not recommended.

The town is home to "Pesto" (actually, it was invented in Genoa). If you don't know what it is, it's pretty simple. You crush together pine nuts, olive oil, basil leaves, garlic, grated parmesan cheese, and presto; that's Pesto. It may come from the words "Mortar and Pestle," which are used for crushing the ingredients. You can purchase it already made, and it's a great gift to bring home from Vernazza. You will find many dishes made with it, e.g., Pesto Pizza, Salmon with Pesto Pasta, and more.

Vernazza also has one of those unique rail stations. The train station itself is quite short. So, most trains stop in a tunnel. Yup, just like the station at Riomaggiori. Don't get shocked if people open the doors and start walking in the tunnel. On another subject, since they didn't have room for the tunnel, it was placed under

151

An Alternative to the Escorted Tour

about 3-4 blocks of the houses in town. So if you are staying overnight, don't be surprised if you hear a very slight rumble as the train passes a hundred feet underneath your bed. Don't worry, it's not a rumble from a mild earthquake.

Hopefully, you will be taking the train to Vernazza. So, after exiting the train onto the platform, you will find stairs and an elevator, which will take you down to the Via Roma. The Via Roma is the main drag of Vernazza. In several blocks, it becomes Via Visconti as it works its way down to the harbor, the beach, and the castle.

The Doria Castle dates from around the 11th Century and was used as a lookout for invading pirates. In 1284, the fortress was taken over by invaders from Pisa during the Battle of Meloria. Ultimately, Genova won. During WWII, the Germans used it as an anti-aircraft position.

If you stand on the jetty at the end of Via Visconti, you can take some awesome pictures of those fishing boats moored together (there are no piers). You can then turn around and take more breathtaking photos of the painted houses, much like Manarola.

If you are physically fit, you can take the ninety-minute hike to Monterosso al Mare.

You will find many restaurants mainly serving seafood on the side streets of Via Visconti. If you want to dine outside (weather permitting) and enjoy a gorgeous sunset, visit Gambero Rosso Restaurant. It's that restaurant with all the umbrellas at the beginning of the concrete walkway to the boats at the end of Via Visconti. But show up early (at the opening time) as the place fills up quickly. Make sure you check the sunset time. Best to visit here in October, April, or May. On now to the resort town of Monterosso al Mare, Monterosso of the Sea.

MONTEROSSO AL MARE (NOT MONTEROSSO)
This is one place you would not expect to be part of the Cinque Terre. It is not like the other towns—first, not enough pretty

ITALY NO TOUR NEEDED
You Can Do It Yourself

houses with lots of colors on the hillside. Secondly, it is a beach resort. You should note that this is Monterosso al Mare, not Monterosso! Monterosso is about 230 miles away near Padua. On the Ligurian Sea, Monterosso is the largest of the five towns and has a population of about 1500.

The town is divided into two areas: the old town and the new town. A pedestrian tunnel of about three blocks connects them.

Vehicles can also pass through this tunnel, so best to be cautious. The northern or most western town, the oldest town of the two areas, is known as "Fegina." It has the longest beach in the Cinque Terre and a lovely beach compared to the other "postage stamp" beaches. Fegina is also home to the stazione.

If you are driving, you should enter from the Genova (northern or western side) and not through the four towns to the south because of the very steep and curvy road, SP38 (Via Roma).

There is ample beach parking for the day in a large muni lot at Fegina Beach. If you are staying overnight at a hotel or a BnB, you need to check with your hotel and obtain a pass; else, you will be ticketed for a ZTL (Zone Traffic Limited) violation. That ticket is pretty pricey; trust me, they have a habit of catching you in a few months. I know from experience. This is another reason to take the train through the Cinque Terre towns.

If you are not too concerned about all those pretty houses perched on the hillsides of the other four towns and want to enjoy a place that is also a reasonable resort, then Monterosso is the place. If you wish, you can pay three times the price a few miles up the road in Portofino, but you would need to get back to the main line to the Cinque Terre for all your day trips. So the best is to camp yourself at one of the many resort-style hotels in Monterosso. You will find most of the hotels in Monterosso lie in the flat area abutting the beach for about six blocks in length.

If you are visiting out of season but in September or early June, you probably will find the beach warm and swimmable. There still

153

An Alternative to the Escorted Tour

will be crowds. Of the other four towns, this one is the liveliest. They do not roll up the sidewalks in the evening.

Here is a little history about Monterosso al Mare:
First, that church on the hill is the church of San Francesco (same as St. Francis of Assisi). It divides Fegina with the new section of Monterosso al Mare. There is an attached Capuchin convent. The church was built in 1619-1622 and was consecrated in 1623. In 1819, Napoleon took it from the friars and converted it into a fort of the Ligurian Republic. After Napoleon's fall in 1816, it was given back to the Monks.

In 2013, a significant landslide destroyed several pieces of the convent, historic wall, etc. Most of the rubble spilled down the hill onto the driveway connecting the two towns. Inside the monastery are beautiful paintings. However, to view the church, the town, and the cemetery, you need to climb about forty steps and negotiate a path with several switchbacks.

Monterosso dates to about the 11th Century. There are remnants of medieval fortresses and watchtowers. These were used to spot invading marauders and pirates. Other than that, not too much history as Monterosso is a "new" town.

>>>TIP<<<   NO BAG SCHLEPPING
Want to do the Via della Amore, or hike those hills in the Cinque Terre but don't know what to do with your roller bags? Simple, these Italians thought of everything. You will find baggage check facilities in all five towns either at the rail station or in the town. The charge is only 8Euros per day. They do have hourly rates. If going by rail and continuing by rail see "Stow and Go" 150 meters from La Spezia station. More info at:
www.cinqueterre.eu.com/en/cinque-terre-luggage-storage

That's it for the Cinque Terre. I do hope you enjoy the five towns as much as others do.

ITALY NO TOUR NEEDED
You Can Do It Yourself

CHAPTER 13

TUSCANY/UMBRIA
HILLTOP TOWNS
CORTONA, SAN GIMIGNANO
PERUGIA, ASSISI
GUBBIO, MONTEPULCIANO

OVERVIEW

You have been to Rome, Florence, Venice, and the Amalfi area and now you are looking for something different to do in Italy. The only problem is, you only have one week of vacation to spare. You would like to leave JFK on a Friday night and return the following Monday. You summarize you will only miss 6 days of work. Secondly, you don't have a lot of money to spend. And, further, you just bought a "mistake" fare ticket for $295 on ITA which you were "birddogged" by GOING.COM. for a round trip basic economy to Rome the first week of November. So now what are you going to do? The Hilltop towns of Tuscany and Umbria are your answer. It's something different.

First, you will need your passports. Check to make sure the expiration date is at least 6 months forward. Secondly, you will need a backpack of essentials. One pair of comfortable shoes (sneakers) will do. Pack lightly. You can always wash your clothing at the laundromat in town. If you are going to rent a car for the week (good idea, it's cheap), you need to go to the AAA or CAA and get an international driving permit. Don't worry about seat assignments. If you arrive early at the check-in counter, you and your partner can have your choice. All you need is a backpack full of your essentials for the week i.e., your clothes, your passport, and of course this book.

My recommendation, for an entire week, is to base yourself in one town, and then move to the second town. My preference is

An Alternative to the Escorted Tour

Cortona. Cortona allows you to visit Montepulciano, Gubbio, Perugia, and Assisi. San Gimignano is between Siena and Florence. It is out of the way of the grouping I discussed. However, San Gimignano is ideal for making day trips to Siena (if you have not been there) and Volterra. I describe Siena in Chapter 9 and Chapter 11. Volterra is also a hilltop town, supposedly the oldest town in Italy. It is definitely worth a visit.

You should consult Chapter 4 for an overview of the hilltop towns. In this chapter, I discuss more of these towns.

CORTONA (TUSCANY)

Before visiting Cortona, it is an absolute must that you watch the movie *"Under the Tuscan Sun"* by Frances Mayes. If you can't watch the movie, then read the book. That being said a site not to be missed is a visit to Bramasole Villa, now known as Villa Laura. You can visit it and even rent it for a wedding if you wish.

I have always found Cortona to look and feel like San Gimignano of course without the towers and the Gelato Dandoli.

The medieval town is perched on a hill overlooking the Val d Chiana (the nearby valley). Very much like the Val d'Orcia. The main square, known as Piazza Garibaldi, allows you to view other places in the area, i.e., Lake Trasimeno, Montepulciano, and, of course, the Val d Chiana. Like San Gimignano, the entire town is surrounded by a wall. Parking in the old town is definitely not available. You will find public parking along the lower ring road around the town. You can reach the center by several staircases which lead from the public parking lots to the square.

As for hotels, I usually recommend only the hotels just outside the walls. However, the Hotel San Lucas is an excellent find. There are more BnBs in the town. However, your problem here is to make sure they have parking, else you must park in the lower level and walk up those staircases. There is lots of good shopping for local items on all the streets; in addition to excellent restaurants. My favorite for years has been the Taverna Pane e Vino. It means bread and wine. The Taverna is very rustic looking and serves up excellent Tuscan dishes. If you have a group of six or more, contact Claudia at "il Sole del Sodo" for a group BnB with meals.

ITALY NO TOUR NEEDED
You Can Do It Yourself

SAN GIMIGNANO (TUSCANY) This unique hilltop town is discussed in Chapter 9, IT-Rome-To-Florence, and Chapter 11 Florence Extra Days.

ASSISI (UMBRIA)

I have always felt that Umbria is the sister province (or land) of Tuscany. Settled by the Etruscans thousands of years ago, it is much like Tuscany. It is loaded with medieval hilltop towns with ancient walls, Assisi, Gubbio, Spoletto, and Todi, to name a few, and vineyards still farmed by generations of families. If it's not grapes, it's olives or both. If you look west from Assisi, across that last valley is Tuscany. Perugia is the hub of Umbria.

If you are driving, I suggest you base yourself in Assisi as your second town. I have been to Assisi so many times you could put a blindfold on me, and I could walk from one end to the other without bumping into anything.

Parking in the old City of Assisi is almost non-existent. However, there are muni parking lots on the lower level. They are all connected to the old City by escalators. You park in the muni lot and then find your hotel, and drag your bags. Two hotels I suggest are the Domus Laetitiae (it's an old convent), and my favorite is the three-star Hotel Umbra. Note the way I spelled it. There is no "i." It is not Umbria. However, you cannot beat the location, just like the Hotel Cisterna in San Gimignano. It is right off the main piazza. Outside the entrance to the Umbra, you will find a lovely café for a light lunch. If booking at the Umbra, book directly and request a view overlooking the valley.

WHAT TO SEE AND DO IN ASSISI

The way you visit Assisi is a walk through the town. You start at one end and finish at the other. So beginning at Porta Nuova (one end) or Giovanni Paolo III parking area (the other end) is best, instead of entering the main street which changes names along the route. If you are arriving late in the day, start at the Giovanni Paolo III parking area and visit the St. Francis Basilica and tomb first (since it may close late in the day), then walk the town till you exit at Porta Nuova. The walk from the Porta Nuova lot to the

An Alternative to the Escorted Tour

Giovanni Paolo III parking lot is about one mile. Start at the Porta Nuova lot. When you finish your walk, you will take the escalator to the parking lot at the Basilica of St. Francis.

Starting at the Porta Nuova parking lot, take the escalator and follow the crowd onto the Borgo Aretino, along the souvenir shops, and under that big stone gate and tower. Look to your left, and you will see the Basilica of Saint Clare. Construction of the church started after the death of St. Clare 1257-1265 around the ancient church of San Giorgio, which until 1230 had kept the remains of St. Francis. Clare's remains were subsequently buried at the church of San Giorgio. The remains of St. Clare were buried under the altar of the new church in 1265. In 1852, they found the original bones of St. Clare and buried her in a new tomb. Saint Agness is also buried at this Gothic church.

Note the flying buttresses which support the walls from outside the structure. The flying buttresses were used for many Gothic churches during the Renaissance period. This is much like the upper Basilica of San Francesco d'Assisi. The church is all late 14th-century design with a façade fabricated with rows of white and pink local stone. The square-based bell tower stands on the side, with mullioned windows and a large single window. In addition to the exterior design, the inside is also worth visiting.

This region of Umbria is a high-risk area for earthquakes. Several have occurred in 2022. However, substantial damage occurred in 1997 to the Basilica di Santa Chiara and St. Francis when the roof caved in. Four people were killed at St. Francis.

After you view the Basilica of Saint Clare, continue walking to the left (on the Corso Giuseppi Mazzi) until you come upon a building on your right that looks like an old Roman temple. It is. That's the Temple of Minerva, which sits in the Piazza del Comune. The Piazza is the main square of Assisi. You can't miss it. Six well-preserved Corinthian columns are supporting the main cross beam. The temple with those columns dates to the 1st Century BC. It was converted to a church in 1539 and later renovated in the 17th century to the Baroque style. The temple housed a court with an annexed jail in the Middle Ages. The Italian painter "Giotto"

ITALY NO TOUR NEEDED
You Can Do It Yourself

depicted the Corinthian columns of the converted temple in a fresco which is in the Basilica of St. Francis up the street. When visiting St. Francis, you will see it, as the portrait of the church has windows and bars.

The central square is home to the Palazzo del Capitano del Popolo, a mid-13th-century design with merlons added in 1927. That tower you see is the Peoples Tower, built in 1305. The fountains with the three lions on the southern side date from the 16th century. About a block to your left en route to the Basilica of St. Francis is the Forum and Archaeological Museum. If you have an extra hour, or if you are staying in the old city, it is worth a visit. There is a charge of nine Euros.

Like many of the other cities in Italy, Assisi was conquered and reconquered by practically every warring people because of its strategic importance as a defensive hilltop town.

When you are finished with your visit to the Piazza del Comune, walk up toward the tower next to the Temple of Minerva toward the Basilica of Saint Francis. It's a good 15-minute walk to Saint Francis. There is shopping on this street (Via San Paolo) as well as BnBs. Continue walking in the direction of the auto traffic until it ends at Porto Giacomo. Take a left here and continue with the traffic for about two blocks until you come upon the Basilica of San Francesco. If you want to grab a light bite or a café, there is a "Ristorante Bar San Francesco," just off that grassy area in front of the upper Basilica. Best to use the facilities at this bar since the main pubic facilities are located on the square below the upper Basilica, known as the lower square "Piazza Inferiore San Francisco."

The Basilica has a lower and upper part. The upper is a beautiful church with paintings on all the walls. The lower contains the crypt of St. Francis. If you enter the lower Basilica to visit the crypt area and view the tomb of St. Francis, you will have to navigate a small stairway of about twenty steps. No big deal, hold onto those wrought iron railings. You will return to the lower Basilica through another staircase on the other side of the crypt area. You should feel free to light a candle. However, there are no flash pictures or talking allowed. So turn your flash off.

After leaving the Basilica, you must work your way down to the Giovanni Paolo III parking lot. If you have parked your car in the Nuova Porta parking lot, you must take a taxi or that local bus. If you are staying in Assisi, all you need do is walk back to your hotel and shopping, of course.

PERUGIA (UMBRIA)

If you did not know by now, Perugia is a medieval hilltop town, better, I should say a city. It is also the capital of the province of Umbria. It is now very commercialized. You should not expect anything like San Gimignano or Assisi. However, the town management has done an excellent job preserving the town and the historic district over the years. There is virtually no parking for any cars in the historic district or the hotels located there. All parking is paid, and most are underground. There are numerous escalators in every underground parking garage. In addition, there is the "mini-metro." You will see this sometimes spelled as "mini metro." It's part cable car and part subway transportation system. You can ride it for 1.5Euros for 70 minutes. Once exited in the historic district, an escalator will whisk you to the surface. However, if you stay close to the historic district, you won't need to use the mini metro.

QUICK HISTORY OF PERUGIA

Perugia is one of the original Etruscan cities. It was an Umbrian settlement around the year 310BC. The town was burned in 40BC, leaving only the temples of Vulcan, Juno, and the Etruscan terrace walls. Whoever wanted to occupy the destroyed City did so. Resettlement of the City occurred in 251AD. The City is surrounded by a mile-long monster double wall. The Romans could not conquer this City because of the size of its wall.

In the 9th Century, control of Perugia was passed onto the popes and Charlemagne. By the 11th Century, the small commune found itself warring against the neighboring hilltop towns, i.e., Assisi, Spoleto, Todi, Arezzo, etc.

ITALY NO TOUR NEEDED
You Can Do It Yourself

WHAT TO SEE AND DO IN PERUGIA

Perugia has the remnants of the Romans and what's left of the medieval and Renaissance periods. There is very little to see of the Roman remains since most are located below the underground City. Fortunately, we are lucky as most remains of the medieval and Renaissance period are in the underground City, not below it. I'll describe more below.

The main square in the historic district is the Piazza IV Novembre. Here you will find the city hall, covered market, cafes, restaurants, and numerous chocolate shops. It's also the central hangout place.

If you do one thing in Perugia, you must visit the underground City known as the "Rocca Paolina. In medieval times, the rulers of Perugia were the lords. The popes took over control in about 1540 and built the Paolina as a fortress. In 1848, the underground City was systematically destroyed. It was not until 1860 that control passed as Perugia became part of the new Kingdom of Italy. It was in 1965 that the underground City was "unearthed" into what we know today. There are four entrances, all with escalators. Tunnels connect the underground rooms. If you are driving, it is easily reached from the Piazzale Partigiani car park or station Via Baglioni on the Minimetro. You will need at least two hours, and it's free! The other places are worth a visit:

The Etruscan Arch (Arch of Augustus or Augustus Gate) is one of eight gates that were part of the Old City. The Arch of Augustus was constructed in the second half of the 3rd century BC. The arch is part of a massive set of walls that are 30 ft (9.1 m) tall and 9,500 ft (2,900 m) long, made of travertine and set without mortar. It covers approximately a quarter of a square mile over three hills.

The other surviving gate is the Arco d'Augusto (Arch of Agusto). It was built in the second half of the third century BC by the Etruscans but took its name from the Roman emperor Augustuo who restored it in 40BC.

The Palazzo dei Priori or Comunale is one of the best examples in Italy of a public palace from the 11th century. It takes its name from the Priori, the highest political authority governing the City in the medieval eras. You will find it in the central Piazza IV Novembre, the town's main square. Now to Gubbio.

A DAY IN GUBBIO (UMBRIA)

The Romans conquered the Town about the 2nd century BC. However, the occupation of the hills around the Town of Gubbio dates to about the Bronze Age, 3300BC. In pre-Roman times the Umbri people occupied the land and the other Umbrian hilltop defensive towns like Assisi, Todi, Spoleto, and Orvieto. Gubbio contains the second-largest surviving Roman theatre in the world. Gubbio was mighty during the Middle Ages and peaked in the first half of the 16th century. It is rumored that Gubbio sent 1,000 knights to fight in the first Crusade.

You need a car to visit Gubbio. Gubbio is built into a hill or, better, the slope of Mount Ingino. Sorry to say there are no escalators, not even stairs. The Roman Theatre is in the flat area at the base of Mount Ingino. By the way, the Romans called this place Ikuvium. I can't even pronounce it!

For six Euros for a round-trip ticket, you can go to the top of Mount Ingino. You need to go from the main square and drive to the end of via San Girolamo where you will find the Colle Eletto Funivia www.funiviagubbio.it. There is plenty of parking at the Funivia. From the top of the Funivia, there are breathtaking views of Gubbio. Once at the top of the Funivia, don't count on a town to visit. There is none.

This funivia is more like a ski lift. The attendants will put two people in a bucket, and you stand for six minutes as it lifts you to the top of the hill. There is a basilica on top of the hill. In the Basilica lie the remains of San't Ubaldo. To reach the Basilica of San't Ubaldo you would need to walk the equivalent of several blocks on a winding path behind the funivia. When they remove you from that basket at the top of the mount, look at the Basilica and see if you are up to this moderately strenuous walk.

After you visit the top of the funivia, you need to take it back down and work your way over to the Piazza del Quaranta Martini, the main square. The square is a semi-circle. Here you can grab a bite before exploring the other highlights of Gubbio. However, before heading down the hill, if you walk across the slope, in other words, not down the hill, you will come across the Palazzo dei Consoli in the Piazza Grande. It's an old palace but looks like a castle with a crenelated top. This place contains the seven Iguvine Tablets with ancient inscriptions from the bronze age. About a block further up the hill is the Duomo of Gubbio.

After lunch, you are ready to view the Roman Amphitheatre. The actual name is the "Teatro Romano d Gubbio." It's a short flat walk of no more than 10 minutes. However, it isn't easy to describe just how to get there. So, I will do my best. All you need to do is go over to that small rotary. Then walk to your right along Route 298 until you see the signs to the Teatro Romano d Gubbio. You can also walk to the right of the Chiesa di San Francesco (the church in the square), down Via Ortracci, and then take a right on Route 298. You can't miss it. Just look for a smaller coliseum on your left.

MONTEPULCIANO (TUSCANY)
Wine, wine, wine, and more wine, it's called Vino Nobile di Montepulciano, but it's not from Montepulciano, or anywhere around this hilltop town. This wine comes from grapes grown in Abuzzo called the Montepulciano grape. Yes, Montepulciano is a wine-producing area, however, what's more important is that it is a hilltop medieval town dating from the 14th Century. There is lots of shopping here along pedestrian-only streets. In addition, there are three churches worth a visit. It's a nice day trip; only 40 minutes from Cortona right across the valley with all those vineyards.

CHAPTER 14

IT-FLORENCE TO VENICE

INTRODUCTION

Hopefully, you have rented your car either in Florence or in Rome. Now it's time to head for Venice. Whether you are going on to Venice from Milan and the Lakes district (Como, Maggiore, etc.) you still need to traverse the same area. I should have noted that if you are flying out of Venice (VCE) you should consider dropping your car on arrival in Venice. You won't need it unless it can also be used as a boat. There are several drop points in addition to the VCE airport. You won't need a car in Venice, so best to save those extra two or three days of rental.

The road from Florence to Venice traverses mainly the agricultural areas of Emilia-Romana and the Po River Valley. The Milan-Venice road traverses the industrial area of Lombardy.

With suggested sightseeing, you should anticipate a full day of travel. So, don't plan on arriving in Venice midday or late afternoon and then heading into the Venice Lagoon.

There are three interesting sites en route. They are Bologna, Euganee Terme (known for its wineries in the Eugan), and Padua, home to St. Anthony's Basilica. You should plan on at least 2-4 hours for wine tasting in wineries in the Euganean Hills and lunch. A swingby in Padua will be at least two hours of shopping and visiting the St. Anthony's complex. To be honest, it is difficult to visit Bologna and see the beauty and history of this city in a few hours. If Bologna is on your bucket list, it is best to plan for two full days here, then continue your travels to Venice with stops in Padua and Euanee Terme for wine tasting.

>>>TIP<<<

If you have to shorten the day for any reason, the best approach is to skip Padua, assuming you are not going to Bologna. The reason I say this is that Padua is easily reached via rail as a nice day trip from Venice. Trains depart the Venice stations (there are two

164

stations) and most of them stop in Padua. It's only about 30 minutes and a round-trip ticket is about $15. You won't need a car in Padua either and everything is within walking distance from the Padua rail station. It is extremely difficult without a car to visit the wine-tasting wineries in the Euganean Hills. Therefore, do your wine tasting en route to Venice.
>>><<<

BOLOGNA
Bologna is home to the oldest university in the world, established in 1088AD. The city is also home to numerous red churches including the Basilica of Bologna known as the Basilica of San Patronio , also made of red brick. It dates from the 13th Century.
If you have time and want to swing through Bologna, this is the place for shopping and lunch.

Here is a quick list of the areas:
The main square is the Piazza Maggiore. It contains the Basilica of San Patronio and the Palazzo d' Accurisio. Both areas are home to numerous shops, eateries, and cafes, not to mention souvenir stands and all that other good stuff you find in Italy.

And, yes parking is a problem in the historic district, and it is best to watch out for those ZTL areas.

>>>TIP<<<
There is no free parking in Bologna. However, it is best to park in one of the attended parking lots or underground garages. Some of these are located in the ZTL area. If you park in one of these garages or lots, you must enter the city through a specific route. A photo of your rental car license plate (tag), will also be sent by the parking garage to the authorities so you will not receive a ZTL fine. You need to plan your visit to Bologna, i.e. where you want to go, etc. For a detailed overview of the parking situation it is best to visit:
https://www.anticopoderesanluca.it/en/visiting-bologna/where-to-park-your-car/

An Alternative to the Escorted Tour

Do not under any circumstance, drive around the city aimlessly. If you don't park in a ZTL controlled garage, trust me on this one, you will get a hefty ZTL ticket as a souvenir of Bologna.
>>><<<

Like Palermo, Sicily, Bologna is filled with outdoor markets of all types. If you are renting an apartment for a few days consider: Mercato di Mezzo and Mercato delle Erbe. There are several other food markets in the City. If you are into shopping for designer brands, you will find them on the Via Rizzoli.

In summary, if you want to just do a swing by, the best is to shop and have lunch around the Piazza Maggiore before continuing on to the wine tasting of the Colli Uganei region.

>>>TIP<<<   CAUTION
Once you are approaching Bologna and are heading north to Padua and Venice, you need to follow the short ring road known as A14 for just a few kilometers before you get on the A13 and head to Padua/Venice. Bologna will appear on the right-hand side of your car. Do not follow the signs for the A1 toward Modena. If you are going directly to the old city of Bologna you still need to exit the A1 on that short stretch of the A14. Just follow the signs to Bologna Centro, or else you will be put on the A13 heading toward Padua/Venice.
>>><<<

WINE COUNTRY THE EUGANEAN HILLS (COLLI EUGANEI)
About 100KM after starting up the A13 in Bologna, and crossing the Po River, you will come across the exit for the Euganean Hills, which is called "Terme Euganee." If you exit here, you will find no less than 40 wineries with most of them offering tours and wine tasting. Once you exit the A13 it's only 10-15 minutes to enter the "Colli Uganei" wine-growing region. Hundreds of vineyards dot the area. The Euganean Hills and Colli Uganei are only about 20KM south of Padua. This is part of the Veneto Region of Northern Italy.

In 1969, the Colli Euganei and the Euganean Hills were declared a national park by the Italian government. You can expect

166

vineyards to grow over ancient volcanic lands. In addition, there are Etruscan ruins and medieval towns. You can certainly spend several days here if you have the time.

There are just too many wineries here to offer any suggestions on wine tasting. You probably will be only able to visit two of them. If you get an early start out of Florence at about 9AM (0900) you should arrive in the area at about 1PM (1300).

If you are hungry, consider stopping first at one of the many places in the villages along the way to your first winery.

When you email the wineries below to check their hours, do ask them which restaurants are open for pranzo, as many are open only for dinner. Also, with plenty of wine tasting coming, you may want to settle for a few slices of pizza and a Coke.

List of wineries offering tours and tastings in Colli Euganei:
https://www.winalist.com/appellations/colli-euganei

https://www.wwcellars.com/our-wineries/italy/colli_euganei/

https://www.winalist.com/s?lat=45.3166667&lng=11.6666667&utm_source=&utm_medium=&utm_campaign=

https://www.winedering.com/wine-tourism_padua_g3171727_colli-euganei_dn34

In addition to the wine-growing area, the hills and the towns are rich in history. Do check out the Agritourismos in the area.

If you are into wine, I would highly suggest spending the afternoon in the wine-growing region and as stated above, go to Padua for the day from Venice.

A VISIT TO PADUA   (ALSO SPELLED PADOVA)
It is best to review all the details about Padua in Chapter 16 Venice Extra Days.

An Alternative to the Escorted Tour

If you have not had lunch yet, it is best to stop in Padua where you will find Europe's second oldest indoor market known as "Sotto il Salone." The market contains about 100 shops and cafes many over 800 years old. It is best to figure a minimum of two hours.

Hopefully, you are driving in. Padua is only 90 minutes after leaving Bologna. If you have stopped in the wine country of the Euganean Hills you should be arriving in Padua about 4-5PM. You can either take the local road (SS16) into Padua or the A13. Either way, it will only take you 20 minutes to reach that parking lot. You need to take the main Padua exit which is Exit 8. There is no problem parking in Padua. The main square, (actually it is an oval) is called the Valle Dell Prato and is lined with beautiful statues of famous people from the Padua area. About two blocks from here you will find a monster parking lot. You can set your GPS to "Parcheggio Prato della Valle".

Once in the parking lot, it is a short walk of no more than 10 minutes to Prato della Valle and St. Anthony's Basilica. Lots of eateries in this area. If you want to get some exercise, the Sotto il Salone is a little over one kilometer (16-minute walk) from St. Anthony's. The nice thing about Padua is that it is all flat and just really a nice walking town.

ONTO VENICE
If you are bound for Venice on my three capitals tour i.e. Rome, Florence, and Venice you need to follow the A13 into the Padua area where the A13 ends. If coming in from the west, Milan, Verona, and the Lakes district, you need to take the A4 in the direction of Venice. Note if you are coming in on the A4 from west of Venice, the city you will be passing known as "Vicenza" is NOT "Venice" in Italian. Venice in Italian is "Venezia."

You should note that out of Paduva you need to get on the SR47. Continue on this road till you pick up the A4/E70 toward Venice. Follow the signs into Venice Mestre and Marghera. You leave the E70 and get on the E57. Watch for this split in the road. You need to keep right, or else you will go inland and north of the Venice area. Follow the E57 till it takes a hard right and becomes the SR11 which will take you right into the Venice area.

ITALY NO TOUR NEEDED
You Can Do It Yourself

You need to read the next chapter for all those details about Venice. However, if arriving by car you need to know what you will be doing with that rental car. I start off the next chapter with the "what to do" with that rental.

VENICE HAS TWO PARTS
Most folks don't know that there are two parts of Venice. The Venice we all know is the lagoon area. And, yes, you can't drive in Venice unless you are in some type of boat or gondola.

The other side of Venice is called "Venice Mestre." This Venice rhymes with pastry. It's pronounced "Mess Stray." You can have your choice of staying in the Lagoon or the mainland (Mestre). Frankly, I enjoy Mestre. Far better than staying in the Lagoon. Here is why:

There are several hundred lodging places in Mestre.
There is a train every 20 minutes to the Lagoon. All trains
    bound for Venice, whether they are Frecce (high-speed trains)
    or "locals" stop in Mestre.
The fare to the Lagoon (end of the line) is 1.5Euros.
The ride into the Lagoon takes about 12 minutes.
There are no noisy crowds in the streets of Mestre, if you want to
take a nap, no problem. If you like noisy streets stay in the Lagoon.

There are also direct buses into the Piazza d Roma.
    Many hotels in the Mestre area provide complimentary shuttle
        service into the Piazza d Roma.
And finally... The price. If your three-star hotel in the Lagoon
    area is 300Euros per night, expect to pay about 120-150Euros
per night in Mestre.
And did I tell you that you won't have to walk up and down all
those bridges, lugging your bags.. oy, oy, oy.

Please see the next chapter for more details on Venice Mestre.

An Alternative to the Escorted Tour

>>>TIP<<< MY FAVORITE HOTEL IN MESTRE
Directly opposite the Mestre stazione, you will find several high-rise hotels.   The American-style, four-star Hotel Plaza (www.hotelplazavenice.com) is my favorite. The rooms are large and an excellent breakfast is offered. Great lobby bar, and a restaurant to boot. So tour the Lagoon, and hop a train back to Mestre for a snooze and dinner. You will find more on Mestre later in this chapter.
>>><<<

YOU WON'T NEED THE CAR IN VENICE
Once you arrive in Venice, you won't need that rental car, unless you are driving to Milan and the Lakes District. It is far better to return the rental in Venice and take the train to Milan. It will cost you a lot less in terms of parking in Venice, tolls, gas, etc., to get to Milan. And, further, you don't need a car in Milan. Your day trip to Lake Como to see Varenna and Bellagio is only one hour from Milan easily reached by an in-expensive train ride of less than one hour.   Trains of the Trenord division of Trenitalia operate every hour to Lake Como (Varenna/Esino) and also to Stresa, home to Lake Maggiore . I describe all these trips from Milan,   in Milan and the Lakes, Chapter 17.

By the way, if you are staying at a hotel in the Lagoon, and you want to park your rental car at that monster garage right off the Piazzale d Roma (Piazza d Roma), it will cost you about 35Euros per day. Now, when you book that rental car in Rome or if you are doing a hopoff in Florence, it is best to specify that you will drop the rental in Venice.

You can rent and drop off your rental car in the following locations: Venice Marco Polo Airport; Mestre train station; Venice Piazzale d Roma (in the parking garage adjacent).   Other locations in Venice Mestre are some of the hotels.
Great, we made it to Venice. Our tour with the details of Venice continues in the next chapter (Chapter 15).

170

CHAPTER 15

VENICE

INTRODUCTION

The beginning of this chapter starts with your entry into the Venice area with your rental or flying into "VCE." You need to know where your hotel is located. You just can't cruise into Venice and say, "Gee, I think I need a hotel for 3 nights." So here is what you need to know in the planning phase of your visit to Italy.

After I describe lodging in Venice, I will give you a brief history of this unique place. Then I will detail each day, what to do, etc.
In addition, I have included a chapter on extra days in Venice to wet your appetite. However, before we get going, let me share with you my thoughts on ARRIVING IN VENICE.

ARRIVING IN VENICE

If you depart Florence by 10AM and you care not to do a swing through of Bologna, wine tasting in the Euganean Hills, or a visit to Padua, you can arrive in Venice by 1PM. The running time from the center of Florence to Venice Mestre is a little over three hours at about 260KM. Therefore, it's easy to arrive in the mid-afternoon. This will allow you to do most of the Venice orientation which you would normally do on a full Day #1 Venice. If your hotel room is not available when you arrive, the front desk will be glad to check your bags for you, while you enjoy the town, or should I say the Lagoon area. It is best to make the proper plans.

VENICE HAS TWO PARTS

Most folks don't know that there are two parts of Venice. The Venice we all know is the lagoon area. And, yes, you can't drive in Venice unless you are driving a boat or being paddled around by a "gondolier", and no he does not sing "oh solo mio."
The other side of Venice is called "Venice Mestre." This Venice rhymes with pastry. It's pronounced "May Stray." You can have your choice of staying in the lagoon or the mainland (Mestre).

An Alternative to the Escorted Tour

Frankly, I enjoy Mestre. I have always felt it is far better than staying in the Venice Lagoon (unless this is your honeymoon).

There are hundreds of lodging places in Mestre. If this is June, July, August, or September and you have a family of little ones, my suggestion is to take a look at Venice d Jesolo. In those summer months, they have frequent high-speed ferry service which goes back and forth to the lagoon area. There are well over 80 places of lodging (most of them in expensive hotels/motels) in Venice d Jesolo which is 20 miles North. This place is great for kids and has an excellent beach being on the Adriatic.

Getting back to Venice Mestre and why I prefer to stay there:
There is a train every 20 minutes to the Lagoon. All trains   bound for Venice, whether they are Frecce (high-speed trains)   or "locals" stop in Mestre. However, you cannot board a Frecci in Venice Mestre bound for the Lagoon (Santa Lucia Station). So you will usually have to wait for a local train. No big deal.

The fare to the Lagoon (end of the line) is 1.5 Euros.
The ride into the Lagoon takes about 12 minutes.
There are no noisy crowds, like in the Lagoon area, if you want to take a nap no problem.
There are also direct buses into the Piazzale d Roma from the
   Mestre rail station and other points in Mestre.
In addition, a light railway was recently built which now makes
   access to additional hotels possible, (see below).
Many hotels in the Mestre area provide complimentary shuttle
   service into the Piazzale d Roma.

And finally... The price. If your three-star hotel in the Lagoon
   area is 350 Euros per night, expect to pay about 120-150 Euros
   per night in Mestre for a four-star hotel!

And did I tell you that you won't have to walk up and down all those bridges? No big deal, unless you are lugging your bags.. oy, oy, oy, and you also get to save that porter fee of $50-$60 to lug your bags and find your hotel in the Venice Lagoon maze.

ITALY NO TOUR NEEDED
You Can Do It Yourself

>>>TIP<<<   MY FAVORITE HOTEL IN MESTRE
Directly opposite the Mestre rail station, you will find several high-rise hotels. The American-style, Plaza Hotel is my favorite. The rooms are large and an excellent breakfast is offered. Great lobby bar, and a restaurant to boot. Excellent reviews and get this... it's a four-star hotel! So tour the Lagoon for the day and hop a train back to Mestre for a snooze and then dinner, or better go back to the Lagoon for a nightcap.
>>><<<

Talking about food....

>>>TIP<<<
There is one restaurant that rates a "10" across the board. It is so good and reasonable that our tours used it for two dinners when we were in Venice. "Ristorante Bepi Venesian" is located directly behind the Plaza Hotel off that small park in Venice Mestre (not in the lagoon). It's a 10-minute walk from the Plaza Hotel or the rail station. "Bepi Venesian" is run by three brothers. You cannot beat the fresh fish dishes. In addition, all dinners are served with crusty bread and, oh, those olives. To find it, all you need do is walk up Via Piave and take a right at the first street (Via Sernaglia) until you come to the end of that park. You will find the "Bepi" one block up. When in doubt, of course, find a local and state "por fay vor ay" or scuzzi... "Doe Vay et Bepi Venesian?
>>><<<

>>>TIP<<<
In 2015, the new T1 Tram Line opened between Mestre and the Piazzale Roma. The T1/T2 Tramline has two branches in the Mestre section of Venice. It now opens the possibility of staying at an additional twenty accommodations in the Mestre area, many with free parking. Note- It does not stop at the Mestre Rail Station. More information can be found at:
https://actv.avmspa.it/en/content/tram
>>><<<

BTW, forgot to mention that if you park your rental in the big garage next to Piazzale d Roma, it will cost you 35Euros per day!

173

An Alternative to the Escorted Tour

AN OVERVIEW OF VENICE

Venice is very much like Rome; this is one city that is undoubtedly unique. Yes, I can say this. I have been to Amsterdam, Bruges, and other places where canals are all over. However, none of these and others can compare to Venice. There is only one Venice in the world. Many say it is the most romantic city in the world. It is great for a honeymoon. I can't think of any other unique place like this. I will take Venice over any place, even Bali or some Caribbean island!

Venice is massive. It sits in a lagoon about 2.5 miles from the mainland. Back in time, it was used to protect the inhabitants against marauding tribes. To conquer Venice one would have to mount an invasion by sea, which would be nearly impossible in medieval times. Today, a roadway and a rail link connect the central lagoon island with the mainland, known as Venice Mestre. The rail system ends about 300 feet before the "Grand Canal" at the Santa Lucia rail (Ferrovia) terminal.

With the exception of the end of the motorway at the Piazzale Roma, there are absolutely no automobiles in the Venice Lagoon islands since there are no roads, only canals. All transportation is via water boats comprised of government (ACTV) operated vaporettos, water taxis, and charter boats. Note gondola rides are not allowed on the Grand Canal. So don't expect one of those gondoliers to take you for those forty minutes down the Grand Canal. Also, they do not sing "Oh Solo Mio," that's strictly in Napoli. However, residents can use the Grand Canal for a few "blocks," and gondoliers making deliveries.

I chuckle every time I am in Venice and see the brown UPS boats making deliveries. Very cool. Oh, and did I mention that Venice is the last stop on the Venice Simplon Orient Express from Paris? If you want to take a look at it and take a few pictures, it usually is at the Santa Lucia train station at about 5PM (assuming it runs on time) or you can see it at 11AM (definitely) when it is ready for departure for its return trip to Paris. Now, back to Venice.

There are over 118 islands in the Venice Lagoon, connected by 400 bridges. Several other islands in the Lagoon are not connected to

174

the main lagoon complex. They are the islands of Burano, Murano, and Torcello; all three are worth a visit. There are several other islands worth mentioning.

The "Lido" is a long barrier island at the end of the Lagoon. It is a resort area with a beautiful beach facing the Adriatic. The Lido is dead in the off-season. From October through May, even the birds head down to Sicily. If you spend extra days in either May or September, a day at the Lido is undoubtedly in order. Here you will find lots of BnBs and smaller hotels. You will find many restaurants and shops on the wide boulevard called "Gran Viale Santa Maria Elisabetta." On exiting the Vaporetto, you need to take a hard right, then walk about one block to the Gran Viale. This boulevard is lined with shops, gelato stands, cafes, and restaurants.

Two other islands border the Grand Canal which are not considered in the six Sestieris (or districts). They are Giudecca and San Giorgio. If you can spare an extra day, these two islands are worth a visit. Vaporetti also reaches these two islands.

A SHORT HISTORY OF VENICE

There is minimal early history about Venice. Roman sources believe fishermen were living in the marshy Lagoon about 421AD. That year, the first church was established by these "lagoon dwellers" as San Giacomo. Warring tribes, mainly in Lombardia (Northern Italy), made their mark on the people until they finally got fed up and fled for safety to the marshes of the Lagoon. In 568AD, the first central government was formed.

More and more Veneti fleeing from the Lombardy region of the north, started to inhabit the marshy areas. For several hundred years, the people in the Lagoon were governed by the Byzantine Empire (Eastern Roman Empire, which survived after 476 AD). In 726AD, the people in the Lagoon broke away from Constantinople, formed their own government, and elected their first Doge (duke). In 810AD, the Franks tried to conquer the Venetians living in the marshes but failed.

An Alternative to the Escorted Tour

In 828AD, the Venetians smuggled from Egypt the body of Saint Mark. The Venetians declared Saint Mark, the patron saint of Venice. Venice became a world trading center as its population swelled. About 1200AD, Venice entered into several wars with Constantinople and Genoa.

In about 1348, the Black Plague destroyed a good portion of the inhabitants of Venice. Ships arriving in Venice had to wait 40 days before they could enter for fear of infected sailors. This 40-day waiting period is where we get the term (Quarantine from, meaning 40). The plague struck again in 1630. Napoleon conquered Venice and dissolved its government in 1797. Austria took control over Venice in 1815.

In 1866, the Austrians were defeated by the Prussians. The Venice city-state became part of the new Kingdom of Italy with other city-states, i.e., Florence, Milan, etc., under the leadership of the key Italian unifier Giuseppe Garibaldi.

CONSTRUCTION OF THE CITY

Now that you know a little about the city, you are probably thinking about how these little islands were connected. First, you need to realize that they did not bring in lots of dirt or what we call "material" from the mainland and fill the marshy areas. Instead, they did something very novel. Sticks of Oak and other durable trees were cut and brought in from the mainland on boats. These Oak sticks were then pounded into the marsh until they reached a solid footing. In addition, they were positioned very close to each other and lashed together to make what we would now call a pylon (piling). Flat boards were placed on these pylons to spread the weight needed to carry the load. Bricks were laid on top of these boards until a foundation was created. The Venetians then bridged together each little island they created to form canals between them.

Now mind you, like Rome, Venice was not built in a day, a month, or even a year. It took several hundred years to make it into what it is now.

So, what is the best way to "see" Venice? Here are my suggestions:

176

ITALY NO TOUR NEEDED
You Can Do It Yourself

WHAT TO SEE AND DO IN VENICE

You will need a minimum of two full days in Venice, better would be three full days or a week. There is much to do here, even in the off-season. Here are the must-dos:

Vaporetto trip down (actually up) the Grand Canal
Shopping at Rialto Mercato and
   at San Marco Piazza:
Visit the Basilica of San Marco
Visit the Doges Palace/Bridge of Sighs
Visit the top of the Campanile
A café in the Piazza San Marco
A gondola ride for 45 minutes
   (not allowed on the Grand Canal)

If you have an extra half day- The Peggy Guggenheim Museum
Extra day trips:
   Morano, Burano, and Torcello
   The Lido- No visit during November-March
   Day trip to Padua

And remember, you can't swim in the Venice canals, unless you fall out of a boat, and are forced to swim.

As a recommendation, you should consider the Vaporetto trip down the Grand Canal toward the Rialto Mercato. From the Mercato, you should walk to the San Marco Piazza.

On arrival in Venice (and hopefully, you have turned in your auto rental) you need to check into your hotel. Or, better, check into your hotel first and then drop off your rental car. This is not a problem if you are staying in Mestre. If you are staying in the Lagoon, you need to "schlep" your bags or obtain the services of a porter who will bring you and your luggage to your hotel.

SELECTING A HOTEL IN VENICE OR MESTRE

Please consult booking.com for a list of hotels in Venice by area. Here is a quick summary of where they are located:

An Alternative to the Escorted Tour

First, some geography about Venice. If you look at a map of Venice, it looks like a coupler they use in railroading to connect two cars. You can also look at it as an open wrench. In summary, best to describe it as two interlocked hands. The main lagoon complex is composed of six districts or Sestieris.

These six districts have their own mayors. Cannaregio is where the Santa Lucia train station is (also known on all the signs as the Ferrovia (way of the iron). If you want to stay close to the locals and don't want to do a lot of walking over big bridges (20 steps up and 20 steps down), Cannaregio is the place. It is also home to the Jewish Quarter. Please take note that many restaurants in the Jewish Quarter are closed Friday evening. You should plan accordingly. Many hotels offer Kosher (Israeli-type) breakfasts and of course Kosher dinners.

The district, known as San Marco, is home to St. Mark's Basilica, the Doge's Palace, The Campanile (that big red brick tower), The Rialto Bridge, and of course, St. Marks Piazza. St. Marks is also home to the gondola fleet. And yes, if you want to take a gondola ride, you will have to get one in front of the Hotel Danieli (actually on the border of San Marco and Castello), where most of the Gondoliers hang out. More on this later.

San Polo is the smallest of the districts. It shares its fame with the western side of the Rialto Bridge.

The Dorsoduro district is home to several well-known art galleries, of which the Peggy Guggenheim is the most visited. I will bet, you didn't know there was a Guggenheim in Venice.

Castello is on the far eastern side of the historic district. It is a mix of one side of tourists and hotels and the other side of the locals. It is worth a stroll if you have an extra hour or two.

The sixth Sestieri is the transportation hub (non-rail) of the historic district. This is the home to the Piazzale (another word for plaza) Roma, where the causeway terminates. It is also home to the terminus of the local buses that go to Mestre and other places on the mainland, including the airport bus. Also of importance is the original car park. However, a monster garage was recently built on one of the abutting piers (at Tronchetto). If you are turning in your rental in Venice, it is best to contact the rental company and find out exactly where you turn in your car.

If you are driving it is best to compare parking prices at the major parking garage on Tronchetto or the parking lots in Mestre.

By the way, don't look for those big modern American-style hotels in Venice. You will find only a few, if any, in the Lagoon area. However, because hotels can have elevators and be built on solid ground instead of marsh, you will find them in Venice Mestre. We are now ready to find our hotel in the Lagoon.

First, here are some quickies on selecting any hotel in the Lagoon. If you don't want to lug all your bags, it is best that you follow my recommendations below. Here is the alternative:

At the parking garage and the Piazzale d Roma, you will find official porters. Look for them in their sky-blue spiffy outfits. They are here, if you wish, to take you to your hotel if you care not to port your bags or don't know where your hotel is located in the big maze. If you don't know Venice, this is the best approach to get you and your luggage to your hotel.

>>>TIP<<<
You must discuss the fixed price (including the Vaporetto fees for you and the porter). You can purchase the Vaporetto tickets at the Grand Canal's yellow and black booths (ACTV) in front of the rail station or at the water level side of the Piazzale d Roma.

Remember, you still may have to walk across that humongous bridge known as the Ponte Degli Scalvi bridge. If you are going to hotels in and around San Marco, you will need to take the Vaporetto anyway and will not have to cross the Degli Scalvi bridge. By the way, those Vaporetti (Waterbuses) tickets are not cheap. You can take any combination of Vaporetti for 75 minutes (except the Lido) after you validate it for 7.5Euros on the boat. So you can figure without the porter fee (which is tariffed, you can't

An Alternative to the Escorted Tour

haggle), it will cost you about $25 (for three people). The porter will take you to the Black and Yellow booth and instruct you to purchase the tickets for him/her and others in your party. The porter fee will run another 40-50Euros. You will have to pay in Euros as no credit cards are accepted. Guys, take it from me; this is not the time to show your other half you are a "hero." Let the porter do the schlepping. You will be glad you did; it is part of the Venice experience. On the other hand if you just have a small roller carry-on bag or a backpack, save your Euros get your map out, and just start navigating the maze. Lots of "Doe Vays" will be needed in negotiating this maze.

If you are fortunate or it's your honeymoon, you can arrange a private water taxi to pick you up at the Vaporetto stop marked "Piazzale d Roma", or the rail station. You still need to get your bags from the garage to this point. However, ensure they will port your bags into your selected hotel. You can figure about 100-200Euros for this water taxi service.
>>><<<

If you are staying in Venice Mestre, logistics become minimal. Just locate your hotel, check in with your bags, and then go and return your rental car. Hopefully, it will be in Mestre. The best turn-in location is the Mestre Rail Station.

>>>TIP<<<
If you are flying in or out of Venice, you should also check out the water taxis, which will come directly to the airport (there are several slips) and take you to your hotel. However, bear in mind that this is pricey but the least stressful. Also, some water taxi transfers are "shared," so be advised that the taxi may make several stops before yours. Best to ask if it will be private or shared. It is also the fastest from the airport to your hotel. One such firm is www.motoscafivenezia.it. I believe they are all tariffed, so there is no price negotiation. If you are flying in and beginning your honeymoon in Venice, the best is to book this private water taxi discussed above.
>>><<<

ITALY NO TOUR NEEDED
You Can Do It Yourself

Consult booking.com for the closest hotels to the Piazzale d Roma and the Santa Lucia rail station. Note, that they are all on the left-hand side of the rail station (as you walk toward the Grand Canal), about 2-5 blocks. However, if you are walking from the Piazzale d Roma, you can add on a few blocks to get over to the rail station. Several are also in the Jewish Quarter, which is excellent if you are a Sabbath observer or enjoy Kosher food. And further, don't worry about hearing those trains. They don't make any noise when they are parked at the station.

YOUR FIRST FULL DAY IN VENICE (OR HALF DAY)
If you are staying around the Mestre rail station, you must walk to the station (about 1-3 blocks) and buy a ticket to Venice from one of those red machines. They will take your credit cards. You cannot board a Frecci, Italo, or the Orient Express, only local trains. You need not worry, as the conductor will not let you board anyway. Make sure you validate your ticket at one of the machines on the platform. Once boarding the train; in about twelve minutes, you will arrive at Venice Santa Lucia station. Make sure you hold on to that ticket, as the ticket collector will inspect it for validation. If you forgot to have it validated just tell the ticket inspector, that you are a tourist, and you forgot. He will initial the ticket and you should have no problem.

DOWN THE GRAND CANAL-VENICE ORIENTATION
On the first day (or that extra half day, after you arrive from Florence), it's best to get a "feel" for the City. So after arrival at Venice Santa Lucia station or the Piazzale Roma, head down to the closest Vaporetto stop and buy a ticket. All the single-ride tickets are the same price, except for the multi-day passes. As stated above for 75 minutes of travel, it will cost you 7.50Euros. And yes, that black and yellow ticket booth at the Vaporetto stop will take your credit cards. Only purchase tickets when you need them, and remember to validate.

If possible, I suggest returning to the Santa Lucia (Ferrovia) train station Vaporetto stop unless you are closer to another stop (taking the train back to Mestre). The Piazzale Roma also has a Vaporetto stop. Get your 75-minute ticket and catch a Number 1 (One)

An Alternative to the Escorted Tour

Vaporetto. Make sure it is heading toward Rialto Mercato. It will probably zig-zag back and cross the Grand Canal. Take photos as you go down (maybe up) the canal, and be prepared to exit at Rialto "Mercato." Note, that I said Mercato. There are two Rialto stops. You want the Rialto "Mercato" stop. You do not want to get off at the Rialto stop. This will force you to go over the Rialto Bridge. You will have a chance to cross this bridge on your way to San Marco Piazza.

You can shop to your heart's content if you get off at Rialto Mercato. Also, you should note that there are public facilities here; however, ensure you have that one Euro coin with you.

>>> VERY IMPORTANT TIP <<<

There are two items to note on your first Vaporetto trip. You need to validate your ticket in that little green or yellow machine on the boat or the pier, and secondly, you need to be real street savvy. Watch out for strangers who may bump against you and force you to part with your wallet. They don't want the validated ticket you are holding. It's worth nothing once it is validated for the ride. Be extra cautious of who you stand next to and keep your hands on your wallet and smartphone and not on the peaches.
>>><<<

Once at the Rialto Mercato, you can buy many "made in Itlay items." However, I find that the Mercato is a great place for buying fruits, candy, and the like. Consider taking some back to your hotel room to munch on before dinner.

>>>TIP<<<   DON'T TOUCH THOSE GRAPES

Italy is a little advanced regarding cleanliness at the supermarket or the fruit stands. You cannot pick up fruit or vegetables with your hands or even feel them with your fingers! Either the vendor will select them and place the product on the scale, or you must put on a plastic glove; makes sense.
>>><<<

WALK TO PIAZZA SAN MARCO

After you have "shopped" the Mercato, it should be about 4PM or Noon, before you are ready to take a short walk, about three

ITALY NO TOUR NEEDED
You Can Do It Yourself

football fields over to Piazza San Marco. You won't have too much time here unless you are going to have an early dinner (it's doable). There are several ways through the Venice maze to get to San Marco. You can follow the crowd. If you think you are lost, look at those black-painted signs on the corners of the buildings. First, you must cross the Grand Canal by going over the Rialto Bridge with your back toward the Mercato. Halfway over the bridge, there are great photo ops. Just don't drop your camera or smartphone in the Canal. Also, if you want a nice photo op, ask another tourist to take a picture. Don't ask a stranger or those little "hopeless" kids. Now, continue over the bridge, and as you exit, take the pathway to the right (Pescaria S. Bartolomio), passing the Rialto Vaporetto stop. You should note that if you go over the Rialto bridge and go toward your left, it will dead-end and you will be forced to turn around and backtrack; sort of like one of those corn mazes. Continue following the crowd, and if you don't make any shopping, pastry, or gelato stops, you should arrive in San Marco in about fifteen minutes. There are several small bridges to negotiate, no big deal. You probably need the exercise.

After arriving in Piazza San Marco, you will understand why I say Venice is one giant maze. Just follow those painted black signs on the corners of the buildings. On arrival in Piazza San Marco, you will only have time to acquaint yourself with the area. On your left, as you enter the Piazza (assume you are walking in from the Rialto area), you will notice the Basilica San Marco and the Doge's Palace to the right. The Doges were the kings who ruled the Venice State.

Directly in front of you at the foot of the lagoon (the Piazzetta San Marco area), you will note two large columns with statues on top (part of the Colonna di San Todaro). Moving to your right, you will note the Campanile, that very tall red brick tower. And, finally, as you move further to the right, you can take in the full Piazza of San Marco. Note, this is where you came into the Piazza; through that arch is the famous clock tower. Those two little "knockers" come out every hour and hit that big bell. So do not confuse this with the massive clock on the top of the red brick tower in the square known as the San Marco Campanile.

An Alternative to the Escorted Tour

>>>TIP<<< WHERE ARE THE TOILETS?
There are public toilets in the Rialto Marcato and in a corner of San Marco Piazza. You should find them relatively clean from my last trip over there. Be advised that each person will need a Euro for entry. There is usually a coin changer next to the turn styles. Those Euros pay for the matron or the attendant to keep the place clean, the toilet paper, and the paper towels. Great idea. To locate them, spin your head around, and you should see some signs. When in doubt, "Doe Vay et Toilette or Banjos."
>>><<<

On your half day, there will probably not be enough time to visit any of the sites in San Marc's. However, if there is a very small line you might want to visit the ornate Basilica of San Marco. The best approach is to take a lot of photos and shop the square. By the way, it is now illegal to feed those pigeons and seagulls in Saint Mark's Square. If you are caught doing it, there is a hefty fine.

>>>TIP<<< AVOIDING PIGEON PROBLEMS
If one of those pigeons or gulls does a number on you, do not attempt to wipe it off. You need to let it dry, and dry hard. Then with a credit card (I'm assuming the one you rarely use), brush it off. You may want to consider this a sign of good luck and purchase one of those lottery (lotto) tickets from a tobacco stand or one of those folks selling them on the street. Good luck, and remember, if you feed the pigeons you risk being fined.
>>><<<

After a snack or a gelato, it is best to make your way back to your hotel. If you are in the San Marco area, it should be a short walk back to your hotel. If you are staying in Mestre or near the rail station you need to take the Vaporetto back. Since it's late in the day, the best approach is to get the #1 Vaporetto going in the opposite direction and exit at the Ferrovia (rail station). Also, note that it may go the opposite way, i.e., toward the Piazzale Roma (where the buses and taxis arrive). Try not to panic. The next stop will be Ferrovia. If you are inclined to get, some last-minute exercise go back through that arch with the clock on top and make your way to the Rialto Bridge. Cross the bridge and follow the

184

ITALY NO TOUR NEEDED
You Can Do It Yourself

signs to the Ferrovia. You will also need to cross that big bridge near the rail station (the Ponte Degli Scalvi bridge). From either stop at Saint Mark's, it would be best to take the Vaporetto #1 back to Ferrovia. Then, you won't have to climb up and down the Ponte Degli Scalvi bridge.

If you are into walking and do not care to cross those two bridges, you can take a leisurely walk through the Cannaregio district. All you need to do is find your way over to the base of the Rialto Bridge (not the Mercato side). Don't climb those steps. Instead, locate about two blocks before the base a wide alley and go directly toward the Burger King (don't laugh). The BK is after that first small canal bridge. Then find through the maze the Strada Nova. Trust me; you probably will get lost several times. Not a problem; a lot to see. Just keep asking those locals, "Doe Vay et Ferrovia" and hope they point you in the correct direction. Also, if you are seeing the sun setting you are going toward the rail station. The Strada Nova will take you to the Jewish Quarter and then the rail station.

DEALING WITH THE ACQUA ALTA
I need to prime you on this one if you have any intention of walking around Venice when there is an Acqua Alta, you need to read the next section. So, just what the 'ell is an Acqua Alta?

THE ACQUA ALTA
Mainly in the winter, many of the walkways, alleys, piazzas, etc., become flooded. Not with sewage backup but with seawater. In addition, most of the canals overflow into the basements of the abutting buildings. Yikes, does this really happen? There are several reasons:

1. The rain, wind, and tide (due to the moon's gravitational pull) will elevate the water level in the lagoon.
2. A very high tide is predicted on certain days. In addition, cruise ships and oil tankers heading for the industrial port of Marghera will also raise the water level in the lagoon. The railroad and the motorway causeways have also done a number on displacing water in the lagoon.

An Alternative to the Escorted Tour

3.   As we all know, the City of Venice is sinking…OMG. The sinking is only a few millimeters a year. All of this contributes to the Acqua Alta problem. However, Venice is partially protected for the time being, thanks to new technology.

When the "Tide Monitoring and Forecast Center" realizes that an Acqua Alta is about to occur, they notify the inhabitants of the City via text message and sirens. At the same time, 79 massive barriers are raised near the three lagoon entrances. It takes about an hour or two to raise them with compressed air. The lagoon is then sealed off from the Adriatic, and only a minimal amount of water will raise the level in San Marco Piazza. Hmmm.. it works.

When the Acqua Alta occurs, an army of city workers in yellow raincoats and boots erect plywood walkways around certain areas. The areas in and around Piazza San Marco, abutting the Grand Canal, are usually hit hard. It's not uncommon for the water to rise 100 cm (39 inches) or more and come ashore. The Acqua Alta may last anywhere from 12-24 hours or more.
You can check the website: https://www.moseveneqia.eu/

>>>TIP<<< MAKE SOME ACQUA ALTA BOOTS
The best tip I can suggest (even if in doubt) is to pack in your luggage a few of those heavy-duty black contractor bags you can buy at Home Depot, Lowes, True-Value, and more. Please don't rely on all those boards to be placed exactly where you want to go; they won't be. In addition, you will need a few quarter-by-3-inch rubber bands. Yes, duct tape will also do. If an Acqua Alta materializes (the front desk will know), all you need to do is borrow a pair of scissors from the front desk, cut two black bags down to knee height, pull them up over your shoes and legs like boots, and run those rubber bands over them like a garter to hold the top of the bags around your legs.

Secondly, the Cannaregio district (the one to the left of the rail station as you come down the steps of the station) usually does not flood. Best to check the City's website. And yes, the Vaporetti do run when there is an Acqua Alta.
>>><<<

ITALY NO TOUR NEEDED
You Can Do It Yourself

Now on to Day Two 2 in Venice:

DAY TWO IN VENICE
This day should be a full one. I assume you made that Vaporetto trip down the Grand Canal, shopped at the Rialto Market, crossed the Rialto Bridge, and did the San Marco orientation. So here we go with Day 2 in Venice.

Best to take a gondola ride before lunch. Make your way over to San Marco Piazza. You should arrive 10-11AM. Head directly to the Gondola parking area in front of the Danieli Hotel. It's on the Riva Degli Schiavoni Strada, which parallels the Grand Canal. Take a 40-minute gondola ride. See below for more info.

>>>TIP<<<   HORDES OF PEOPLE
In case you didn't notice by now, Venice is filled with people. The daytime working population is 250,000. At midnight it dwindles to about 55,000. Now add to this 250,000 people about 50,000 cruise ship visitors, 100,000 day visitors coming in from as far away as Florence and Milan, 100,000 coming in by tour coaches for two or three days, and, you probably have almost one-half million people on the "sidewalks," or more. Even the Riva Degli Schiavoni Strada is bumper-to-bumper with people from all over the world. It is even rumored that one of the reasons Venice is sinking, is the hordes of people trampling around.

If you want to avoid these massive crowds, consider going to Venice early in the morning. I get to the hotel buffet breakfast about 15 minutes before they close so this is not for me. However, in this way, you avoid the cruise shore excursion people, the day trippers who arrive by coach or train, and all those tour people having breakfast. So, best to arrive before 10AM. If you are staying in the lagoon area, just roll out of bed and hit those sidewalks by 9AM.

There is another way to avoid the crowds. Consider hitting the streets 3-4PM when all the day trippers flea the Lagoon to get home. Or better, what about a romantic gondola ride at about 6PM

187

An Alternative to the Escorted Tour

(or sunset) before dinner? BTW, I do not advise gondola rides right after lunch or dinner. No explanation is needed on this. If you are taking day trips to the other islands in the Lagoon, you should not have any problems.

>>>TIP<<< GONDOLA RATES

Those gondolier rides are tariffed. They all charge the same rates, which the City of Venice approves. For a 40-minute ride, the charge is 150Euros. So if there are two in the gondola, you will be charged 150Euros. However, if you get three more, to make it five, the cost will still be 150Euros. So the best is getting three other people who want to share the fee, and each would pay 30Euros. Best to look for a party of three people who may be interested in a gondola ride.

You should know the following: First, you can't haggle on the price. Second, they don't take credit cards; third, they are not compelled to find three other people for you. So, best you arrive and meet some "friends" who want to join you. BTW, the maximum now is five people in the gondolier because the gondoliers were complaining that the people were getting too fat (yes, this is not a joke), and for safety concerns, six was too much weight for the gondola. And as stated before, they don't go in the Grand Canal because of the waves, for the standard gondola ride.

After your gondola ride, it should be time for lunch. Lunch in this area is an easy one. As you exit the gondola mooring area, directly next to the Hotel Danieli is an alley (pathway) known as Degli Albanesi. Go down this alley for almost three blocks, and on your left, you will find #4250, The Taverna Dogi. You can't beat the food, the price, and the service. Do try the fish soup or stew. After lunch, you are ready to visit the other sites in the San Marco area. By the way, avoid the restaurants and bars directly on the Grand Canal (Riva Degli Schiavoni Strada), they define the word "Very Pricey." A glass of wine and a bottle of water will cost 30Euros. The waiter, however, will take your picture with a background of the Grand Canal. There is no extra charge for taking the picture. I don't think they charge for a dish of potato chips.
>>><<<

ITALY NO TOUR NEEDED
You Can Do It Yourself

>>>TIP<<<
I always recommend a tour of the Doge's Palace and the Basilica in Piazza San Marco. You probably won't be able to get in. So the best is to look online and buy those timed tickets on Tripadvisor, about a month or two before the date you wish to visit. It will be time spent well. The Doge's Palace is one big museum with painted ceilings and walls; the likes you have never seen. I should note that you can always cancel on Tripadvisor 24 hours prior and receive a full refund. In addition to the Doge's Palace and the Basilica, you need to view the "Bridge of Sighs." This, supposedly, is the most romantic bridge in Venice, connecting the Doge's Palace with the prison next door. The bridge was built in 1600. The best view is from the bridge on the Riva Degli Schiavoni Strada; be street savvy here.
>>><<<

If you are still not tired after this point, your next and final stop should be that massive red brick tower known as the Campanile di San Marco. There is usually no waiting at the end of the day or early when it opens up; see below.

THE CAMPANILE
Yes, it's a bell tower. However, before becoming a bell tower, the Campanile was a watch tower. The belfry was added in the 20th century. And get this: it collapsed in 1902. What you see is the reconstruction effort of 1912. If you want to bring home an interesting souvenir, see if you can locate the black and white photo of the bell tower as a pile of brick rubble. The original tower was built in 1514. It is one of the symbols of Venice.

The bells were rung to announce the start of the workday, the end of the day, an execution, meeting commencement of the city fathers, and other functions. The tower now stands 323 feet tall. At its base, it is 120 feet wide. On the top of the Campanile is a gold weather vane in the form of Gabriel, the angel. There is a charge of ten Euros to enter the tower, which includes your elevator fee. More at:

An Alternative to the Escorted Tour

http://www.basilicasanmarco.it/?lang=en.
Tickets run 10-13Euros, depending on where you purchase them. In the off-season, you should not have any problem purchasing them on-site. The best time is probably first thing in the morning. Check opening times. This is absolutely the best place to take pictures of the entire City.

EXTRA DAYS IN VENICE SUGGEST DAYS 3 AND 4 --THE LIDO

If you have extra days to spare and are visiting Venice from April through October, consider an afternoon at the Lido. I discussed the Lido in depth at the beginning of this chapter. There is lots of flat walking, shopping, and of course, a nice lunch at one of the outdoor cafes. If you are of the Jewish Faith, you might want to visit an ancient Jewish cemetery that dates from 1386. It is known as the Jewish Cemetery at San Nicolo. As you exit the Vaporetto pier, you will find it only one block to your left.

If it is a beach day, consider bringing your swimming attire. Some concessions will rent you umbrellas, lounge chairs, etc., on these beaches: San Nicolo, Alberoni, Murazzi (rocks), and Blue Moon. They are within a few blocks of the ferry terminal. All of them have changing facilities and restrooms. In addition, many of them sell hamburgers, paninis, and other nourishment goodies. So best just to bring your bathing attire (you can also go in the Adriatic in your shorts) and a towel. Also, best to bring Euros as many may not take your credit cards. And, with any beach, do remember to watch your items.
There are two excellent websites:
https://www.veneziaunica.it/en/content/beaches
https://www.visitlido.it/en/experiences/a-venetian-beach-holiday/

THE ISLAND OF MURANO

There are three islands worth visiting, or at least one. They are Murano, Burano and Torcello. If you can only spare a half-day, I would favor Murano. There is enough time for a whole day here. It would be best if you figured arriving about 11AM and departing about 4PM. There are seven small connecting islands.

ITALY NO TOUR NEEDED
You Can Do It Yourself

It won't cost you a penny to go to Murano. You can check with your hotel concierge, the internet, or with one of the small glass shops around the Piazza San Marco. It's simple. A boat takes you over to the island (it's about a mile away), drops you off, and picks you up later in the day. The boats run approximately every hour. Hopefully, you will purchase some of the hand-blown pieces of glass as a souvenir. This is how they make their money. However, it's still a free boat ride even if you purchase nothing.

If you wish, you can take one of the Vaporetti over and back to the island. The Vaporetti depart the San Zaccaria stop about every hour, costing about two Euros. San Zaccaria is one of the Piazza San Marco stops. Also, that same Vaporetto goes on to Burano. You should check the ATCV schedules as they change throughout the year.

BURANO AND TORCELLO
I discuss these two islands in the Lagoon because they are very similar. As for Burano, most tourists go here for a few hours to take pictures of those gorgeous houses on the local lagoons. The main product, in addition to tourism, is hand-woven lace.

Romans settled Burano in the 6th Century. Because lace-making was labor intensive, it declined until the 19th Century, when it was revived. If you visit Burano, the best souvenirs are the lace doilies and those fantastic photos.

Torcello is the third island in the group. The island was first settled in 452AD. They believe Torcello was the parent island from which Venice was populated. The island even had a cathedral and bishops before there was St. Mark's Basilica. In the 10th century, Torcello had a population of almost 20,000. In pre-medieval times Torcello was a more extensive trading hub than Venice. Its primary product was salt. The black plague and other factors lead to a total decline in the population.

As of 2018, the population was reported at 12 (yes twelve). Most of the material used to build the many palazzi, parishes, and cloisters disappeared as they were recycled to create other structures in

An Alternative to the Escorted Tour

Venice. That basilica and the campanile were later rebuilt in 1008AD. There is also a small museum there. The main attraction is the Cathedral of Santa Maria Assunta. It was founded in 639AD and has many Byzantine works, including mosaics from the 11th and 12th centuries.

Torcello is also home to Attila's Throne (nothing to do with Atilla the Hun) and the "Devil's Bridge," a stone bridge. It is believed the original bridge was built during the 13th Century and a new bridge replaced it in the 15th century. As recently as 2009, the bridge received an overhaul. If you go to Torcello, the Cathedral and Campanile, along with the Devil's Bridge, are worth a visit.

GIUDECCA AND SAN GIORGIO

There are two historic islands across the Lagoon that you may want to visit. They are Giudecca and San Giorgio. However, you won't find a lot of souvenir shops here. These two islands are primarily residential. There is not too much activity on San Giorgio as the church occupies most of it, along with the new Vatican Chapels built in 2013. There are, however, some very historic churches. The best known and often photographed is the Basilica of San Giorgio Maggiore. If you are looking at pictures of Venice, you can't miss this one. The Basilica sits on a triangle of land jutting into the Lagoon.

Consider having lunch at one of the many cafes on the island of Giudecca, where you will find the five-star Belmond Cipriani Hotel. You should note that the Island of San Giorgio is not connected to Giudecca. There is no connecting bridge. You must take a Vaporetto about three minutes from one island to the other. So plan your day if you visit the Basilica of San Giorgio and the new Vatican Chapels. BTW, there were never any Jewish people who lived in Giudecca (pronounced Ju-Decca). The source of the name of this island is unknown. Giudecca is worth a visit for a stroll and lunch in any one of the numerous cafes.

PEGGY GUGGENHEIM MUSEUM

Peggy was the daughter of Benjamin Guggenheim. Benjamin was one of seven sons born to Meyer Guggenheim. As we all know the Guggenheims are right up there with the Carnegies, Rockefellers,

ITALY NO TOUR NEEDED
You Can Do It Yourself

Rothschilds, and all the other famous people who made their money around the "gilded age of America," 1870-1900. Peggy's father died on the Titanic in 1912. Her mom was Florett Seligman, who came from a wealthy banking family. In summary, Peggy inherited a lot of money. So what did she do with all this money? Simple, she bought works of art.

Peggy moved to Paris in about 1920. In 1938 she opened a modern art gallery in London. Peggy collected contemporary art at the rate of one piece a day. When WWII ended, she moved everything from the south of France to Venice, where she opened a gallery after purchasing a home on the Grand Canal. It was open to tourists every summer. In 1976, she donated the house and her entire collection to the Solomon G. Guggenheim Foundation. The foundation now owns the museum. It is one of the Guggenheims, just like New York and Bilbao, Spain.

The Peggy Guggenheim Museum is worth a visit. It contains originals of all the famous modern artists of our time: Jackson Pollack, Dali, Kandinsky, and more. Over 600 pieces of work mostly range in style from Cubism, Surrealism, and the Abstract school. If you are a lover of art, this is the place.

The current entrance fee is 16Euros. In the off-season, I believe you can purchase tickets at the museum. However, plan your visit and buy your tickets online to play on the safe side. You should figure a minimum of two hours at the Guggenheim. The museum is closed on Tuesday. More information can be found:
https://www.guggenheim-venice.it/

If you still have extra days in the Venice area, best is to read my next chapter Venice Extra Days, Chapter 16.

*** EXTRA SPACE BELOW IS FOR YOUR NOTES ***

CHAPTER 16

VENICE DAY TRIPS
PADUA AND VERONA

INTRODUCTION

This chapter supplements my Chapter 14. If you have selected more than four days in Venice, you might be interested in two excellent day trips. Padua (often spelled Padova) is about 30 minutes away by train, and Verona is a little over an hour. Both cities offer lots of history. What's nice is the trains are very frequent and extremely inexpensive. I won't steal the thunder on Padua, which I describe below. Few know about Verona.

Where can you view (and stand on) the actual balcony where Juliet said to Romeo: "Romeo, Romeo, where art thou Romeo?" Yes, it was Verona. Verona has more than just that balcony; given the time, you ought to consider a day trip here since there is more to see and do than the balcony.

Another interesting fact, Shakespeare wrote about seven plays set in Italy: *Romeo and Juliet, The Merchant of Venice, The Taming of the Shrew*, and *The Two Gentlemen of Verona,* to name a few. However, Shakespeare never visited Italy! Go figure that one out? It has been a topic of discussion by Shakespeare's followers for several hundred years.

PADUA DAY TRIP

If you did not know, Padua is best known as the home of St. Anthony (Antonio). Saint Anthony is the patron saint of lost, stolen, and forgotten items. Padua lies about 25 miles due west of Venice on the Bacchiglione River. The Basilica and the complex are the number one draw to Padua. It is also home to one of the oldest universities in Italy. If you make it a leisurely day trip, you can plan on arriving about 10AM or 11AM and returning about 6PM for a snooze before dinner at 7:30PM.

ITALY NO TOUR NEEDED
You Can Do It Yourself

I won't go into all the details of Saint Anthony's life, but suffice it to be, that he was a Franciscan monk, born in 1195 in Portugal, and died in Padua in 1231. He is one of the most famous and revered Saints, right up there with Saint Francis of Assisi.

Padua is one of the oldest cities in Northern Italy, dating from 1138BC. It predates ancient Rome by about 500 years. It is interesting to note that this city, for almost 3,000 years, has gone back and forth under the rule of so many conquerors. Far too many conquerors have invaded Padua, even to mention here. It is probably well over a hundred.

What's important, about 50BC, Padua allied and became a part of the Roman Empire. You can still find Roman ruins in Padua. There are ruins of an amphitheater and bridge foundations. In 899, Padua was sacked by the Magyars. The city had to be rebuilt after the fire in 1174. In 1214 Padua went to war with Venice, which Venice won in 1216.

In medieval times Padua, in the year 1405, came under the rule of the Republic of Venice. This domination by Venice lasted about 400 years until 1797. In 1814 with the fall of Napoleon, the city became part of the Austrian Empire. Under Austrian rule, Padua entered the Industrial Revolution by laying the first railroad from Venice to Padua in 1845. In 1866, Padua was annexed to the Kingdom of Italy by the Battle of Koniggratz. As Italy was an ally of Prussia, Padua and the Veneto region cities (Venice, Verona, Vicenza) became Italy.

Padua is an enjoyable day trip from Venice, even if you are driving. Almost all trains bound for the west and south of Venice will stop in Padua. It does not pay to board a "Frecci" with a reserved seat for that 30-minute ride. It will cost you about 20 Euros. The best way is to take a local train from Mestre or Venice Santa Lucia for about 5-10 Euros. Remember to validate your ticket in that small red, yellow, or green machine on the platform—also, no need to purchase tickets before you go.

On arrival in Padua, it's a little more than a mile to the Basilica of St. Anthony. I would not suggest the walk even though it is all flat.

195

An Alternative to the Escorted Tour

It is much faster to take a taxi from the rail station unless you can use the exercise. It will cost you about seven Euros. You are lucky because in the same area is the old square (Piazza del Santo) and "The Prato della Valle" along with the University. Here you will find lots of shops, eateries and the like.

If you are walking to St. Anthony's, you might want to visit the Scrovegni Chapel and the museum. The chapel has exquisitely painted frescoes on the walls and ceilings. These paintings are one of the highlights of the fresco artworks of the 14th century.

The "Chapel" is en route to St. Anthony's. You can view the chapel paintings only on Mondays. However, it is also available with a combination ticket for the museum on all other days. If you need to purchase a timed ticket (not advisable in the off-season), plan to visit 45 minutes after your train arrives from Venice. You can also take your luck at grabbing a ticket for time slots later in the day.

On arrival at St. Anthony's, I suggest first viewing this magnificent Basilica and then the tomb of St. Anthony. The Basilica took about 78 years to complete (1232-1310). It's a combination of Romanesque, Byzantine, and Turkish designs. It is unique, and you would never think this structure is a church.

Then after a light lunch, proceed less than a football field (a two-minute walk) to The Orto Botanico di Padova. This is the oldest botanical garden known. It was founded in 1545 by the then-Venetian Republic to cultivate herbs and unique plants for healing. It is still in its original location and is part of the University of Padua.

Statuary adorns most of the botanical garden. It is just a stone's throw from St. Anthony's. It is worth a minimum of a one-hour visit. Tickets are about 10Euros. You can find more information at: www.ortobotanicopd.it/it/biglietti.

Also, just a quick note, at St. Anthony's, you will find the facilities to the right of the entrance, about 100 feet near those gardens. And yes, remember to have that Euro handy.

ITALY NO TOUR NEEDED
You Can Do It Yourself

Within a stone's throw of the botanical gardens is the "Prato della Valle." This is the largest square in Italy and one of the largest in all of Europe. It is unique because it is not a square. It occupies about 900,000 square feet (about 22 acres) and is oval. A trough or canal runs through it. Or shall I say within it?

The "ill Prato," as they call it, is the central gathering point for concerts and other festive events. Here is a quick history.

The Prato was a swampy area used for horse riding events, i.e., jousting in medieval times. The monks of Santa Giustina owned it. The city of Padua purchased it in 1767. There are a total of 78 statues in the inner and outer rings. They are originals carved by artists of the area. All are carved from stone mined in nearby Vicenza. All this work was accomplished between 1775 and 1883. Most statues are of local politicians of Padua, Popes, and famous people of the Venice and Padua area. However, you won't find any Michelangelo or Da Vinci sculptures here. This is an excellent spot for picture-taking.

If you are up to walking and care not to visit the botanical gardens of Padua, you might enjoy a leisurely lunch in the Piazza Dei Signori. There are numerous places around the Piazza and en route from St. Anthony's.

DAY CRUISE VENICE TO PADUA- THE BRENTA CANAL

As a point in passing, I should note that a canal connects Padua with Venice. In season (March through October), there are daily sailings between the two cities. However, with the tours of the abutting mansions, you will have very little time to view the highlights of Padua. If you are staying a week in Venice, this day tour on the Brenta Canal makes another excellent day trip. My suggestion is to take the train back to Venice or overnight in Padua and return to Venice the next day in the afternoon after visiting St. Anthony's and Padua.

An Alternative to the Escorted Tour

VERONA DAY TRIP

While Venice represents medieval times and the Renaissance, Verona is a mix of history. On entry to the city, you are thrown back into Roman times. Verona lies on the banks of the Adige River about 75 miles west of Venice, on the way to Milan, and is surrounded by hills. Verona is a city made for walking.

Ask anyone who has visited Verona, and they will tell you "Romeo and Juliet" and that "big stadium" like the Colosseum in the center of the town. Here is a quick history of Verona:

Little is known about the early history of Verona. We know that the area became Roman in about 300BC and officially became a Roman colony 49BC. The city became important because it was at the intersection of several crossroads to the other cities in the area, i.e., Milan, Venice, Florence, and the towns north of the Italian Alps. The city went back and forth between several powers in the area until King Alboin of the Lombards took it in 569AD. That's about 100 years after Rome fell.

The Holy Roman Empire took over Verona under Austrian control. In 1135 Verona became a free community and integrated into the Lombard League. Many wars continued into the Middle Ages. And, of course, the black plague of 1346-1353 took a toll on the population.

In 1260 the "Della Scalas" rose to power, and the arts and architecture flourished in Verona. Mansions of the wealthy were built. The Della Scalas were also responsible for building the Castelvecchio. If you have extra time you might want to consider visiting the Castle. Castelvecchio is a humongous castle on the banks of the Adige River. It is now a museum. In 1405AD, Verona became part of the Republic of Venice. It became home to more wealthy merchants as trade flourished. Finally, in 1866, Verona became part of the Kingdom of Italy. The entire city is also a UNESCO World Heritage Site.

ITALY NO TOUR NEEDED
You Can Do It Yourself

WHAT TO SEE AND DO IN VERONA

Verona is the second largest city in the Veneto region, second only to Venice. In 89BC it was a Roman settlement. Most of the history of the City is wrapped up in its medieval past. Parts of the medieval wall and its gates remain.

By now, it should be evident that the home of Juliet "Casa di Giulietta" is a must-see. The actual balcony is located at Via Cappello 23. Note- Parking is difficult in the area, and there are few paid parking lots. If you are coming by train, you need to hop in a taxi for a 2.5-mile ride to Juliet's house. Also, watch out for BnB's name Juliet House, or something similar. Using this location may lead you to the wrong place.

William Shakespeare (the Bard) wrote Romeo and Juliet in 1597. To put things in perspective, that's only 23 years before the Mayflower dropped anchor in Plymouth, Massachusetts. As the Bard wrote, the 13th-century house belonged to the Cappelletti family, not the Capulets. The small balcony where supposedly Juliet uttered the words "Romeo, Romeo where art thou" was installed on the house in the 20th century. She spoke those famous words from an open window. Also, there was no Juliet. The Bard made it all up. The house of the Cappelletti (not the Capulets) is now a museum with a small entrance charge. I don't know who invented the "balcony scene."

You must now purchase tickets for the Juliet Museum: https://www.museiverona.com/

There is a bronze statue of Juliet under that balcony. The saying goes, if you rub her right breast, you will be blessed with love and fertility. There is a side of the walkway into the courtyard where you can post a note to Juliet. You might want to consider belonging to the Juliet club. You will find it across the street. One of the staff will write a note to Juliet on a piece of old parchment and post it on that wall for you.

An Alternative to the Escorted Tour

There are many gelato shops in the area, and this is a great place to take some photos, especially with your "significant other," friend, or a family member on that balcony.

In case you missed it. As I said, the Bard never visited Verona. So how did he write this masterpiece? No one knows. Now on to the Arena, the number one ancient attraction in Verona.

The Arena was built outside the walls of the City of Verona. It is now inside the walls of the old city. I don't think they moved the Arena. However, the best bet is they built a new wall. A ten-minute walk from Giuletta's house will bring you to the Arena. The Arena was built in 30AD, about fifty years before the coliseum of Rome i.e. Colosseum. Since they did not have the term coliseum yet, they called it the Arena. An alternate name could have been the Amphitheater of Verona. Now, it's just called the "Arena."

The Arena is about 1.5 football fields in length and a little more than one football field across. Gladiators fought here, like the Colosseum, for over 400 years until the Roman Emperor Honorius ended the games in 404AD. For over 400 years, the Arena stood empty. At one time, the structure stood four stories until an earthquake in the 12th century caused so much damage the Arena had to be reduced to three stories in height.

The Arena is almost round and held 30,000 people in ancient times. Today because of the stage, it holds about 20,000 people. The façade of the building was decorated in pink limestone from nearby Valpolicella (the extensive wine-producing area).

The earthquake of 1117AD almost destroyed the Arena's outer ring. There are vestiges of the outer ring still standing.

Because of its outstanding acoustics, the Arena has been used to host numerous operas since the Renaissance. It continues to this day with about 4-6 productions per year. It's worth a visit. However, you should watch the traffic around the Arena. There are several sites worth seeing in the old or medieval city: The Piazza Delle Erbe and the Piazza Bra are excellent places to enjoy lunch and shopping.

ITALY NO TOUR NEEDED
You Can Do It Yourself

If you are into medieval castles, consider an hour of viewing at the Castle Vecchio (Castelvecchio) and its bridge across the Adige River. Just look for a castle with a crenelated roof. The castle dates to 1354. You can't miss it. The Castle is on top of a hill. As usual, the Castle is closed on Mondays; admission fee is six Euros.

You may want to visit two of the many medieval churches of Verona. They are the Basilica of San Zeno Maggiore and the Verona Cathedral. These two churches and many others are beautiful examples of the Italian Renaissance. Not only are the exteriors magnificent, but also the interiors.

The largest church is the Basilica of Sant' Anastasia. It is only a five-minute walk from the Piazza Delle Erbe.

The best approach is to visit Juliet's Balcony first, then have lunch in the Piazza Delle Erbe, and then walk about three blocks to the Basilica. The Corso Sant' Anastasia is lined with shops, so best to visit the area on a weekday since many shops may be closed on Sunday. After you see the Basilica, I recommend visiting the Arena if you have not done so. These visits should round out the day.

>>>TIP<<<   RENT A CAR FOR THE DAY
Compare the price of the train from Venice to Verona and the time it takes. If you have a party of 4 people it will pay to rent a car for the day. You can rent a car for the day from any rental location in Mestre. The best place is the Mestre stazione. Another good reason for staying in Mestre.

I always suggest "ORBITZ.COM." The present rate for a one-day rental in mid-July 2024 from Venice Mestre, out at 10AM and returned by 8PM is less than $60! You can't beat that, even with the tolls and the gas fillup. Plus, you get to stop at those Autogrills and purchase all those Italian food products (yes, you can bring them all back to the USA, as long as you do not open them) and other souvenirs before you leave Italy. It's best to buy them inbound to Verona at that first Autogrill you spot!
>>><<<

CHAPTER 17

MILAN & THE LAKES
COMO & MAGGIORE

INTRODUCTION

The lakes of Northern Italy are a must for second-time visitors. If you are on your first trip and have another week available, I recommend spending it in the Lakes region. This region of Italy comprises two areas: Lombardy and the Piedmont. Since the lakes region is above Milan (except for Lake Garda, which is northeast), I suggest flying out of Milan back to the USA or Canada. Plenty of non-stop flights are available with all the major carriers. Also, pricing is quite reasonable since the Milan route to major North American cities is very competitive.

Milan has two airports, and most of the North American non-stops fly out of MXP (Malpensa), not Linate (LIN).

There is a lot to do and see in Milan. For one thing, it is one of the fashion capitals of Europe, second only to Paris. So don't think you need to spend $150 on a pair of shoes! And, unlike Rome, there is something for everyone when it comes to shopping. All of metro Milan is flat. So walking is easy.

Concerning the lakes, there are two ways to visit them. As we all know, checking in and out of hotels is a pain. It consumes time, and you must check your bags until 4PM when the rooms are available. It's a real drag, literally and figuratively. It is far easier and less stressful to base yourself in Milan for about four days and make day trips to three lakes; Como, Stresa, and Garda. On another point, Lake Garda presents a minor problem and is best visited with a rental car out of Milan and an overnight stay. If you are starting your Italian experience in Milan, you won't need a car until you head to Venice or drive south to Bologna, Florence, and Rome. I will explain later.

ITALY NO TOUR NEEDED
You Can Do It Yourself

MILAN AS A BASE

If you base yourself in a hotel around the "Centrale" rail station, you will find it easier to visit the lakes since you will not have to take a taxi, a tram (street car trolley), or the Metro (Milan's subway) to the Milano Centrale rail station.

If you are coming in from Venice on a train, you can easily walk 5-10 minutes to your hotel from the Milano Centrale rail station. If you are driving in with your rental from other points, the best place to turn in your car is at Milano Centrale.

If you are starting your Italian vacation with a flight to Milan Malpensa airport you will not need a car as there is excellent public transportation to Milano Centrale or better, consider a taxi directly to your hotel in the Centrale area. When you are ready to leave Milan, you can easily rent a car at Milano Centrale.

I should point out that when you use ORBITZ.COM or other search engines (OTA's, Online Travel Agencies) and specify Milano Centrale as a pickup point, many pickup points are a block or two away from the train station.

>>>TIP<<<   THE HOTEL COLOMBIA

My favorite hotel is only three blocks away from Milano Centrale on a quiet side street, the Hotel Colombia. It's a four-star boutique hotel with the breakfast of a five-star hotel, and it will cost you about $170 or less (2024 rates). Book directly to get the best possible rate and the best cancellation privileges. On another note, if you get one of the smaller rooms, do inform the manager and perhaps they can upgrade you to a larger room. Also, it is best to request a room overlooking the courtyard as opposed to the street, since there is usually less noise. You will find additional hotels around "Centrale" on booking.com.
>>><<<

Now let's get to those day trips.

An Alternative to the Escorted Tour

The Lakes (sometimes just called the Lakes District) have become a real tourist draw in the last 25 years. They were once and still are, where the real wealthy live. It's just beautiful. The lakes were formed in the last ice age, about 22,000 years ago, and have a backdrop of rock formations ranging from 800 to 2,000 feet in height. These lakes are gorgeous!

DAY TRIP TO LAKE COMO, VARENNA AND BELLAGIO

This town, along with the Cinque Terre and Positano, has become one of Italy's three most photographed towns. Everyone raves about Lake Como, not to mention George Clooney. There are numerous paintings of the homes abutting Lake Como in Varenna and those small walkways along the Lake. These pictures and photographs are why people love Varenna. Oh, sorry, but you won't find any remnants of Roman civilizations. Here's how we get there:

Walk to Milano Centrale and purchase a ticket on the next local train to Varenna-Esino. You do not want to go to "Como" unless you take a whole day cruise with lunch on the Lake. The tourist spots for Lake Como are in Varenna and Bellagio. This is not on the CITY of Como line. The City of Como is on the rail line to Lake Lugano, which is mostly in Switzerland. Make sure you don't purchase a ticket to Lake Como. You need to buy a ticket to Varenna-Esino. Tickets are good anytime.

>>>TIP<<<

Do not purchase your rail tickets from the red machines. Go directly to the ticket agent for "Trenitalia-Trenord" (note there is no service on the competitor "Italo"). BTW, Trenord is part of Trenitalia and operates all the local trains in the Piedmont Region. Ask for two round-trip tickets to Varenna-Esino and then ask for the Senior Discount if you are 50 and above. There is a train every 45 minutes. You might want to walk over to Milano Centrale the day before, note the train times, and purchase your tickets. All seats are unreserved. Even though the ride is only 60 minutes, arrive early to grab some munchies to go. Also, you will be required to clear security to gain access to the rail platforms. All trains have very clean facilities on board.

>>><<<

204

ITALY NO TOUR NEEDED
You Can Do It Yourself

>>>TIP<<<
Make sure you sit on the left side of the train as you face the locomotive. The left-hand side will give you lots of photo-ops as Lake Como comes into view about 30 minutes out of Milano Centrale.
>>><<<

When you arrive in Varenna-Esino, note the return times, so you can plan your return trip, and follow the crowd down those few steps, or better that ramp. You'll see most people walking down to the Lake on that street to your left. It is known as Via Per Esino. In a few blocks, take that left on the major street known as Via Venini, then take the next right on Via Imbarcadero. You will see the Hotel Olivedo on your left in a few hundred feet. You should note that a taxi stand is just in front of the hotel and outside the restaurant. You will need this as there is a long and strenuous "hike" up to the train station. A taxi will cost 7Euros.

Directly in front of the Hotel Ristorante Olivedo is the ferry slip to Bellagio and other points in the Lake. Leaving the Olievedo and going to your left will bring you into the village of Varenna.

However, before leaving the Olivedo, you need to make some strategic decisions. Should you explore Varenna and have some lunch, or would it be better to take the 15-minute ferry to Bellagio have lunch there, and return to Varenna for shopping in the late afternoon? My feeling is that there is a lot of walking in Varenna. As they say, it's six of one, half a dozen of the other. So I would favor Varenna till you are shopped out, then spend the afternoon having lunch on the Lake next to the ferry terminal or in the village of Varenna. It would be best if you planned to get to Bellagio at about 2-3PM.

CAUTION- Make sure the ferry is going to Bellagio. They all look the same, and some of them go to other points on the Lake. The ferry fare is relatively cheap, at about 6Euros a ride.

An Alternative to the Escorted Tour

On arrival in Bellagio, in season, you will find a 30-minute tram tour around the town. I don't know if it operates in the winter months. However, it's only ten Euros and certainly worth it.

The ferry terminal and the area around Bellagio are all flat. However, there is a steep hill area behind the ferry terminal. If you are considering an overnight in Bellagio, you should be aware that many of the accommodations are up several flights of stairs, and you won't have to worry about using the hotel fitness room. It would be better to stay in Varenna or across the lake (a 12-minute ferry ride) in Cadenabbia, where the hotel prices are lower than Varenna. Make sure you request a lake view and check the proximity to the ferry terminal.

There is not much to do in Bellagio unless you have several days. So it is best to enjoy lunch, the shopping and of course gelato.

When you are done for the day, work your way back to the ferry terminal in Billagio and get the ferry going to Varenna and not to some other point on the lake, e.g., Cadenabbia. On arrival in Varenna, take a taxi for seven Euros back up that hill to the stazione and return to Milano Centrale via the Trenord train. Make sure you validate your ticket in the red or yellow machine.

DAY TRIP TO STRESA (LAKE MAGGIORE)

This is my favorite lake in Italy. You probably never heard of Stresa and Lake Maggiore. It does not get the play that Lake Como does. George Clooney does not live here. Ernest Hemingway made Stresa and Lake Maggiore famous in his novel *"A Farewell to Arms"* (1929 by Scribner). Like the other lakes, it was formed in the last ice age about 22,000 years ago. It is a beautiful lake which is part of Italy and Switzerland. Hotels and parks line the shoreline in the village of Stresa and continue three miles up the Corso Umberto to the town of Baveno.

The major draw to Lake Maggiore, Stresa, and Baveno is the Borromean Islands. There are five islands less than a half mile offshore. Two are worth visiting as the fifth and smallest, "Malghera," contains lush vegetation and a small beach. Isola Madre and Isolino di San Giovanni are the third and fourth islands, only if you have another day to spare. San Giovanni was the home

ITALY NO TOUR NEEDED
You Can Do It Yourself

of Arthuro Toscanini, the famous Italian orchestra conductor during the 1930s and 40's this leaves two remaining islands that are a must to visit: Isola Bella and Isola Pescatore (also called Isola Superiore). BTW, Maggiore means "major."

Inexpensive combination ferry tickets are sold for departures from Stresa and Baveno to visit each island separately or two (Isola Bella and Isola Pescatore) together. A government authority operates the ferries. You can see both islands in one day with no problem. There are no roads, only pedestrian walkways. The Islands are small, less than two football fields long and about one wide.

If you are driving out to Stresa, you will find a good amount of parking near the ferry terminal. It is all metered and strictly enforced. You can figure at least 90 minutes to get out to Stresa after you get lost and navigate through the Milan traffic. So, I always advocate the train for a short one-hour journey of about $15 roundtrip. There are trains every hour from Milano Centrale to Stresa and Baveno. And, you don't have to worry about finding a parking space and worrying about that meter.

Just a point in passing. Avoid going to Stresa and the Borromean Islands on a weekend when it is crowded with locals.

If you are looking for a resort-style hotel and have a family. Your best bet is the Hotel Dino in Baveno, within one block of the Baveno ferry terminal, with frequent departures to Stresa and the Borromean Islands. I have personally stayed at this excellent four-star hotel. More information can be found at: www. grand-dino.hotelslakemaggiore.com. You might consider a day or two in Baveno before departure from Milan's Malpensa airport. You can turn in your rental car there.

If you take the train to Stresa, it is best to exit the station and follow the signs to your right. Take a left on that main street known as "Via Duchessa di Genova" and follow it till you get to the lake, then go right to the ferry terminal. You should note a slight slope (as opposed to an uphill gradient) as "Via Duchessa" goes down to the lake. On your return from the Borromean Islands, it would

An Alternative to the Escorted Tour

be wise to take a taxi back to the Stresa rail station. It will cost you about 5-7Euros. Trust me, you will be bushed from walking all day, or else you can walk through this lovely Italian village.

You should anticipate arriving at the rail station in Stresa at about 11AM. From here, best to walk to the ferry terminal and purchase a combination (yes, they will take your plastic) ticket to Isola Bella and Isola Pescatore/Superiore. I always advise everyone to visit Isola Bella first. You can figure with the grounds and the tour of the Palazzo Borromeo, it will take about two hours. So, make sure you bring some snacks to munch on since you won't be in Isola Pescatore until around 2PM for lunch.

I should note that there are about six places to grab a bite on Isola Bella. However, you will find many more restaurants and lots of shopping on Isola Pescatori, even a hotel. You will have a greater selection of eateries if you can hold off the hunger.

If you want to stay on Isola Pescatore for the night at the Albergo Ristorante Belvedere: I believe the island is shut off late in the evening till sunrise, so if you have any medical conditions that may require emergency attention, it would be best to stay on the mainland i.e. Stresa or Baveno.

Here is a quick history of Isola Bella:
The main attraction is the gardens and the palace. There is an entry fee, and well worth it. I cannot tell you how incredible the gardens and the palace are. There is no comparison if you have been to places like the DuPont estate in Wilmington, DE, the Biltmore Estate in Asheville, NC, or any other famous gardens. Both Isola Bella and the smaller Isola Madre (where there is also a small palace) are mentioned in *1,000 Places To See Before You Die* by Patricia Schultz. And by the way, there is more to these gardens besides the fauna and flora! It is a MUST-see!

In 1632 Carlo III of the House of Borromeo started construction on a barren island, about four football fields off the shores of Stresa, a palace dedicated to his wife "Isabella" (hence the name of the island is Bella, for the beautiful one.) Construction stopped about 1650. Milan was struct by a plague. Further work started

208

after the plague by Carlo III's sons, Giberto III and Vitaliano VI. However, the gardens were not completed until 1671. Construction continued for almost 400 years. They definitely took their time.

In the 1800s, the palace hosted Napoleon and Josephine, the Prince of Wales, and others.

In 1935, the palace hosted representatives of Italy, France, and the United Kingdom, resulting in the "Stresa Front."

You should depart the ferry terminal and make your first stop the Isola Bella. If the first stop is Isola Pescatore (Superiore), stay on the ferry till the next stop. They are less than 10 minutes apart. Visiting Isola Bella first is the easiest way to see both islands. It would be best if you went to the ticket booth, bought your tickets, and took a tour of the palace and gardens.

>>>TIP<<<
On exiting the ferry at Isola Bella, ask the attendant (with the white hat) when the next ferry is to Isola Pescatore. He usually carries a card with him and will tell you when ferries are usually in about two hours. Knowing the departure time for Isola Pescatore will give you time to plan your stay on Isola Bella, and further, you won't wait at the ferry terminal for a long time for the next ferry to Isola Pescatore.
>>><<<

The Isola Pescatore (or Superiore) is just what it is. It is an island of fishermen and working people. You will find many restaurants, souvenir shops, and other shops selling fine goods here. And, yes, gelato. After lunch, do your shopping and walk around the whole island. Once again, when arriving on the island best to see when the return ferries are to Stresa about 4-5PM.

Some quick facts about Isola Pescatore:
It is just a charming place. As a New Englander, it's very much like Nantucket. Cobblestone streets, shops, and houses line the streets. The island was first occupied in the 10th Century. The chief "industry" was, fishing. There still are fishermen here.

An Alternative to the Escorted Tour

However, in the past 70 years, tourism has taken over. If you have a few minutes, visit the church, which dates to the 11th Century.

On arrival back in Stresa around 4-5PM, time permitting, consider taking a walk over to the Grand Hotel Des iles Borromees. Have a drink at the lobby bar and think about how it was for young Hemingway (Frederic Henry) and Catherine Barkley as they contemplated rowing across Lake Maggiore to Switzerland the following evening. And yes, they did it in the dark of night; it was cold and raining, and would you believe she was pregnant? Great job, Ernest! You will have to read the book (*A Farewell to Arms*) to see how it ended. It was one of Hemingway's best books and a true story. Well, mostly true.

>>>TIP<<<
It will cost you 5-7Euros to take a taxi back to the railway station from the Grand Hotel Des iles Borromees. Take a 10-15 minute walk back to where you parked your rental and return to Milan. Oy, and that Milan traffic, better you should have taken the train.
>>><<<

If you are staying overnight in Stresa or Baveno, several other attractions are worth visiting. First, if any of your friends advise you to take that cable car up the mountain in Stresa, it is still closed due to that horrific accident in May 2021 which killed 14. You can check with the local tourist information booth in town if the cable car has re-opened. However, it is still possible to hike the mountain the cable car served. It is known as Monttarone. Here you will find breathtaking views of Lake Maggiore. Also, check with the ferry people about illumination tours of Lake Maggiore. More information can be found at:
www.isoleborromee.it

I address Lake Como and Maggiore since I find them to be the most popular. You can find more on the internet on Lake Garda. However, it is a two-hour run out of Milan. Further, once you get to Lake Garda it will take you about four hours to circumnavigate the lake. This leaves little time for shopping at the small villages abutting this beautiful lake. In summary, it is a long day. It is best to stay overnight at Sirmione, the major town.

ITALY NO TOUR NEEDED
You Can Do It Yourself

WHAT TO DO AND SEE IN MILAN

Milan is great for shopping. On Saturday there is a massive outdoor market selling everything. Two blocks away is the major shopping street known as Corso Buenos Aires. If you care to do some upscale shopping with lots of designer shops, check out the Galleria Vittorio Emanuele II.

No trip to Milan is complete without a visit to its Gothic Cathedral of Milan. This magnificent church is the largest in Italy and took 600 years to build. If you take a walk over to the Santa Maria delle Grazie church, you will find one of Da Vinci's most famous paintings *The Last Supper.* For an opera, do consider a visit to the La Scala Opera House (purchase tickets online).

The Sforza Castle is another big draw in Milan. It is a converted castle that now contains ten separate museums. There are not too many Roman ruins here. Milan is an "affordable" shopping town.

If you are flying out of Milan Malpensa (MXP) there is direct train service from Milano Centrale, otherwise, taxi service is available. You should note that there are two types of express trains from Malpensa to the City. One train goes to Centrale the other goes to another station in the city knowns a Cardorna. Make sure you get the closest train station from your hotel. If going to Milano Centrale, no worries. There is bus and taxi service to LIN (Linate) airport; sorry to train. May have to email your hotel.

CHAPTER 18

THE AMALFI COAST & NAPLES AMALFI DRIVE & CAPRI POSITANO, SORRENTO, RAVELLO, AMALFI, POMPEI PAESTUM, HERCULANEUM

INTRODUCTION

Outside of the three capitals tour i.e. Rome, Florence, and Venice, I don't know of any area of Italy which draws more tourists than Positano and the Amalfi Coast. Is it the colorful houses perched on those hills overlooking the Tyrrhenian Sea (part of the Mediterranean)? Or is it the famous Amalfi Drive with all those twists and turns as it hugs the cliffs from Sorrento to Amalfi? Officially the road is called STRADA STATALE 163 AMALFITANA (SS163) or as we know it "The Amalfi Drive."

>>>TIP<<<   CRITICAL TIP – YOU MUST READ

Enacted in April 2023, the governing authority of the Sorrento and Amalfi areas has instituted a policy aimed at controlling the traffic on Amalfi Drive. Here it is: If your license plate ends in an even number you cannot be on Amalfi Drive on an even day. Likewise, if caught on the Amalfi Drive on an odd day, and you have a license plate ending in an odd number you will be fined and escorted off the road by one of Italy's finest, the Carabinieri. This only applies to rental cars. Not taxis, residents, etc., who possess stickers.

Now, if you are going or coming from a lodging establishment, you can drive. However, if pulled over by the Carabinieri you must show your reservation documents.

So, what do you do if you want to drive this crazy road? Simple, before you leave North America, plan your day of travel down the Drive. When you rent your car either in Rome or Naples, make

ITALY NO TOUR NEEDED
You Can Do It Yourself

sure the license plate is "okay" for your day of travel through Sorrento and Amalfi. If you want to traverse the road on August 23, you cannot have a license plate that has the last digit as an odd number. You may have to go back to the rental counter and exchange the car. However, most rental companies are now using a "just pick any car in Row B or whatever." So, you need to get the correct car if you plan on *traversing* the Amalfi Coast.
>>><<<

With respect to this new regulation, you need to check the internet. It is quite complex. However, once again, you don't have a problem if you are checking into or out of your hotel:
https://www.amalficoastrentalsupport.com/traffic-regulation-amalfi-coast

I have included many details on the Sorrentine Peninsular under Chapter 8: "Rome Extra Days." If you are basing yourself in Sorrento and plan on just taking it easy or visiting the ruins of Herculaneum and Paestum, you will need an additional two or three days in the area.

First, if this is your final destination on your visit to Italy, consider flying back to the USA or Canada from Naples. As of now, United Airlines is the only operator with a non-stop to and from Newark, New Jersey, USA. However, you will pay a premium for this non-stop service. Other than that, you will have to fly to a European hub, e.g., Paris, Rome, Munich, Lisbon, and then fly home non-stop. If you are starting your Italy visit in the Naples area, the same holds, i.e., you would probably fly to one of the hubs mentioned, if not flying on United Airlines.

WHERE TO STAY - POSITANO, SORRENTO, OR AMALFI?
The steep hills in Positano make it difficult to stay here with an auto rental. Sorrento is best since it is all flat and easy to drive. Amalfi would be my second choice. Why? First, unlike Positano, Sorrento is pretty much flat and easy to walk. Second, it's clean, with many pedestrian-only walkways selling everything, including wine and cheese of the region, to all those Italian souvenirs. It's

213

An Alternative to the Escorted Tour

also excellent for finding an apartment for 4-6 nights. And finally, it's centrally located for day trips. You can't ask for anything better.

If you elect to stay in Positano, remember that it's all walking up and down that beautiful hill dotted with buildings of different colors; very much like the Cinque Terre towns. Most bed and breakfasts will offer to port your bags from a convenient drop-off point. However, they won't carry (transport as they say) you, even in a rickshaw!

Hotels on the "water," or the lower side (below the SS163 road), will take your bags and may port you via a golf cart. If you base yourself in Sorrento, you can always go to Positano for the day.

If you have a rental car, before you commit to a hotel in Positano check the location on Google Earth and see if you can make it up those steep hills with your rental. Many have narrow streets and will only allow taxis. Booking.com also provides a map of the area with the hotels indicated on the roads and the paths. Those small dotted lines are paths not streets. Also, be aware that in most cases, you will do a considerable amount of "inclined" walking to access restaurants and shops.

Consider the ferry service to Positano from Naples. In this way you won't have to use the Circumvesuviana railway to Sorrento and then the blue mini-buses to Positano. This only applies if you have turned in your rental at the Naples rail station as the Naples-Positano ferry does not take cars. You can get more detailed information at www.naplesbayferry.com.

If you want to get excellent photos of the town of Positano, make sure you take the ferry after 1PM. Positano faces west and looks great when the sun sets, and there is no cloud cover. So if you can time your ferry departure from Naples, you may be able to get incredible photos. The fast ferry is only $20 and makes the journey in about one hour and 20 minutes. In summary, if you are in excellent shape, I say, "go for it," and stay in Positano!

ITALY NO TOUR NEEDED
You Can Do It Yourself

>>>TIP<<<

If you are driving a rental car and wish to stay in Positano, be aware that you will have to negotiate the Amalfi Drive. You also need to contact the hotel for parking accommodations, if any. In this case, you may want to reconsider and stay in Sorrento. Also, you need to carry your hotel documents per the new regulations.

>>><<<

CONSIDER STAYING IN AMALFI OR SORRENTO

If you want to take it easy and live with the locals, consider staying in Amalfi. There are many hotels in what I call the "Flat Area" abutting the main road, SS163. There is not much walking unless you stay at one of those touristy hotels in the hills. Further, the town is not that touristy, and you can find excellent restaurants, dine with the locals, and spend a lot less.

Like Positano, you should also note that there is a ferry service from Naples to Amalfi. During the off-season, the ferry schedule is minimal. This is one boat you won't want to miss, or you will spend the night sleeping in Naples. Also, remember that you will probably do your sightseeing in reverse, i.e., Amalfi to Positano, then Sorrento in those Blue SITA vans. Not much to do in Amalfi but enjoying the locals, is not a bad idea.

There are two areas of Sorrento with hotels. If I had to design the town again, I would have placed the central railway station closer to the center of the city, known as Piazza Tasso.

Later, when you walk through the town, you will see that statue of Tasso. Torquato Tasso was a latecomer to Italian history.

The current rail station of the Circumvesuviana, the only rail station in town, is located about five football fields from the Piazza Tasso. It's not a big deal and an easy short walk of about 10 minutes from Piazza Giovanni Batista de Curtis station to Piazza Tasso. The best way is to walk down the Corso Italia. Hopefully, the hotel you have selected will be closer to the Piazza Tasso, where all the action is.

An Alternative to the Escorted Tour

You should note the last stop on the train (Circumvesuviana) is called "Sorrento." If you don't know where your hotel is and prefer not to walk, there are plenty of taxis at the station. And, as I have stated before, it's best to hire a car and driver for Naples Centrale or the airport to Sorrento. See my notes on Sorrentocars.com.

Most hotels in Sorrento have public (paid) parking. Or they will direct you to an off-site parking area located a few blocks away. Most of them are located on the Via degli Aranci.

>>>TIP<<<
If you base yourself in Sorrento, you won't need a car for a few days, unless you are going to Paestum for the day or "doing" the Amalfi Drive—yourself. Yikes! Positano, Capri, and Pompeii are easy day trips without the hassle of a rental.

Also, once you exit the A1 (follow signs to Sorrentine Peninsular) onto the local road to Sorrento (SS145), you will find lots of traffic. It's a pretty drive, sort of like the Amalfi Drive with several pull-off points. However once you get down to Castellammare di Stabia (they make the cruise ships here), it's a two-lane road through the local towns with bumper-to-bumper traffic. So it's best to just park that rental in one of the lots in Sorrento for a few days, or else be prepared to take a lot of aspirins for that headache.
>>><<<

WHAT TO DO IN THE AREA
Here are my choices, based on the order of popularity:
1. The Amalfi Drive, Sorrento to Amalfi, with a stop in Ravello for lunch and a visit to the Rufolo Villa.
2. Full day visit to the Isle of Capri
   with a visit to the Blue Lagoon or
   a 90-minute tour of the island
3. A half day in Pompeii can be included in Day 4 below
4. Visit to Herculaneum (Ercolani) and shopping in Naples
5. Visit to the ruins of Paestum (a full day)
6. Shopping and relaxing in Sorrento
   Forget the relaxing; you can do that when you
   get home and really need a vacation.

ITALY NO TOUR NEEDED
You Can Do It Yourself

WHERE TO STAY IN SORRENTO

If you are going to stay in the Sorrentine/Amalfi area, I recommend that you stay in one of the hotels in Sorrento. My favorite is the Hotel Antiche Mura. My discussion on where to stay in Naples (with a rental car) would take at least ten pages. However, I do favor one, the Hotel Signorini. It's a rare find.

Staying in Sorrento allows you to do a lot of shopping, eat at great restaurants, and enjoy a beautiful place perched high above the bay of Naples, with breathtaking views, especially at sunset. By the way, do have dinner one night at "Da Filipo." Have your concierge or front desk person call them, and they will pick you up and deliver you back to your hotel at no charge. What a deal!
Oh yes, do remember to tip the driver both ways; a Euro or two per person is acceptable.

If you are taking the train down from Rome, on arrival in Napoli Centrale, you can take the Circumvesuviana (about 8Euros) to the last stop and then take a taxi for 4-7Euros to your hotel. Otherwise, you can drag your bag or better contact www.sorrentocars.com and arrange for a pickup at Napoli Centrale. It's best to email "Ugo" at Sorrentocars.com. It will be about 100-150Euros per car. Rates vary, contact directly.

Back to places to stay in Sorrento. Here are the areas: In a hotel on that large cliff overlooking the Bay of Naples. Trust me on this one, all those hotels with a view will be expensive. The further you stay from the Piazza Tasso will determine the price of your overnight lodging. You will find hotels and BnBs off the SS145 and the Via Degli Aranci. It is best to spot them on Booking.com.

Several years ago, my friend stayed at a hotel about a block away from the "Piano" train station. You will find lots of places to stay, shopping, and eateries in the Piano area of Sorrento and they are not expensive. All you need do is hop the Circumvesuviana from "Piano" to the next stop (end of line, Sorrento) for five minutes at a cost of about two Euros, and you are where all the action is. The trains run every 20-30 minutes.

An Alternative to the Escorted Tour

>>>TIP<<<
Parking is somewhat difficult in Sorrento. When you book (hopefully directly) with your hotel, do ask them where you can park your rental. Sorrento is a walking town. You can walk anywhere within 10-15 minutes.
>>><<<

** DAY 1 ** AMALFI DRIVE, SORRENTO TO AMALFI

Trust me on this one. You may want to reconsider driving your rental car down Amalfi Drive. I say "drive." The better term would be negotiating the Amalfi Drive. Notice I say "negotiate" and not drive. I have driven down the Amalfi Drive twice over the past 30 years. Two times were enough. In California, the Pacific Coast Highway from Monterey to San Simeon is a straight line compared to the Amalfi Drive from Sorrento to Amalfi (and on into Salerno). Life is short, don't make it shorter. Here are my suggestions:

HIRE A PRIVATE CAR (VAN) SERVICE FOR THE DAY

On my last visit to the area, about three years ago, I emailed "Ugo" at Sorrentocars.com (Leonardo Travels) and asked him to send over a driver to my apartment rental in St. Agata (near Sorrento). The driver arrived promptly at 10AM and brought us back at about 5PM; no hassles. She parked the car, dropped us off for shopping in Positano, and took us to lunch (on our own). Then she picked us up and took us to the town of Ravello to see the Villa Rufolo and estate. This place is awesome and takes about 45 minutes to view. It's not a lot of money and you can enjoy a gelato in the abutting piazza.

A private car (or van) and driver will cost you about 250-300 Euros for the day, depending on the number of people. Best booked directly at Sorrentocars.com (email Ugo at Sorrentocars or Leonard Travels), or other private car service in the area. Suggestion, do not book with an OTA. It is too costly. If you have 4 or better 6 people it will not cost you a lot. Why do I say go for the private car? First, they are familiar with the road i.e., the twists and turns, etc. Secondly, they know the rest stops for those necessary body breaks. Thirdly, they know the souvenir places where you can get the best deals. Fourth, they know where to park

ITALY NO TOUR NEEDED
You Can Do It Yourself

(we even had a reservation). Try parking in Positano, at the Garage Mandara (see below) at 11AM, hah!

TAKE THE SITA #5070 BLUE BUS (VAN)

If you are just a couple or a single and don't want to spend more than 5Euros to see the Amalfi drive you can use public transportation. Yup, you read that right.

The blue SITA vans leave the Sorrento Circumvesuviana train station roughly every 30 minutes. A one-way ticket to Positano, get this, is only 2.40Euros. It takes about ONE hour and MAY make 32 stops if needed to drop passengers. It fills up fast. Driving down to Positano, you need to be on the right side of the bus (not the driver's side) for that great view of the Tyrrhenian Sea. Make sure you validate the ticket (with the date and time) at the Sorrento train station or on the bus. Also, you can buy your ticket on the bus. Make sure you have the correct change. The best is a 5Euro note for two people. Make sure you use the facilities at the station before the bus leaves. You can also get off at several other locations and reuse the ticket if you can find a seat, else enjoy. It is best to get off at the second Positano exit, right in the heart of the town, or else a lot of steps to walk down.

On the return, my suggestion is to take the 30-minute ferry back, Positano to Sorrento. This cost is about $25 per person. This is great if you are only two people. However, if you are four or more it justifies the private driver option. Also, you need to take a ferry at about 4PM or 7PM depending on the sunset. Note, as Positano faces west you will see the sunset against the Amalfi coast and you would need to be on the right (port) side of the ferry as the starboard side faces the Tyrrhenian Sea. Also, make sure you are at the ferry dock 30 minutes before departure.

WHAT TO DO IN POSITANO

This is another reason I like the private car and driver. He/She will drop you off in Positano and pick you up in 60 or 90 minutes. If you are having lunch, all you need do is text your driver that you are leaving the restaurant. It's only a 15-minute walk up that

An Alternative to the Escorted Tour

shopping path to Garage Mandara where your private car/van will probably be parked, and waiting for you.

>>>TIP<<<
Paths/and narrow vehicle roads emanate from the SS163 road down to the sea. My suggestion is that you bear left as you leave the Garage Mandara and follow the crowd to the main shopping district. You can also just ask any shopkeeper "Doe vay et Mar" and they will respond in English "just keep walking."
>>><<<

The next stop would be Amafi for lunch (if you didn't do lunch in Positano) and then Ravello to see the Rufolo Villa.

Positano is synonymous with shopping, shopping, and more shopping, and I don't mean magnets for the refrigerator. In addition, most tourists take incredible pictures of the houses perched on the hills.

You can also walk past all that shopping and find your way to the beach where there are several restaurants. If you came by private driver suggest you notify him/her when you start that walk up the hill from the beach area. The next stop is Amalfi and Ravello for a one-hour visit to the Rufolo Villa.

ON TO AMALFI AND RAVELLO
Amalfi has a lot of local shops, not too touristy. However, it is a nice place to have lunch, or better buy some sandwiches (ask a local "Doe Vay et Alimentaria?") and have them in the park near that rotary (with a glass of wine of course). If you took the SITA bus #5070 from Sorrento, it will be the last stop. Afterwards, it's on to Ravello, home of the Rufolo estate.

RAVELLO AND VILLA RUFOLO
No visit to the Amalfi area is complete without a 45-60 minute visit to the Villa Rufolo and its garden's. This without question is the main draw to Ravello. This place is a must if the sun is shining and it is nice out even after a light rain with a rainbow in the sky. The Villa was built in the 13th Century and fell into disrepair until about 1850 when it was purchased by a Scotsman named Reid. The

220

complex and gardens are magnificent. In addition, there are breathtaking views of the Tyrrhenian Sea. The Villa and gardens are a bargain at only six Euros.

If going to Ravello you need to change buses in Amalfi to #5110 since the #5070 ends in Amalfi.

If you came by bus, you need to take the #5110 back to Amalfi and connect with the #5070 to Sorrento Circumvesuviana.
You return to Naples Centrale for a train back to Rome at about 8-9PM. Else, your driver will take you to your hotel in Sorrento.

Here is the bus schedule:
https://www.ravello.com/sita-bus-schedule/amalfi-positano-sorrento/

For the ferry schedule back to Sorrento consult:
Directferries.com (note time is in 24-hour clock)

>>>TIP<<< ALTERNATE DRIVE HOME
I have done this once and am passing it on as a tip. If you have a rental car, instead of going back the same way to Sorrento over The Amalfi drive consider going SOUTH TOWARD Salerno over the SS163. Just before Salerno (about 10KM), pick up the A3 (near the town of "Vietri sul Mare" heading toward Pompei (not Salerno). According to Google Maps, it shows as only one hour and 45 minutes, but you don't have to navigate The Amalfi drive late in the day with all that traffic i.e., bumper to bumper!!! Oh, and don't think about a shortcut. There is no shortcut across the national park known as "Riserva Statale Valle delle Ferriere."

As another alternative, you can also take the SP1 out of Ravello. However, I do not advise this as there are numerous mountain switchbacks. Check it out on Google Maps as the road looks like your "small intestine." It is far better to take the coast road (SS163) with that beautiful blue water on your right-hand side.
>>><<<

An Alternative to the Escorted Tour

On return to your Sorrento hotel, take a snooze and request that "Da Filipo" pick you up at about 8:00PM for dinner. No need to drive anymore. Now on to Day 2.

** DAY 2 ** THE ISLE OF CAPRI
If staying in Sorrento, there are ferries every two hours from the Marina Piccola in Sorrento to the Isle of Capri. You need to take a taxi or else a short walk. If you are walking, there is a very steep staircase off the Corso Italia leading you down to the marina area. However, you still need to walk down a dangerous slope several blocks to the ferry terminal. Take a look at my tip below.

>>>TIP<< THE SORRENTO LIFT TO CAPRI FERRY
Here is a hot tip. There is a park abutting the marina area known as Villa Comunale Park. If you are on the Corso Italia, you will find the park to the left (as you face Naples Bay) of that steep staircase. Once in the park, you will find the SORRENTO LIFT, which will take you down to the marina ferry terminal for only one Euro; from there, it's a two-block stroll to the ferry ticket booth over flat terrain. This is the only way to go, besides a taxi, to and from the Marina Piccolo ferry docks. Suggest you do not attempt to negotiate the steep stairs from the Corso Italia and then that steep walk down the switchbacks. The best, once again, is the SORRENTO LIFT.

It is best to ask your hotel concierge exactly where the lift is and what the ferry schedule is for the day. It's about 20Euros each way on the high-speed ferry, which operates every two hours. More information at www.naplesbayferry.com
>>><<<

If you are driving into Sorrento for the day and taking the ferry to Capri, there is parking next to the Marina Piccolo ferry docks at the base of the switchbacks. It is in a garage carved into a tunnel. You need to get there no later than 10AM, as the garage fills up fast. It's on your left-hand side at the end of that last switchback.

You should note the following: There is a ferry service to Capri from the Naples docks (parking is available) and also Positano. There is no parking at the ferry dock in Positano, and further this is one place where you cannot get here from anywhere! Best to park in the "Garage Mandara" (on the Amalfi Drive in the heart of Positano), fill up on the Agip, and grab a cold drink. It's a long walk to where the Capri Ferry pulls in. You should be at the Garage Mandara at least one hour before ferry departure.

ON ARRIVAL IN CAPRI- WHAT TO DO

We have just pulled into the dock in Capri, so what do we do? First, you need to pronounce this place the way the Italians do. It is Kah-Pree, not Capri. It's an island about 19 miles off the coast of Naples. There are two towns on the island, Capri and Anacapri. The island dates to pre-historic times. Villa Jovis, one of the best preserved Roman villas, dates from 27AD. Emperor Tiberius ran the Roman Empire from here till he died in 37AD.

After the end of the Roman Empire, Naples controlled Capri. Pirates raided the island, and the French took it in 1808. Before World War One, the island was a haven for gay men. The most famous who lived and vacationed on the island were Oscar Wilde, Somerset Maugham, Alfred Krupp, and more.

The island is now a haven for the A-list and the ultra-wealthy. It's worth a visit for the beautiful views, the shopping, the food, and visiting Anacapri and the Blue Grotto. The only problem is you only have a few hours to do it and you don't have a boatload of money to live on this beautiful island.

You should note, that cars are off-limits in the Town of Capri except for the Marina Grande and the "top-side" town of Anacapri. So all you will see are golf carts running around with luggage and supplies in Capri town.

You can also follow the paparazzi, but they don't technically come out until sundown when the "well-knowns" leave their villas and yachts to go out to dinner.

On arrival (see below), it's best to take an island tour for 60-90 minutes or visit the Blue Grotto. Make sure the island tour goes to Anacapri. See my comments below on the Blue Grotto.

223

An Alternative to the Escorted Tour

I recommend an island tour without the Blue Grotto. The Blue Grotto is a cave down the island where you take a boat to the entrance, then you must transfer to a tiny boat that takes you into the water-filled cave for about five minutes. You can check the reviews before you go.

If you are into shopping, this is the place. One of the best souvenirs is to visit the shop which sells "Capri" watches for men and women. The watches are made in Italy and are pretty reasonable and fashionable. There are lots of restaurants off the main square (the Piazzetta). You should note that most of the shopping is on well-paved walkways. Some walkways do have a slight incline. There are lots of places to sit and take in a gelato.

On arrival at the Marina Grande in Capri, exit the ferry and follow the crowd to the funicular ticket booth. It will be on your right, just past that last concrete pier. All the visitors will be lining up here. Make sure you purchase a round-trip ticket on the funicular, as the return walk from the top down is quite a long way. The ticket is about three Euros round trip. Even if you are taking an island tour or a Blue Grotto tour, you will still have to purchase a funicular round trip ticket since the taxi, and the Blue Grotto boats take you back to the marina, where the island taxis hang out. After your island tour or visit to the Blue Grotto, you must go up the funicular to visit Capri as no taxies can take you to the main square.

Unless you are going on a boat to the Blue Grotto or taking an island tour, after you purchase your funicular ticket, turn around and go across the roadway to the funicular, which will take you to the main square of Capri, the "Piazzetta." From this square, all roads, or should I say walkways emanate. Lots of restaurants and if you keep walking you will see the shops and fancy hotels.

>>>TIP<<<
On exiting the funicular, you will find numerous restaurants if you take a hard left down that walkway (Via Roma). My favorites are Al Capri and Villa Jovis.
>>><<<

224

ITALY NO TOUR NEEDED
You Can Do It Yourself

AN ISLAND TOUR OR A VISIT TO THE BLUE GROTTO

On arrival in the marina area, you will find the "hawkers" or what you may call the "greeters." They will be offering two options. One is an island tour (best to get another couple to join you or some other singles), and the second is a visit to the Blue Grotto. I do not recommend the Blue Grotto. You need to climb from one boat into another boat the size of a small rowboat and then wait in line (upwards of 40 minutes) to gain access to the Grotto, where you will be for about five minutes. The boat which takes you down to the Blue Grotto usually includes entrance to the Grotto. You should check, as many do not. Also, I do not believe there are any facilities on the boats that take you down to the Blue Grotto area. So best to use the facilities at the ferry terminal in the Capri marina. It is best to read Tripadvisor's reviews and make up your mind. My personal preference is to take the island tour with a taxi.

After you return from the island taxi tour or your Blue Grotto experience, you will have to take the funicular to the main square in Capri Town. I then advise lunch on the Via Roma. You can then shop your heart out, and stop at the Capri Watch store (their watches are not expensive), have a gelato, and take a lot of pictures; then, you will be ready to start your journey back.

If you are visiting Capri on a day trip from Rome, it would be best if you allowed at least three hours from the time you go down that funicular before your train departure time back to Rome. The fast ferry would be two hours and the slow ferry three. Remember, you could always hang around Napoli Centrale for an hour. By the way, Italians don't like to rush. So if you arrive early, except for the local trains, it may be difficult to hop on an earlier Frecci or Italo train. Most earlier trains "close out" an hour or two before departure and there may be penalties for changing. Remember all Frecci's and Italo's have reserved seats.

If going back to Sorrento (advisable) you can certainly take a later ferry. It's best to go back to your hotel, shower, take a snooze then go out for dinner at about 8PM.

An Alternative to the Escorted Tour

** DAY 3 ** THE RUINS (SCAVI) OF POMPEII

>>>SUPER TIP<<< POMPEI & AMALFI DRIVE

If you book a private car and driver (sorrentocars.com or alternative) it is possible to visit Pompeii in the morning and take the Amalfi Drive in the afternoon. Your driver will pick you up in Sorrento or at the Naples rail station (Centrale) at 10-10:30. You visit Pompei Scavi at about 12Noon, and depart for the Amalfi drive at about 2-3PM. Plan on a late lunch at about 4PM, or grab a slice of pizza after you exit the Pompeii Scavi at one of the stand-up bars. "Ugo" at Sorrentocars.com or Leonardotravels.com can assist you. It may cost you a little more, but certainly worth it.
>>><<<

SHORT HISTORY OF POMPEI

All the historic details on Pompei, entrance fees, etc., are discussed in detail in Chapter 8, Day Trips from Rome. The sections below only address how to get to Pompei.

TAKING THE TRAIN FROM SORRENTO TO POMPEI

It's simple. Just go to the Sorrento or Piano Circumvesuviana rail station buy a ticket from the machine or the attendant for about 5Euros and exit the train in about 40 minutes at Pompei. Follow the directions from above. Oh, make sure you validate it in the yellow or red machine.

IF DRIVING TO POMPEI

From the Sorrento area or coming down from Rome, take the Pompei exit. There is plenty of parking if you arrive early. My favorite place is the alley leading to the Ristorante Pizzeria Turistico. It is shaded. Look for the signs "Ristorante Pizzeria Turistico." The attendant will have you part with about 20Euros and further, you get to just walk into the Ristorante (not walk into the hotel). If you can't find parking here, try opposite the rail station abutting the scavi. If all else fails, follow the hawkers waving those flags, just like a Yankee baseball game in the Bronx. Oh, make sure you lock your valuables before you leave your hotel in the morning and not on arrival in Pompeii.

ITALY NO TOUR NEEDED
You Can Do It Yourself

** DAY 4 ** HERCULANEUM AND SHOPPING IN NAPLES

Herculaneum (also known as Ercolano) is also a nice day trip from Sorrento, and it costs very little, no more than twenty dollars per person (Circumvisuviana and entrance fee). There is a major street market daily on the streets abutting Ercolano Scavi (Herculaneum) and you can shop here for anything and then have lunch in several local restaurants. For some reason, Herculaneum does not get the play that Pompeii receives. Perhaps because it's part of Naples? I don't know. I don't know anyone who jumps up and down and says, "I want to go to Italy and see the ruins at Ercolano," but they do with Pompeii. Don't count on Herculaneum being on the same magnitude as Pompeii. The current excavated size is about a tenth of Pompeii. Herculaneum is on the south side of Naples.

If you are staying in Sorrento, there is no need to drive your rental car through all that local traffic, even though part of it gives you a beautiful view of the Bay of Naples. Just hop the Circumvesuviana and exit the station marked Ercolano Scavi. See my note below about the two Ercolano stations.

If you are staying about four blocks from Ercolano at the Villa Signorini Hotel (a wise idea), all you need do is take a short walk.

>>>TIP<<<
If you still insist on taking your rental car for the day to Ercolano Scavi, you will find the abutting market area so crowded that it is doubtful that you will find a parking spot, even if you have a Smart Car. I might note that the abutting residential area has extremely limited parking. However, it does have nice restaurants and shops.
>>><<<

Ercolano is easily reached from Sorrento in about 50 minutes and from Naples Centrale (Garibaldi Square) by taking the Circumvesuviana railway for about 20 minutes. Trains run every 20 minutes. If you leave your hotel in Sorrento at about 11AM you should be at Herculaneum at about Noon. If you are coming from Sorrento, it is the first stop marked "Ercolano Scavi." If you are coming from Naples, make sure you get off at the Scavi stop. You

227

only need 30-60 minutes to take photos of the ruins and head for that massive street market. After you are shopped out, consider lunch with a return back to Sorrento at about 5PM with enough time for a nap, of course, before dinner at 8PM.

Here are some quick facts on Herculaneum:
It was buried in the same Mount Vesuvius eruption of 79AD, which also buried Pompeii. There are few ancient cities preserved intact. Ercolano was discovered by accident while drilling a water well in 1709, compared to Pompeii in 1748. Unlike Pompeii, Ercolano was covered by pyroclastic material, not lava and ash. This material preserved more "organic material," i.e., wood, papyrus, etc. Ercolano had a population of only 5,000. Because it was located close to the sea as opposed to Pompeii, Ercolano was a vacation spot for the Roman elite. The eruption covered the city to about 60 feet. Only a fraction of the city has been unearthed. The heat (480 degrees F) of the eruption, which occurred on October 17, 79AD, had a radius of seven miles and killed everyone in sight, even those sheltered.

The entrance fee is 13Euros per person. You do not need to book tickets online. You should figure one hour here at most. I should note that the rail ticket from Pompei to Ercolano (Naples) is about 3Euros.

>>>TIP<<<
If you plan your day accordingly, you can visit Herculaneum and Pompeii on the same day since they are on the same Circumvesuviana rail line, only 20 minutes apart. I would visit Pompeii first, then about 2PM go to Herculaneum for lunch and shopping. BTW, some parts of Herculaneum can be seen from the street. You may want to save that 13 Euros and just visit the street market. On the other hand, if you are an archaeologist this place is a must.
>>><<<

** DAY 5 ** THE TEMPLES OF PAESTUM
First, I have stated: "The Temples at Paestum." However, the entire complex is an architectural park sprawled over about 300 acres. It is massive and not only contains three of the best-

ITALY NO TOUR NEEDED
You Can Do It Yourself

preserved temples in the world but also the ruins of the ancient city of Paestum. Most of the city walls are still intact; at least, their foundations are. In addition, there is also a museum worth a visit. Admission is about ten Euros and includes the museum. You should note that the park closes at 1:30PM on the first and third Monday of the month. So, best to plan accordingly.

None of the temples in the ancient world, including the Parthenon in Athens, and the Valley of the Temples in Agrigento, Sicily, compare to these temples. Why? They are mostly still intact, and secondly, they are a marvel of construction. Unlike Stonehenge and the Acropolis of Athens, you can enter all the temples, sit on those ruins, and take as many photos as you wish with no security people chasing you.

Some quick historical facts: Way before the Romans arrived, Paestum was part of ancient Greece. The territory was Magna Graecia and dates to about the 8th Century BC. The region of Salento in Southern Italy still speaks a Greek dialect known as Griko, a blend of Italian and Greek. On my most recent trip to the heel of Italy (Salento), I was amazed that there are over 30,000 Italians who speak Griko in this region.

Yes, after the Greek god of the sea, Poseidon, the actual complex, now known as Paestum, was originally a Greek colony known as Poseidonia. While the complex is also Greek and Roman ruins, most people visit it because of the three well-preserved temples.

Here is a basic recap of the three temples: Hera One was built about 550BC, Hera Two about 450BC, and the Temple of Athena about 600-500BC. These temples were built by the ancient Greeks and later taken over by the Romans. They were constructed as all temples were built to honor the gods, i.e., the god of the ocean, Neptune, Polaris, etc.

A quick overview. First, the two temples are about half a football field apart. They are Hera One and Hera Two. By the way, Hera was a Greek Goddess. She is best known as the goddess of marriage, women, and family and the protector of women. As you

An Alternative to the Escorted Tour

enter the complex, you need to take a quick left-hand turn, and you will see the two temples. If you take a right-hand turn about five blocks up, you will find the Amphitheater of Paestum. After exiting the amphitheater, go right for another five blocks, and you will come upon the Temple of Athena, which also dates to about 500BC. The Romans took over the entire area at about 237BC and renamed it Paestum.

About these three ancient temples, there are two interesting facts to note. First, observe the columns. They are all tapered as they rise to the top, where there was probably a roof. Secondly, the one on your left (the most southern temple) is called Hera I (Hera One). Inside, there are seven columns down the center. The one on your right is Hera Two, initially thought to be the Temple of Poseidon.

As for the Temple of Athena, it was also built in about 500BC. The architecture is known as transitional. Some of the columns are Doric in nature, and some are Ionic.

Of an interesting note, the amphitheater you see is only half of the remains. In 1930, a local builder, built a road right through the center, burying the eastern half. The locals stated that the responsible civil engineer went to trial, was convicted, and received a prison sentence that was described as wanton destruction of a historic site.

You will need 2-3 hours to take in the entire complex, including an hour in the museum. You will not be able to exit the complex via that restaurant abutting (The Netunno). You will need to leave where you came in and walk around the entire complex.

To get to Paestum, you have two alternatives. I assume you are staying at a hotel or an apartment in Sorrento. Taking the train and the Circumvesuviana is NOT an option. This is one place you need to hire a private car and driver. Otherwise, if there are just one or two of you, I strongly recommend renting a car for the day in Sorrento or Naples and driving the 90 minutes down to Paestum. If you don't want to rent a car your only other "doable" option is a private car and driver. Best to pick you up in Sorrento or the Naples station.

Just like you would spend some good money for a nice day trip down the Amalfi drive, you ought to consider the same for a trip to Paestum. It will be a few dollars less on what you leave your kids. The best approach is to contact www.sorrentocars (www.leonardotravels.com). His name is "Ugo", and trust me, he is very reliable, having done work for Bob Kaufman and National Travel Vacations in the past.

As in your Amalfi day, he can pick you up at about 10AM, take you to Paestum, take you to Agropoli for lunch, and return you to your Sorrento hotel at about 5PM. If you would like to stop and take a one-hour tour of a mozzarella factory (funny, no joke) in Paestum (Annulli Farms) before your visit, I suggest you leave at about 9:30AM. It would be best if you invited another couple(s) to join you, thereby splitting the cost.

Annulli Farms is only open in the mornings for tours. If you don't like cheese, there is ample time to have lunch in Agropoli and then do about one hour of shopping before starting your drive back to Sorrento. The best is to contact Ugo on the website.

** DAY 6 ** SHOPPING AND RELAXING
AN AFTERNOON AT THE BEACH - RELAX

If your hotel does not have a pool, no worries. There are several opportunities. So, grab your towel and your beach attire and head out after breakfast for a dip in the ocean. If you have a rental the nicest place is Mary's Beach; you can Google it. There are other beaches around, but the locals agree this is "the place." There is no charge to use it and no fee to park your car.

You will find Mary's Beach at the end of a road abutting the Hotel la Certosa in a section of the Sorrentine Peninsular called Massa Lubrense. Here you can rent beach chairs, an umbrella and the like. There are changing facilities, etc. If you didn't have time to stop into an Alimentaria in Sorrento or Sant' Agata (you will pass through it) for some rustic bread, cold cuts, and a bottle of wine (or better a cold six-pack of your favorite brew), you will find a nice in-expensive restaurant on the beach. If you can get all that sand off of you and look presentable i.e. no bathing suit, etc. you can certainly find a nice pranzo (lunch) in the Hotel La Certosa. Plenty of parking and if you forgot your SPF50, there is a nice convenience store abutting the hotel. The best is to spot the Hotel La Certosa on your GPS. This will lead you there.

You will find Mary's Beach about 30 minutes from the Piazza Tasso in the center of Sorrento. I am also sure a taxi (or an Uber) will take you there. Best to split the fare with another couple. On the return back to your Sorrento hotel, there are usually taxis next to the Hotel La Certosa or I am sure they will be able to call one for you. Avoid taking the #5070 bus. There is a long walk down a steep hill loaded with switchbacks, easy down, but you need to be an "iron man" to make it back up the hill, not recommended.

>>>TIP<<<
In Sorrento, there is a small beach next to the Marina Picola where you get the ferry to Capri. Definitely avoid this place, even if your hotel desk clerk says it's "nice." I could tell you a lot, but the proof of the pudding is in the viewing. A swim in the Grand Canal in Venice would be healther and better. Nicest place is Mary's Beach. Please see my write-up above.
>>><<<

SHOPPING IN SORRENTO
When it comes to shopping, Sorrento has everything. The main shopping street is the Corso Italia. Here you will see shops selling high-end designer apparel, i.e. Colors of Benetton, etc.

As you work your way toward the Bay of Naples you will find other side streets which run parallel to the Corso Italia. Here is where you want to buy those souvenirs that only you can buy in Sorrento. Lemons, lemons, and more lemons are grown in the region. And, guess what? They make lemon liquor from those lemons, peel and all. It's called Limoncello. I always suggest those small bottles (nips) as souvenirs. You can easily pass through US

ITALY NO TOUR NEEDED
You Can Do It Yourself

Customs and Agriculture inspectors at the USA ports of entry. Just make sure you don't bring a case for resale.

Also, remember that anything that is not opened i.e. it is shrink-wrapped can be taken into the country. You run the risk of that mozzarella cheese and those Italian oranges you were munching, on the flight home, being confiscated by the Department of Agriculture people. They don't want another "Med Fly" epidemic! So, get ready to give up those oranges.

Getting back to shopping, there are numerous other items for purchase on those side streets. I tend to stay away from T-shirts and the like. However, we do have a craving for refrigerator magnets. Also, I might note that there are also plenty of cafes and gelato shops in the shopping area. So enjoy it all!

If you are going further South you will find my discussion on the "Heel" of Italy, called Apulia and Salento in Chapter 19.

CHAPTER 19

THE HEEL OF ITALY
APULIA (PUGLIA), SOLENTO,
BARI, LECCE, TARANTO
ALBEROBELLO & MATERA

INTRODUCTION

This chapter is unique. If you have been to Italy a few times or have a third or fourth week to explore this beautiful country and its people, I strongly suggest you explore the highlights of Matera, Alberobello, Bari, and Lecce. I really can't group them into one province since they lie in Basilicata (Matera), Alberobello (Puglia), Bari (Puglia), and Lecce (Lecce).

Several pieces of information in this chapter have been duplicated. Since I do not know exactly where you are going or where you came from, you may find some of my advice redundant.
Here is your itinerary, which will minimize check-ins and maximize your site-seeing time:

You can certainly drive across the spine of Italy (Naples to Bari) in one day. However, take it from me: you will be exhausted after that overnight flight from North America and may not want to drive with toothpicks holding your eyes open.

The best thing you could do is drive to Arpino (not the one in Naples but the one in Frosinone) and stay at the Hotel il Cavalier. You can take a look at the chapter entitled Arrival At Rome FCO for more details on staying overnight in Arpino.

Since Apulia and Salento are "vast" the best thing you could do is base yourself at one or better two towns and take day trips from there. What I mean, is that all those sites you will be visiting, are all over the place. They don't exactly "line up" like Orvieto, Siena,

ITALY NO TOUR NEEDED
You Can Do It Yourself

San Gimignano and Florence. Here are my suggestions for a base.
I recommend two bases, however one is fine:

BARI AS A BASE
Where to stay- The 4-star Excelsior Hotel
Closest to the downtown area and rail station - paid parking
What to do - Walking tour of the old city, port, etc.
Day trips to –
 Polignano a Mare - 33 mins
 Monopoli - 37 mins
 Ostuni - 65 mins
  Above all, on the Adriatic with beaches

 Matera one hr, 15 mins inland
 Alberobello 48 mins inland

LECCE AS A BASE- STAY WITH THE LOCALS
Where to stay - Villa Domus Salento – Free parking
      - Hotel delle Palme
Why- Walking distance to the old city:
  Porta San Biagio Gate, Roman ruins and many
  Baroque Churches
What to do - Walking tour of the old city, ruins, shopping, etc.
Day trips to   Otrano   - 39 mins on the Adriatic Sea
     Gallipoli - 30 mins on the Ionian Sea
     Santa Maria di Leuca - one hour
      The southernmost tip between the Ionian
      and Adriatic seas of the Mediterranean.

TARANTO AS A BASE- STAY WITH THE LOCALS
Where to stay – Hotel L'Arcangelo
     In the historic district, free parking
Why – because it's a historic old city, why would you want to
stay in the new section with all those high rise buildings?
Day trips to - Alberobello – 50 mins
     Matera - one hour 15 mins

An Alternative to the Escorted Tour

ALBEROBELLO AS A BASE
Where to stay - Grand Hotel Olimpo
  If you can get into one of the Trulli hotels,
  I would definitely go for it. Otherwise the Olimpo.
  Why go to Alberobello? Home of the Trulli's houses
  Day trips to - Matera - one hour 15 minutes
  Relaxing days off the E90 in direction of
  Reggio Calabria – LOTS OF BEACHES AND RESORTS

My suggestion is always to base yourself at two of those towns/cities I mention above and then take day trips after visiting the town itself.

For example, spend a day in Alberobello. Then make a day trips to Matera and spend your final day in Salento on one of the excellent beachs on the Gulf of Taranto. One of these areas with beach front hotels is Castellaneta/Lido Trocadero, less than 30 minutes from Taranto. If you are in to relaxing for 2-3 days this might be the place for a base with a side trip to Matera.

Here is a short itinerary for the Heel:

Day 0 - Overnight flight to Rome from North America.
Day 1 - Rent a car and drive to Arpino. That's enough. Check in to the Hotel il Cavalier and recover.

Day 2: Explore Cicero's ruins and arch, which still remain. Then, at about 11AM, head for Bari. Overnight at the 4-star Excelsior, and make day trips below.

Day 3 - Walk the old City of Bari o/n Bari.
  Day trip to Polignano and Monopoli
   Note they are only 4 minutes apart by train.

Day 4 and Day 5 after Bari, base yourself in Lecce, Taranto
  or Alberobello and make day trips from one of these bases.

Note both Lecce and Taranto allow you to go to excellent beaches either on the Adriatic or the Gulf of Taranto.

236

ITALY NO TOUR NEEDED
You Can Do It Yourself

I have done this trip twice and based myself in Lecce on one trip and Alberoello on another. There is no simple answer. It's your choice. Take a look at my diagram in the Appendix.

Here is an overview of those sites, not to be missed in Puglia/Salento :

OVERVIEW OF SOME OF THE PUGLIA TOWNS

Bari is the hub of the northern part of Apulia (sometimes called Puglia). Bari is quite cosmopolitan, with excellent shopping, good restaurants, and history. Secondly, it's a rail hub featuring trains to Rome, Milan, and Italy via the Trenitalia and the new Italo systems. There are frequent daily flights to Rome, Milan, and other European hubs. It's a place I would rent an apartment for a month to get out of the harsh winter in the USA or Canada.

Alberobello is home to over 1,500 cone-shaped houses. Unlike Bari, Alberobello and Matera are unique historical cities.

Matera is also a unique city. The place is "ancient". You will not believe this place when you visit it. It is nearly impossible to describe. This place is massive, and the recent James Bond movie only shows a small part of Matera. Matera has been featured in numerous motion pictures, the most recent being *"No Time To Die"* (2021, by producers Barbara Broccoli and Michael G. Wilson.) The first well-known film was "Ben-Hur" (1959, Charlton Heston). To date, there have been over 137 movies filmed in some parts of Matera. If you want to visit Matera, I would suggest you see the film *"No Time to Die"* before your visit.

If you want to visit these towns, I have constructed your visit that you do not have to overnight in historic Matera. It's a hassle. There is a lot of walking and numerous ramps and flights of stairs in and around the historic district of Matera. It's like negotiating a three-dimensional maze. In addition, most of the streets and walkways are cobblestone. The historic area where the caves are is called the "Sassi." There is a modern section of the town which is not the Sassi; here you will find hotels, shops, and restaurants. Please see below for more information on historic Matera.

An Alternative to the Escorted Tour

Using the rail system is not an option for visiting Matera. It takes too long to get there from Bari and other key points. In addition, the entire historic area (The Sassi) is a ZTL (Zone Traffic Limited) controlled area, and you cannot drive around or even park in it. Do not even attempt to enter the Sassi area. If you care not to drive, I suggest hiring a car and driver.

Another idea, instead of a private car and driver, is to go back to the Bari Airport and rent a car for two or three full days. It's easy and inexpensive. I should note that there are only rental locations at the Bari Airport. There are no in-city Bari rental locations.

>>>TIP<<<
If you rent a car at Bari Airport, a taxi from the City will cost you $38. However, there is a train every 30 minutes to the airport from the Bari train station, and it will cost you only $5 per person. Also, remember that when you drop off the car and return to your hotel in Bari, you can take the train back. If you stay at the Hotel Excelsior, it's just across the street from the rail station. So, if you would like to rent a car, just hop on the train to the Bari Airport and bring it back to your hotel in Bari. Load up, and away you go. A better idea is to just take your bags to the airport, it's easy.
>>><<<

You can extend the above five-day itinerary by adding two or three days in Lecce, another historic town, and making day trips to Otranto, Gallipoli, Santa Maria di Leuca, and other places in the Salento region. However, using Lecce as a base in what is known as the Salento region of Apulia (or Puglia) would be a plus.

BARI - POLIGNANO A MARE AND MONOPOLI
If you arrive in Bari by rail (you are doing a hopoff and will rent a car), you can walk to the four-star Hotel Excelsior. It is only one block from the station. The only negative about this hotel is that it is in an intense graffiti area. This area will be a real plus if you are into modern art. You may be able to take pictures of all that graffiti and convert them to excellent wall art.

238

ITALY NO TOUR NEEDED
You Can Do It Yourself

To reach the Hotel Excelsior, take the elevator down to the under-tracks tunnel and exit to Via Giuseppe Capruzzi; follow the signs. Parking is available at the Excelsior.

There are other fine hotels within walking distance of the rail station. The rail station's other (eastern) side defines the words "the other side of the tracks" with parks, fountains, shops, restaurants, etc. Other hotels within walking distance are the Hotel Cristal and the Hotel Colibri. I might note that all of Bari is flat, so walking is easy. After you drop your bags at one of the downtown hotels, you are ready to explore the City. If you take the fast train from Rome, you will find taxis at the station.

If you walk across from the rail station, you will come to the main walking street (pedestrians only) known as Via Sparano da Bari. It's lined with parks on both sides. Follow this until it crosses the Vittorio Emanuele II, a major boulevard. Here, you will find at least eight outdoor cafes to enjoy lunch or dinner. The old City and its medieval walls lie just behind all those outdoor cafes.

Once in the Old City, bear to your left. Follow the signs to the Castello Svevo di Bari in a few blocks. This castle (the moat has been filled in) was built in 1132 by the Norman King Roger II. It is also known as the Swabian Castle. At one time, the castle extended to the port but was filled in to make way for the Corso Antonio de Tulio boulevard. The castle was destroyed in 1156 and rebuilt in 1233 by Fredrick II of the Holy Roman Empire and was later acquired by Duke Ferdinand of Aragon and later donated to the Sforza family, who returned it to the King of Naples. The Aragon walls remain along with the Hohenstaufen tower. The castle is now used for exhibitions.

If you have another full day in Bari, I suggest driving down (or taking the train down for $4) to Polignano a Mare. You probably don't know much about Polignano, but you have seen many pictures of the famous restaurant under that massive rock or cave. It's also a hotel. The official name of this five-star hotel and restaurant is "Hotel Ristorante Grotta Palazzese." And if you want

239

An Alternative to the Escorted Tour

to spend those big bucks to have dinner there or stay overnight, you need to make a reservation 3-6 months in advance. I might note a "guard" or, better, a "bouncer" who will not let you into the restaurant or hotel, even to take a few pictures. You would probably have to be a member of the "A-List" club and arrive in a Rolls-Royce with a private driver. In addition, you would need to have a write-up in Wikipedia. However, I'm not sure if that bouncer would know what Wikipedia is. That bouncer denied us entry. Would you believe Bob Kaufman, author of books on Italy, was denied entrance?

I usually suggest taking the train down to Polignano. It's only $8 round trip and takes about 30 minutes. On arrival, you can walk down to the old town or take one of those Tuk-Tuk three-wheeled taxis for 10 Euros from the station to the old town. Parking for your rental car is "tight" or nearly non-existent.

The old City is perched on a limestone mesa. There is excellent shopping and great spots for lunch. Two other things worth doing are the beach and the cave boat tours. The beach is small but very nice, sandy with that turquoise green water. So, do pack a bathing suit and a towel or two. You can also sit on the beach and enjoy the view. If you want to spend about $30 per person, there are one-hour tours of the caves by speed boat.

If you make an early start, say 10AM, out of Bari to Polignano, another 15 minutes down the Adriatic, you will find the town of Monopoli. After having lunch in Polignano, take the train to the next major stop or drive down 15 minutes to another fascinating town, Monopoli. It will cost you about two Euros on the train, only four minutes. If driving, consider the coast road for great views of the Adriatic and an excellent view of the City coming up in front of you. If you are smart, consider packing your swimming attire and a towel. There are beautiful beaches where you can pull off and take a dip with no charge for parking.

Like Polignano, Monopoli also sits on a mesa or "bluff" of stone. It's flat walking, and there is municipal parking. If arriving by train, consider a Tuk-Tuk tour or a transfer to the old City half a mile from the train station. A taxi will cost you about 6 Euros to

ITALY NO TOUR NEEDED
You Can Do It Yourself

the old City. Before leaving Bari or arriving at Monopoli, check the return times for the Trenitalia trains or the new sleek-looking regional trains. All trains stop in Bari. Trains operate about every half-hour and make stops at all the coastal towns.

Okay, now we are in Monopoli, so what will we do? First, like many of these coastal cities on the Adriatic, they went back and forth between all the conquering entities over 2000 years. Just too many to name. The town dates to 500BC. The new Italian Kingdom chased the Spaniards out in 1860.

Monopoli is a walking city. Lots of small quaint streets, the real Italy I love. Monopoli has many squares abutting whitewashed buildings, well over 100 years old. Two places worth visiting are the Castello di Carlo and the Palmieri Palace. Like so many places, the Castello was also a prison and barracks. The Spaniards built it for coastal defense in 1552. In later years it was abandoned until the 1990s, when it was reconstructed and turned into an exhibit.

With no heirs to the Palmieri family's succession, the Palmieri Palace was turned over to the government in 1921 to be used as a museum and school of art. You can't miss it. When in the Centro Storico, you will find it on Palmieri Piazza. The Palace is modeled after the palaces you see in historic Lecce.

The old town consists of many Baroque fountains, plazas, and other ornamental designs of the mid-1700s. Most of the design comes from the mid-1800s, known as the late Baroque. The Palace is worth a visit unless you are heading to one of the beaches. Most of the excellent beaches lie south of the town; however, unless you are here during the summer or shoulder months best to skip them. So best to enjoy that gelato while you stroll the Old City.

I would suggest the Basilica of the Madonna della Madia as another place to visit. Construction started in the 12th Century; however, it stopped when they ran out of wood beans for the roof.

It would be best to have a pastry (Il Pasticcino) and café before heading back to Bari at about 6PM.

An Alternative to the Escorted Tour

ALBEROBELLO

If you have not done so, you will need to check out of your hotel in Bari and go to the airport to rent a car. I should note that there are no rental car pickup points in Bari. You need to go back to the Bari airport via the fast shuttle train (from Bari Centrale) or take a taxi (about 35Euros). As discussed, taking your luggage with you would be best so you don't have to return to Bari and can get on the main road to Alberobello. Just a word about Bari airport and the train from Bari Centrale. The airport has elevators and a new escalator system outside the south door. It's not like Rome. You don't have to walk a lot. If you are taking a taxi, you still need to be deposited at the terminal building to sign up for your car at the rental counter. If you have luggage, spend the extra bucks and go by taxi from your Bari hotel to the airport instead of "schelping" your luggage on the train.

It is a four-block walk from the rental counters to the car location. If you care not to drag your bags, have your partner watch them outside arrivals as you bring up the rental car.

It's less than an hour to Alberobello, and your rental car will also be used the next day to visit Matera (from Alberobello). Alberobello, like Matera, is one of my favorite towns in Italy, and in fact, in the world. It is so unique. You may have seen pictures of Alberobello (pronounced AL-BER-OH-BELLOW) with the town and the countryside filled with all those cone-shaped houses. Those cone-shaped houses are called "Trulli." The singular is a Trullo. The town and the outlying villages are UNESCO World Heritage Sites.

On arrival, I suggest you check into your hotel for the two nights. If the room is not ready, check your bags with the bellman. Do not leave them in your car since you will park and walk 3-4 blocks into town. There is plenty of muni parking; you can drive into town.

My favorite hotel in the area is the four-star Grand Hotel Olimpo. It is exceptionally reasonable and includes breakfast as usual. Before booking at the Hotel Olimpo, check if you can stay at one

ITALY NO TOUR NEEDED
You Can Do It Yourself

of the Trulli hotels in town. However, they are usually booked up months in advance. BTW, the Olimpo does have free parking.

So, what's with these funny-looking Trulli houses? First, they are only found in the southern region of Puglia. They are examples of mortar-less (no cement) drywall construction. They are a pre-historic building technique that has stood the test of time in this area. The Trulli are made of chiseled blocks of limestone boulders that came from the neighboring fields. There are several types that, when placed together, form a domed building. They were built for "Thermal Balance." They keep the inside cool in the summer heat and warm when it gets cold.

There are two sections of Alberobello: The section Rione Monti has 1,030 Trulli, and the Rione Aia has 590 Trulli. There are four specific locations (Casa d'Amore; Piazza del Mercato; Museo Storico; Trullo Sovrano).

The houses with the "corbelled roofs" are still being constructed today. They serve as temporary field shelters, storehouses, or permanent dwellings for small-scale landowners or agricultural laborers. The domed (corbelled) roof rests directly on the structure's walls. The walls are double-skinned with a rubble core (probably for insulation against the hot sun). The buildings are whitewashed. Water is collected from the roof's runoff to a cistern beneath the structure.

How restoration and maintenance of the Trulli are undertaken is prescribed in local legislation, and it is illegal to demolish, reconstruct, add floors, or construct fake Trulli. So much for the local HOA (lol). Now that you know about the Trulli houses, what do you do?

Alberobello is a shopping town. The central shopping district is on Via Indipendenza (yes, that's the spelling) and extends for about ten blocks. Here you will find everything, including all types of food and a supermarket. It is all flat walking. However, paralleling Indipendenza is Via Colombo, which is a traditional shopping area (non-Trulli). There are stairs of about 10-12 feet every so often leading up to Via Colombo. Between the two main streets, there are also shops.

I might note that since you will be overnighting here for two nights, you might want to scope out a place for dinner before you go back to your Alberobello hotel and snooze. Our favorite is the Ristorante Terminal Pizzeria next to the large municipal parking lot on Indipendenza on your right as you enter the commercial section of Alberobello. Don't let the name scare you. This place is a lot more than a pizza place! Also, it is owned by the same folks who own the Grand Hotel Olimpo.

Remember, tomorrow is a day trip to the ancient (and I mean ancient) City of Matera. So, if you missed a good dinner, you will have a second shot at it.

MATERA- A SHORT HISTORY
You may have noticed that I have saved the best or most interesting for last.

The original settlement of Matera lies between two canyons carved by the Gravina River. The "Sassi" is a complex of cave dwellings dug into the canyon walls. Matera was occupied by the Romans, Longobards, Byzantines, Saracens, Swabians, Angevins, Aragonese, and Bourbons. All these people made their homes in those caves. There are several hundred of them.

By the way, "Sassi" is Italian for stones. Here is a quick history of the Sassi: Archeologists believe the caves were dug out of the soft stone walls about 10,000 years ago during the Paleolithic era. These caves are almost "pre-historic" history. To put this timeline into perspective: The digging of these cave homes was accomplished during the time of primitive man when he was the hunter and the gatherer. It would be almost 10,000 years before Ancient Rome would come along. This is also several million years after the dinosaurs became extinct.

In the 1800s, cave dwellings became houses of poverty, with poor sanitation, meager working conditions, and rampant disease. The Italian government evacuated these "modern" cave dwellers in

ITALY NO TOUR NEEDED
You Can Do It Yourself

1952. The Sassi area of Matera lay abandoned until about 1980, when the government and private sectors started converting many caves into hotels, restaurants, museums, shops, and an art community. In 1993, Matera was declared a UNESCO World Heritage Site.

The actual town of Matera (not the Sassi) was founded in 251BC by the Roman Lucius Caecillius, who named it Matheola. As stated above, the control of Materia over the centuries passed between various warring peoples. In the 15th century, Matera was controlled by Aragon (Spain). In 1806, Bonaparte assigned Matera to be held by Potenza, also in the province of Basilicata.

In 1927, Matera became the capital of the new province of Matera. On arrival in Matera, don't get surprised. Matera is a modern city with shops, restaurants, hotels, and the like. The new and modern section of Matera is not the Sassi. You need to follow the signs to the Sassi, then park in one of the muni areas.

>>>TIP<<<
Here is another way to see Matera. If you can fly into Bari by 11AM, there is a one-hour bus to Matera. You can visit Matera and then, at about 5PM or 6PM, take the bus back to the Bari airport. No car is needed. However, timing is critical here, and it may be a stressful day. Obviously, you need not bring your luggage, just leave it in Naples or wherever. If you miss that bus back to Bari airport, you will need to check into a hotel (all within walking distance) and find a pharmacy for a toothbrush and toothpaste. And, yes, you will need to wear the same clothes tomorrow.
>>><<<

>>>TIP<<<   DEFINITELY WORTH IT
The best way to see Matera is via a 40-minute "Tuk-Tuk" tour. Tuk-Tuks are small three-wheeled mini-taxis that accommodate two people behind the driver. Some of them are like golf carts and can accept four people. The government sets the rates. You will see them all over Matera. However, the best way to get one is to go into any bar or hotel and ask one of the staff to call one for you. The cost is 50Euros (total for two people) if you want an English-

An Alternative to the Escorted Tour

speaking guide. An Italian-speaking guide with no English will cost you only 40 Euros. And if you are going into a bar, thank the barista and order a café. If at a hotel, please tip the one who called the Tuk-Tuk. There are not that many Tuk-Tuks and the best is not to wait. So, you might want to email "Cosimo" at menavento@virgilio.it. His phone is 39-329-619-3820. Best to give him a time frame for your arrival. In this way, he will provide you with a priority once you arrive.

All Tuk-Tuks are privately owned by the drivers, most of whom have been driving in Matera for over 30 years; also, **CASH ONLY**, no plastic.

Usually, the Tuk-Tuk guide will stop at one of the famous churches in a plaza and allow you to visit it if you would like. One such church is the Cattedrale di Maria Santissima della Bruna e Sant'Eustachio on the Piazza Duomo. I might note that the driver will stop a few times for picture-taking of the entire Sassi area. After you complete your tour, ask the guide to bring you back to where you parked your car. You can grab a bite before returning to Alberobello or Bari.
>>><<<

LECCE AS A BASE
I just love Lecce. Maybe it's because I stay with the locals and not in those commercial hotels in the non-historic district. The residential area around the Villa Domus Salento and the Hotel delle Palme are real Italy. Cafes, fruit stands, alimentaria, a fish store, a few grocery stores, and yes, a laundromat line, the Viale Marche, Viale Vittorio Alfieri, and the Viale Gioacchino Rossini. I love a morning walk in this area or perhaps having a nightcap in one of the local stand-up bars, my Italy!

Here is a quick history of Lecce. First it was founded about 200BC. The Roman ruins make this city as well as the Baroque buildings and the churches. The City is best known for that massive sunken Roman ampitheatre, great for photo ops. BTW, unless you have a permit this entire area is a ZTL. So, don't drive your rental around. Just walk over. BTW, there are excellent, inexpensive restaurants in the area.

And a final word: Before you leave the area, make sure you take a dip or just walk in the water of that blue Adriatic or the Gulf of Taranto. It's all free; just pull up to any parking lot and enjoy!

If you are staying in Taranto, you are only 3.5 hours from Reggio Calabria. So consider moving on and visiting Sicily for a few days or even a week. Check out my Sicily chapter. By the way, you need to take the ferry to Messina. The ferries run every hour. And you can make it to Taormina or Syracuse without any problem. Hurry, the new bridge is being built! Now on to Sicily.

CHAPTER 20

IT-SICILY

AROUND THE ISLAND

INTRODUCTION

For some reason, Sicily doesn't get the play or promotion it ought to get. I spent almost a month in Sicily, circumventing the entire island. You can't beat the history of this island. The people are warm, and the food has a little different flare than the "mainland." And, if you like seafood and fish, Sicily is the place.

What I like best about Sicily is that it can be visited in winter and will feel like a mild spring day. Would you believe that in December and January, they are growing tomatoes? If this is a subsequent visit to Italy, you can't beat the weather in the winter months. January and February temperatures can reach 70 degrees during the day. If you plan to visit Italy during the winter months, plan to spend 10-14 days in Sicily.

The island's terrain and ancient sites vary. Not to mention Mount Etna (a not-so-dormant volcano) in the Catania area, that blows up every few years and spills lava all over its slopes.

Sicily requires a minimum of 14 days. You can make the highlights by following my itinerary below. About six years ago, we circumnavigated the island for a week at the beach resort of Letojanni. It is about 10 km from Taormina on the way to Messina. The best way to see the whole island is with a car rental. If you don't want to rent a car, you can base yourself in Palermo for 6 days, Syracuse for 5 days, and Taormina for 3 days. I am assuming you are flying into Palermo and out of Catania. In this way, you do not have to backtrack to Palermo, which will consume an entire day. When you rent that car in Palermo, make sure the rental car company knows you will be dropping it off in Catania. Many people do this.

248

ITALY NO TOUR NEEDED
You Can Do It Yourself

>>TIP<<<
Be smart. Consider your trip to Sicily a trip unto itself. Only visit the mainland of Italy if you have an additional two weeks.
>>><<<

Sicily is best seen by car. However, there is an option to see major sights by rail. Some of these are addressed as the Valley of the Temples, Taorminia, Syracuse, etc., can all be visited by rail. More information can be found in my book *"ITALY The Best Places to See by Rail."*

SICILY BY CAR (Not the Rent-a-Car Company)
Day 0 Enjoy your overnight flight to Palermo (PMO) via Milan (MXP) or Rome (FCO). Connect with an ITA flight about 2PM-6PM. ITA is the new airline that replaced Alitalia after its bankruptcy. You may also choose a connection via a European hub using several other carriers.

>>>TIP>>> GETTING TO SICILY
With the competition from North American cities, i.e., New York, Chicago, Toronto, etc., to Italy, you may find you will get a better fare to Palermo by flying to Milan or Rome and then buying a "local" ticket to Palermo with a return fare to Milan or Rome from another (discount) carrier from Catania (CTA). From North America, with an overnight flight to Rome or Milan, you need to connect in the afternoon, about 2-3 PM, for a flight down to Palermo. For better pricing and schedules, you can also check other major European hubs, i.e., Amsterdam, Zurich, etc. It is best to take a look at Momondo.com.

You must claim your bags upon arrival in Italy or another European hub city and recheck them to Palermo. You can also try it in reverse, i.e., fly to Catania and back from Palermo.

There is one major problem: You may not be able to get to Rome or Milan in time to board the flight back to North America the same day. Trust me on this. Most flights to North America from Italy or the European hubs depart 10AM – 2PM. This means that you will need to check in 8AM-Noon. It will be difficult or nearly

An Alternative to the Escorted Tour

impossible to do this. The best approach is to go to your hub, i.e., Rome, Milan, Zurich, the day before. If you stay at the Isola Sacra Hotel at Rome FCO airport, it will cost you about $170. Staying there the night before your flight back to the USA or Canada will ensure you get on your flight with little or no stress.

If you want to be a "hero" and drive to Sicily from Rome or Naples, it will be a whole day and at least a full gas tank. Figure the gas alone (at $7 a gallon) will be $100. Then add on another $50 for tolls. Oh, I forgot the ferry from Reggio Calabria. Figure another $50. Once again, driving to Arpino (in Frosinone) and recovering there is best. Before continuing to Sicily for that entire day of travel and that great backache when you arrive in Messina or Taormina. Oh, one more item: You may have to do this in reverse since the rental car company may "sting" you to return the car in Sicily. It is best that you run the numbers vs. the aggravation. In summary, fly down and rent a car in Sicily.
>>><<<

>>>NOTE<<<
This itinerary is what I call counter-clockwise. That is, you start in Palermo, you go south, then east and circumvent the island, finishing in Catania or back in Palermo. There is no problem going the other way. I like this since the sun is not in your eyes most of the time. By the time you are heading South or East the sun is overhead or toward the West i.e. behind you.
>>><<<

** DAY 1 ARRIVAL IN PALERMO
Day 1—Your flight just arrived in Palermo, and you need to rent a car. It is best to visit the City at the end of the trip since you won't need your rental for the last 3-4 days. Further, you don't have to negotiate with the City when it is dark in the evening, and you can't see the streets and the traffic.

The best place to layover before you start your trip around the island is Mondello Beach. It is a suburb of Palermo, about 6KM before you get to the City. Here you will find the Conghiglia D'oro Hotel. It is only a 3-star hotel, but it is excellent. It is a 10-minute walk to the resorts across from the beach. The hotel serves an excellent breakfast, offers free parking and a pool, and is very comfortable. A block from the hotel, you will find several restaurants, including pizzerias, which are perfect for a late bite.

** DAY 2 DRIVE TWO HOURS TO ERICE
Depart Mondello Beach for the hilltop medieval town of Erice (pronounced Err-Ree-Chee) and neighboring Trapani. Set your GPS unit to Erice, but make sure you follow the bus route from Trapani. If you are going to Erice, do not take the "Strada Provincial 3." The SP3 is loaded with short switchbacks, and buses can't make those hairpin turns. Many GPS units route you on the SP3. If the road looks "dumpy," you are probably on the wrong road. If you follow a taxi or a bus up the hill, you are on the correct road. No worries, you will still get up the hill on that dumpy road. Overnight, we will be in the village of ERICE. Check in and relax. Suggest you have dinner at the hotel. See more below.

WHERE TO STAY IN ERICE AND TRAPANI
First, there are about the same number of hotels in Trapani as in Erice. Parking is relatively easy in Trapani. It's all flat walking with lots of shopping and restaurants. If you want to stay in an Italian village with lots of history, then Erice is the place.

However, on the other side, Erice has limited parking, stone streets (sampietrini), a half-dozen hotels, and some of the streets have slight inclines. However, if you have no major mobility impediments, it is best to stay in Erice. It's a medieval town perched on top of a hill. Also, if this is your first stop from an overseas flight, staying two nights is a must since you will need a full day for recovery to just sleep and work that jet lag off. You will also need to use Erice as a base for your day trips to Trapani (for shopping) and a visit to the ruins at Segesta.

One hotel I recommend is the Hotel Moderno. I have stayed here, and for the price and location, you can't beat it. However, you must park temporarily in the main square, about two blocks away, and summon the hotel bellman, who will lug your bags up the slight hill to the hotel. The problem is that he won't carry you up the hill in a rickshaw. Also, be advised that to go to any restaurant, you must navigate the slight inclines or eat in the hotel, which is excellent and very reasonable.

You can find parking after you check in by moving your car about 5-7 blocks up the incline. It's not a big deal. Also, there is free parking on the street. Your bellman will direct you where to park your chariot. It is not a big deal. Further, if you are staying at the Hotel Moderno, request a room with a balcony overlooking the Via Vittorio Emanuele. It's like a Romeo and Juliet balcony. And, yes, the Moderno Hotel has an elevator. If you are booking late and need to "get a room" somewhere in Erice, ask about a private or en-suite bathroom.

>>>TIP<<<

If you cannot make calls in Italy on your smartphone and if you are overnighting in Erice, you need to ask the hotel to help you with your bags. From the square, I suggest you ask any of the taxi drivers or one of the locals to do you a favor (por fay vor ray) and call the Moderno. Make sure you have a piece of paper with the phone number and Hotel Moderno's name. It would be best to offer that person a Euro for a café and a "Grazie."
>>><<<

There are some three-star hotels in Erice and Trapani. However, many hotels, such as Albergos (just a term for a small hotel) and BnBs, may not be rated. Readers are encouraged to check the reviews. Also, many may not offer breakfast. However, there are places to purchase pastry goods, coffee, and cafes.

One more item. If you intend to stay at the Moderno or the Elimo, you should book directly and book early. These two places fill up very fast. Remember, you can always cancel your booking several weeks in advance. You should check with the hotel about their policies.

A word about Trapani. This is not a touristy town. Expect to find inexpensive restaurants and 99% locals. If you want to live with the locals, this is the place. If you want to visit the medieval hilltop town of Erice, you can go for a few hours via the inexpensive

ITALY NO TOUR NEEDED
You Can Do It Yourself

Funivia. It's a cable car system between Trapani and Erice. And, yes, they take credit cards, and it's cheap.

If you are wishing to stay in Trapani. You will find a list of hotels in booking.com. Unlike Erice, Trapani is 100% cosmopolitan. A bustling main boulevard (Corso Piersanti Mattarella/Via Giovanni Battista Fardella) is loaded with shops, hotels and restaurants.

** DAY 3 EXPLORE ERICE AND TRAPANI

A SHORT HISTORY OF ERICE
The Phoenicians founded the ancient hilltop town of Erice (2500ft above sea level). It was destroyed in the First Punic War by the Carthaginians. In 831, it was ruled by the Arabs and renamed the Mountain of Hamed. In 1167, the Normans invaded and renamed it Monte San Giuliano. In the mid-20th Century, the town took on its present name of Erice from the ancient Greek name of Eryx.

Two well-preserved castles remain and can be visited. The Pepoli Castle dates from Saracen times, and the Castello di Venere (Venus Castle) from the Norman period. This temple was built on the ancient Temple of Venus. The city walls remain. Both are no more than a 10-minute walk from any hotel.

A SHORT HISTORY OF TRAPANI
The Elymians founded Trapani, originally called Drepana, and still serves as the port of Erice. The City sits on a peninsula, surrounded by water on all three sides jutting into the Mediterranean Sea. Like many medieval towns, control of Trapani went back and forth between at least a dozen warring tribes. Carthage seized control in 260BC until the Romans took it in 241BC. It was taken by the Vandals, Ostrogoths, and Byzantines until 827, when the Arabs took over. Roger I of the Normans took control in 1077AD.

In the 17th Century, the City decayed rapidly from plagues, famines, and revolts. However, the population grew from 16,000 to 30,000. Because of its strategic natural harbor, Trapani became a

An Alternative to the Escorted Tour

jumping-off spot for the Crusades to reach the Holy Land. Trapani continues to be a large fishing and processing port. Later, the City became part of the Kingdom of Naples.

If you are visiting Trapani, i.e., coming down the hill via the cable car system, make sure you have your cameras out.

WHAT TO DO IN TRAPANI – SHOP, SHOP, SHOP

There is lots of shopping in Trapani. The town is split into two sections: the new section and the old section. However, you will come upon the old section when you reach the park at the end of "Fardella." After you work around the post office, you will find bakeries, pastry shops, restaurants, and churches as you stroll the streets toward the end of the peninsular. If you make it to the end of the peninsular in the old city, you can take a photo of the Torre di Ligney. It houses an architectural museum that dates to about 1670. I like the bakeries on the abutting streets.

It's a long day of walking. If you are bushed, you can always take a taxi or one of the buses back to your hotel from the old section or the railroad/bus station opposite the park. If you stay in Erice and come to Trapani for the day on the Funivia, you can ask any taxi to take you to the Funivia (about 8-10 Euros as it's only about 2.5 miles) or ask any bus if they go up to the Funivia. If they do, jump on and buy a ticket. The driver will advise you when you get up to the Funivia entrance. If you care not to take the Funivia back up the hill to Erice, I am sure the taxi driver will take you back to your hotel in Erice. I should note that the bus takes about 30 minutes. So you might consider spending the extra five Euros and just taking that taxi. You can usually pick up a taxi at a hotel or ask a bar to call one. If all else fails, you probably can "hail" a cab on the main boulevard. You should be able to return to your hotel at about 5PM for a snooze and shower before going to dinner at about 7:30 or 8PM.

If you are staying in Erice, an excellent restaurant is "Osteria di Venere" on Via Abatti, just up the street to the right of the Hotel Moderno. It is best to make this your second night of dining as you will be bushed with all that walking your first day in Erice and Trapani. Overnight is either in Erice or Trapani.

ITALY NO TOUR NEEDED
You Can Do It Yourself

** DAY 4 - DAY TRIP TO THE TEMPLE OF SEGESTA

You probably never heard of Segesta. No one knows anything about it. It is only speculation. This temple predates Greece and Rome. You probably never learned about it when you studied the Punic Wars in high school history. Who studies the Punic Wars anyway? Suffice it to say this temple has been here 2500 years.

Segesta is only 25 miles from Erice or Trapani and will take 45 minutes. It's a short day trip without beating your gums out. It's best to leave Erice or Trapani by 10AM, and visit the Temple and the abutting Greek amphitheater. After the visit, you can have lunch in one of the towns, then head back about 3-4PM.

The Temple at Segesta is so eerie and steeped in history that I don't know where to start. The Temple of Segesta is a well-preserved Doric Temple. Here are some quick facts: It dates from 420BC and is of Greek design, but the ancient City of Segesta had no Greek population. Go figure that one out. The view amongst historians is that it was built by the indigenous people known as the Elymians. The Temple sits on a slight mound in a valley of tall grass backed by hills with moderate outcroppings of rock.

The Temple has six columns in the front and fourteen on the side. It measures about 65 feet on the short side and 175 feet in depth and is on a platform about three steps in height.

The Temple was never completed. Indications are that the bosses in the blocks were never removed after the columns were assembled. Strangely, the Temple lacks a roof. Also, there is no altar site. It is believed that the construction of the Temple halted when Segesta went to war against Selinunte. The Carthaginians in the 5th Century AD spared the Temple's destruction.

In addition to the Temple of Segesta, there is a Greek Amphitheater (Teatro di Segesta) located about a quarter mile away in the same complex. The amphitheater is built into the side of Mount Barbaro, which lies about 300 feet higher than the Temple of Segesta. It is still well preserved and has been

An Alternative to the Escorted Tour

constructed (the latest renovation) in the 2nd Century BC. The theater held about 4,000 people.

To visit this Greek theatre, you must walk about a third of a mile up Mount Barbaro over several switchbacks. However, no need to worry. The park authorities provide a mini-bus that will take you up and down Mount Barbaro.

>>>TIP<<<
If you take the mini-bus (there is a charge of 1.5 Euros), it is best to sit on the right-hand side as you go up the mountain. This way, you can take excellent photos of the Temple of Segesta on the right, off in the distance.
>>><<<

On arrival at the complex, tickets are offered for a combination of a visit to the Temple and the Greek Amphitheater. The price is only six Euros. The Temple lies about a football field behind the ticket booth and the facilities. It is easily walkable; however, you should note that there is a very slight grade.

If you have extra time, you can visit some of the ruins of the ancient Segesta dating to about the 2nd century BC. Another village was recently discovered from Muslim times in addition to a Norman settlement with a castle on Mount Barbaro. After the expulsion of the Arabs, the Normans built a castle on Mount Barbaro. The entire site of the ancient city of Segesta was found in 1574 by the Dominican historian Tommaso Falzello. Ruins unearthed to date are available for viewing.

For lunch, 2-3PM, you will find two excellent restaurants on the OLD main road SP68, less than a mile from the Segesta Architectural Park entrance. Follow the SP68 going west toward the ocean. The SP68 is the road that leads you into the Sagesta Architectural Park from the main highway. Just before the E933, you will find the Ristorante at the Tenute Pispisa Segesta, and after you pass under the bridge of the road, the Ristorante Mediterraneo Segesta. So you can choose either one. Making your lunch (pranzo) the day's main meal is best.

ITALY NO TOUR NEEDED
You Can Do It Yourself

You should arrive back in Erice or Trapani at about 5PM for a snooze before dinner at 8PM.

** DAY 5 - TO AGRIGENTO (VALLEY OF THE TEMPLES) WITH A STOP AT THE TEMPLES AT SELINUNTE

If you are staying at the Hotel Moderno, see if they will let you drive your car up to the side street entrance or help you down to the taxi plaza. You will have to bring your car down from your overnight parking spot.

Here is a quick recap of the day. We visit the temples at Selinunte in the late morning. Then, head to Agrigento in the afternoon. We overnight in a suburb on the Med and then view the Valley of the Temples the next day before heading to Syracuse. You should check out of your hotel by 10AM and head for Selinunte. You will be in Selinunte for a couple of hours.

What I like best about Selinunte is that it sits on the Mediterranean. The ocean makes a great backdrop against the ruins of the still-standing temples. And you can take selfies with yourself perched on top of those ruins.

The temples at Selinunte are a 90-minute run, about 60 miles due southeast of Trapani (or Erice) on the Mediterranean. Covering almost 700 acres, Selinunte is the largest archeological park in Europe. It was founded as a Greek colony in 628BC, perhaps as early as 700BC. It was an extensive Greek city founded by a Greek colony (about 20 miles from Athens) known as Megara. At its peak, it had a population of over 30,000. It was destroyed and abandoned in 250BC and never reoccupied. Many temples are on the site, with the earliest dating to 550BC.

The name Selinunte is a Greek word for celery. It's no joke. Wild celery grew in the area, so the Greeks named their city after it.

Now that you know the background of Segesta, you should know the following facts: First, Segesta (you probably visited it yesterday) and Selinunte always fought each other. Then, the Carthaginians aided Selinunte only to come back later and

An Alternative to the Escorted Tour

conquer Selinunte. This went on for several hundred years. Wars went on and on. It is believed that as early as 580BC the Selinuntines were engaged in hostilities with the non-Greek Elymian people of Segesta, whose territory bordered their own, so much for a short history. To visit Selinunte, there is a six-euro admission fee and no parking charge. The tram is additional.

It's a fast drive down the A29. Then, take the Castelvetrano exit and follow SS115 to Marinella di Selinunte. You will be there in a few minutes. Before entering the park, you can pick up a panini and some soft drinks in Marinella if you have not purchased one in Erice/Trapani. At the entrance, there is a moderate-sized museum and very modern facilities. You can tour the complex on a tram for an additional fee. Please see below.

There are paths connecting all the ruins. It is best to bring your water, snacks, and that fresh panini with you. You may even want to get your hotel or an "Alimentaria" (convenience store selling cold cuts and crusty bread) to make you a sandwich or two. It makes a great photo op, downing a sandwich on one of those ancient Greek columns in the grass.

You should note that the park closes at 6PM. So don't arrive about 5PM and expect to spend several hours here since there are two clusters of ruins and temples about a kilometer apart (a little more than a half mile). You may want to take the mini-tram around the park for 12 Euros or better, 3 Euros between stops.

Here is what you need to see: Most of the ruins were discovered and excavated in the 19th Century. In the 20th Century, the temples on the eastern hill were excavated. Temple E was reconstructed in as little as 1950. At the same time, excavations of the Acropolis in Athens began.

First, the ruins and temples are addressed with an alphabetic charter: A-B-C-D and O are right up against the water. The other cluster, E-F-G, is near the entrance and the museum. Once again, all these temples were built to honor the gods: Zeus, Dionysus, Apollo, Hera (Goddess), and more.

ITALY NO TOUR NEEDED
You Can Do It Yourself

>>>TIP<<<
The best approach is to take the tram from the entrance, where they always hang out to the temples on the water A-B-C-D and O, and then either take the tram back or walk back to the entrance. Also, you may want to visit one of the necropoli and view the foundations, which date back several thousand years.
>>><<<

A rather large necropolis of part of the old city is also located about a kilometer from the entrance. It lies at about two o'clock as you enter the complex. All temples and ruins are located in this massive park. You cannot compare Selinunte with Pompeii or any of the other ruins in Italy or even Greece. This archeological park is spread out and huge.

On my entrance to Selinunte, my jaw dropped as I viewed temples E, F, and G for the first time. It was an "OMG."

After completing your visit to Selinunte, you are ready to make your way over to Porto Empedocle, a suburb of Agrigento and on the Mediterranean. There are lots of hotels in Agrigento. However, my favorite area is Porto Empedocle. There are lots of good restaurants abutting the beach and a fabulous four-star hotel at the end of the beach road. Villa Romana is on the beach and also has an excellent restaurant. If you want to stay here the night before your visit to the Valley of the Temples, do request a room with an ocean view if you are arriving during daylight hours to see that gorgeous sunset. Overnight is at Villa Romana in Porto Empedolce, just a few kilometers from Agrigento.

** DAY 6 AGRIGENTO- THE VALLEY OF THE TEMPLES
The Valley of the Temples is a must-see if you visit Sicily. Like many of the archeological sites in Italy, it is also one of the 58 UNESCO World Heritage Sites.

After checking out of your hotel at about 10AM, it's only a 15-minute drive on the SS640 road to Agrigento. Once in Agrigento, follow those signs to the Valley of the Temples.

An Alternative to the Escorted Tour

On arrival, there is a free parking lot before you gain admission. You should note that there are two entrances. A shuttle bus goes between them for three Euros. So, if you walk to the other end (about 2.5 miles), you can take that shuttle back.

If you decide to base yourself in Palermo, there are trains every few hours to Agrigento, and the journey only takes two hours. If you are in Catania, the journey will take around five hours, and at least two or three trains will change; this is not advisable.

First, if you are attempting to visit June-October, be advised that you need to purchase a timed ticket, or else you won't be able to gain admission. Secondly, if going during this time frame, I can tell you from experience that this place is beastly hot.

You can purchase tickets directly from the Italian Government-authorized website: www.ecm.coopculture.it/index. The entrance fee is 12Euros. However, if you want to go to the museum, it will cost you an additional 3.5Euros. Also, at the entrance, a map of the complex is advisable for one Euro.

Now, on to the history of the Valley of the Temples:

First, this place was originally called Akragas. Like many communities in Sicily, it was founded about the 6th Century BC as a Greek colony, actually an outpost. The complex does not lie in a valley but on a bluff. All the temples, or what I would say, the remains of the temples, are on like a boulevard. It is strongly recommended that you pick up an audio tour and headset.

It is better if you are with another couple or can arrange with another couple to take a guided tour for two hours; this place is also mind-boggling. An ancient wall surrounds the entire complex of about 2300 acres.

The most famous and best preserved is the Temple of Concordia. When you see pictures of the Valley of the Temples, this is the photo they often show you, indeed not a pile of rubble with a few standing columns as many of the other temples are. Here is a quick overview from Wikipedia:

ITALY NO TOUR NEEDED
You Can Do It Yourself

The "Valley" contains the remains of seven temples. They are all of the Doric Greek style. The names you see here are from the Renaissance period. They had Greek names originally.

The Temple of Concordia was built in the 5th Century BC. The name Concordia comes from a Latin inscription found nearby. It probably had a different name when it was built. The Temple of Concordia was converted into a church in the 6th Century AD.

The Temple of Juno was also built in the 5th Century BC. It was burnt down by the Carthaginians in 406BC.

The Temple of Heracles was one of the most revered deities of the ancient city of Akragas. An earthquake destroyed it. Today, only eight columns remain standing.

The Temple of Olympian Zeus was built in 480BC to celebrate the victory over Carthage. Only four columns remain at the Temple of Castor and Pollux, which is the symbol of Agrigento.

The Temple of Hephaestus (Vulcan) also dates from the 5th Century BC. It is now one of the most eroded.

The Temple of Ascipepius (I can't pronounce it either, but I know it's Greek to me) is located far from the town's walls. It was the goal of pilgrims seeking cures for illnesses.

Also in the Valley is the Tomb of Theron. It was built to commemorate the Romans killed in the Second Punic War. Oh, those Punic Wars again!

You will need 2-3 hours to digest the temples fully, take pictures, etc. After you visit the Valley, you have several options. On exiting the Valley, it's best to obtain some nourishment.

If you are bushed, best is to overnight in Agrigento or Porto Empedocle and head to Syracuse and Taormina in the morning. It is a slow two lane road and will take you about three hours to reach Syracuse. If you drive to Syracuse after seeing the Valley of the Temples, you will have the sun in your eyes for a few hours. So

An Alternative to the Escorted Tour

it is best to drive back to Porto Empedocle, take a snooze and enjoy dinner, and go on to Syracuse after breakfast the next day.

** DAY 7 DRIVE TO SYRACUSE (FROM AGRIGENTO)
If you are circumventing the island or this is your second time visiting Sicily and you are visiting what I call "THE EAST COAST," then Syracuse and Taormina are a must. Both of these towns deserve a minimum of two full days each.

** DAY 8 & 9 SYRACUSE (SIRACUSA) FIRST FULL DAY
First you should know that there are two parts of Syracuse. There is an island called "Ortigia," separated by a canal which connects it from the mainland portion of Syracuse. The canal is spanned by two small bridges, no more than 200 feet in length. Ortigia as well as the mainland contain Greek and Roman ruins. Please see my history below.

There are hotels on both Ortigia and the mainland side. Syracuse is a small place compared to Palermo or Catania. You can walk the entire place in less than an hour or two.

My favorite place to stay is on the island of Ortigia. First it's rather quaint. Second, there is a major food and street market everyday (except Sunday). There are lots of restaurants and gelato shops. And finally, it's a small place to walk around as compared to the mainland portion of the town. No question, Ortigia is the best place to stay.

One small point. Parking is like Manhattan. You may have to drive around till you find a "non-resident" parking spot. However, there is overnight free parking in a municipal lot overlooking the canal. Just make sure you move your car in the morning or better feed the meter.

My favorite hotel in Ortigia is the three-star La Posta. It is quite reasonable, and you can request a balcony overlooking the canal (channel). If you want to spend the big bucks, best is to stay at the five-star Grand Hotel Ortigia; do request a water view.

262

ITALY NO TOUR NEEDED
You Can Do It Yourself

If you can't find a place in Ortigia to sleep, one of the best places on the mainland section of Syracuse is the Grand Albergo Alfeo. It's an easy walk to Ortigia and central to everything.

If you are arriving by train, there are lots of hotels within a few blocks of the rail station. The entire mainland of Syracuse and Ortigia island are flat. So, no worries if you enjoy a long walk.

Ortigia is an island made for walking. So best to park your car here and if necessary move it each day. The mainland is auto friendly. However, you can walk it with no problem on the main boulevards of Corso Umberto I and Via Malta. If you are bushed, you can taxi back to Ortigia or take one of the buses.

>>>TIP<<<
The Corso Umberto is a one-way boulevard going away from Ortigia and the Via Malta goes the other way. Best to walk one way on one of the boulevards and return on the other.
>>><<<

A QUICK HISTORY OF SYRACUSA (SYRACUSE)
The city of Syracusa dates back to about 2,700 year ago. It was found by the ancient Greek Corinthians and Teneans and became a powerful city-state. Later it became allied with Sparta in addition to Corinth. It was part of what was known as Magna Graecia. By the 5th Century BC it equaled Athens in size.

It wasn't until 663AD that it became part of the Roman Republic and the Byzantine Empire under Emperor Constans II. In fact, it was the capital of the Byzantine Empire from 663-669AD. Palermo took over later as the capital of the Kingdom of Sicily.

Syracuse is one of the UNESCO World Heritage sites, along with the Necropolis of Pantalica, a few kilometers away.

Syracuse is mentioned in the New Testament in the Acts of the Apostles book 28:12 as Paul stayed there. The patron saint of the city is Saint Lucy. She was born in Syracuse on December 13.

An Alternative to the Escorted Tour

So, if you visit Syracuse over this time frame, you should be aware that hotel rooms may be in short supply. I included more history of what to do and see in Syracuse.

WHAT TO SEE AND DO IN SYRACUSE

With the exception of that great street market in Ortigia, you will find most of Syracuse wrapped up in either Greek or Roman history. Oh, I forgot to mention Syracuse is the home of Archimedes (287BC-212BC). He lived here all his life until being killed accidentally by a Roman soldier during the siege of Syracuse by the Romans in 212 BC. He is best known for his laws of buoyancy, mathematics, and the Archimedes Screw.

Syracuse was founded in 734BC by Greek settlers from Corinth. There are several origins of the name. Some say it came from the Phoenicians, who used the words Sour-ha-Koussim, which meant "Stone of the seagulls."The Phoenicians lived in what is now the seacoast region of modern Lebanon. In ancient times, various villages in and around what is now Syracuse were also occupied by other peoples from the Mediterranean. The center of the city was on the island of Ortigia. Native tribes farmed the land outside of the island.

Under Greek rule, the city grew and prospered until it became the most powerful Greek city in the Med. There is so much history here that I would need a book of at least 600 pages to describe it.

THE OUTDOOR MARKET

This is a place you want to visit in the morning. Grab some olives (or bruschetta), a loaf of bread, a wedge of cheese, and some slices of prosciutto, and head on down to the harbor, where you can sit and have lunch. If you are too early for lunch, grab your goodies and stash them in your Ortigia island hotel. Oh, and don't forget that bottle of wine you need to stash in the Frigo bar. Oh, if you forgot to bring one of those Swiss army knives, now is the time to purchase one at the outdoor market and make sure it has a corkscrew. And, remember you can't pack it in that carry-on bag for your flight back to the USA or Canada.

ITALY NO TOUR NEEDED
You Can Do It Yourself

TEMPIO OF APOLLO (TEMPLE OF APOLLO)

As you cross that small canal on Via Malta, take note of the flower cart and café; you will see the Temple of Apollo straight in front of you. I should really say "the remains of the Temple of Apollo." It, like most other Greek temples, is of Doric design and was built in the 6th Century BC to honor Apollo. The Greek and Roman deity "Apollo" is probably the most revered and best known of all the Greek and Roman Gods. He was the god of archer, music, dance, truth, prophecy, healing and diseases, the Sun and light, and more. There are remnants of temples built to honor Apollo all over the ancient Western world.

Since hopefully, you have been to the temples of Segesta, Selinunte and Concordia in the Valley of the Temples, you will find this temple to Apollo a letdown. It's mainly ruble with about six column stubs remaining. Would you believe this was a smaller temple compared to the others of the ancient world? The Temple was only six columns in the front by seventeen columns in length.

The temple had several transformations. It became a Byzantine church in the late Roman Empire. You may be able to make out the old iron gate in the front. Later, it became an Islamic Mosque when the entire island of Sicily was ruled by the Muslims 831-1091AD. When the Normans defeated the Saracens, it was turned back into the Church of the Saviour in the 16th Century.

The building was built with 42 monolithic columns, which were probably delivered via the sea and erected on site. The temple had a wood roof. Monolithic columns are made of one piece of material, chiseled from one solid piece of marble or stone, then fluted. A hole was bored in the center to aid in its lifting and manufacture. Other temples are made of disks, which are then piled on top of each other to reach the desired height, and then the Doric supporting block is placed on top. The temple and its remains are free to view. The balance of the remains of the ancient world is on the mainland. Please see my discussions later.

An Alternative to the Escorted Tour

THE MANIACE CASTLE

The Maniace Castle sometimes called the citadel, is located at the far point of Ortigia island after you cross through the Piazza del Duomo and head due south past the small university. You can't miss it, there are plenty of signs. It sits on a promontory with water to each side except for the connection to the island. At one time there was a moat, but it has been all filled in. It was constructed 1232-1240AD by Emperor Frederick II.

The first fort was built on this site by an Armenian general by the name of George Maniakes. He captured Syracusa from the Arabs on behalf of the king of Sicily.

The Castle was used by the queens of Sicily until the 15th Century. It later became a prison. In the 16th Century, it became a harbor defense for the city. In 1704, a huge explosion damaged the fort, and it was then renovated to incorporate guns.

It now houses a museum. However, you should take note that it is only open in the mornings. The entrance fee is a small two Euros. You need no more than one hour here.

PIAZZA DEL DUOMO

As you work your way to the Piazza del Duomo, you will pass a small rotary. That's the Palazzo of Archimedes. It also contains the statue of Diana in a fountain. In a few blocks, you will come to the Piazza del Duomo. This is Ortigia's central square (it's not really a square). It contains the Cathedral of Syracuse (the Duomo), the Town Hall, and the Archbishop's Palace. Here, you will also find the Chiesa di Santa Lucia all Badia church. In addition to the historic buildings, there are cafes and shopping.

What I find most interesting about the cathedral is the fact that it is a mix of Gothic with Greek columns. I find this kind of odd.

If you look at the history of this UNESCO World Heritage Site (within the Syracuse UNESCO site) you will understand.

266

ITALY NO TOUR NEEDED
You Can Do It Yourself

About the 5th Century BC, the great Temple of Athena was built on the same site as the Cathedral of Syracusa. Like many other Greek temples, it had six columns on the short side and 14 on the long side. Excavations around the Duomo 1907-1910 showed that the ancient Greek Temple was built on even older foundations.

The present cathedral you now see was constructed in the 7th Century. The Doric columns of the original temple were incorporated in the walls of the church. And in 878AD the church was again converted into a mosque. And further in 1085 the mosque went back to being a church.After the 1693 earthquake, the cathedral was rebuilt 1725-1753. The style is called High Sicilian Baroque. If you see that small rotary, that's the Palazzo of Archimedes. It also contains the status of Diana in a fountain.

There are so many sites in Ortigia; again, I could write a book about them. However, if you have visited the places I have described, you will have visited the major ones. Oh, I forgot to mention that this little island, which was only 2.5 miles long, also had an old Jewish Quarter. It no longer exists, but in 1998, while excavating for a house, a Jewish Bath (Mikvah) site was unearthed. It is now below the basement of the "Residence Alla Giudecca," which is a 3-star hotel. Supposedly, this is the largest and oldest Jewish ritual bath in Europe. If you care not to stay at the hotel you can take a tour of the baths for only five Euros.

Now, on to the mainland section of Syracuse. The number one must see site, is the massive Archaeological Park.

ARCHAEOLOGICAL PARK AND PANTALICA

The archaeological park in Syracuse is one of the most important archaeological sites in all of Sicily and one of the largest in the Mediterranean. It spans several eras of the history of Syracuse. The park is located in the Neapolis (the new city as opposed to Necropolis) section of Syracuse, which is entirely situated on the mainland sections (not on Ortigia island). What is interesting to note is that the park is relatively new. However, the "finds" date back several thousand years.

An Alternative to the Escorted Tour

To see this entire complex and the "Pantalica," you probably need two full days. However, you should spend 2-4 hours just seeing the highlights. The Necropolis of Pantalica is located 25 miles from Syracuse. It is best to drive or taxi over. By the mid-1800s, most of the monuments at the park had been unearthed. It was only around 1950 that a master plan was developed to protect the park. Would you believe, outside the park's core, homes were being built over ancient temples, baths, and streets? This rampant building over precious antiquities had to be protected, and by the 1980s, the park was fully established. Turning toward the park in Syracuse.

ARCHAEOLOGICAL PARK OF SYRACUSE

The park is located on a hill known as the Temenite Hill. The hill divides the park in two. The quarries are to the North, and the South contains most monuments. The park is located near the Anapo River (or what used to be a river).

For the details and locations of all the monuments, it would be best to pick up a map/plan at the ticket booth. Note the ticket booth is located in the park on Via Francesco Saverio Cavallari.

There is plenty of parking on the Corso Celoni in the public parking lot and in all abutting streets. You may want to take a minibus tour; check with the ticket booth. On a positive note, the Greek Theatre is located just across the street from the ticket booth (Biglietteria booth). There is not a lot of walking to visit the Greek Theatre. The Greek Theatre was built in the 15th Century BC on the southern slope of the Temenite hill. It was subsequently rebuilt in the 3rd Century BC. It was renovated once again, now by the Romans. Later, in about 1500AD, when the Spaniards controlled the area, they spent no time taking the Theatre apart and shipping those blocks of stone back to Spain. What you see now is pretty much a rebuilt Greek theatre. Do not confuse this theater with the Roman one across the way.

If you see an odd-shaped structure off the side of the road with people walking around it, that's the "Ear of Dionysos," known in Italian as "Orecchio di Dionisio." If you are curious about the "Ear," I suggest you visit it. The ancient Greeks carved this limestone cave into the Temenite hill. It was given the name in 1608 by Michelangelo. It supposedly looks like the shape of a human ear. It is said that people's voices can echo up to 16 times. I suggest you visit the Ear because of the unique acoustics. The cave's actual purpose was to be a water storage tank. It was dug in Greek/Roman times. An earthquake struck the area and caused severe damage, so the water tunnel is not useable. In the medieval period, it became a prison. This "Ear" is massive. It is about 70 feet in height and extends about 195 feet from front to back. It is tapered from top to bottom like a teardrop. The Ear is definitely worth a visit.

The Church of San Nicolo ai Cordari dates from 1093 and was constructed during the Norman period. It can be seen when entering the Neapolis. The church is a building made of stone blocks. However, I never understood why a Catholic church would be built in a Greek amphitheater area. The church is closed right now. When it is open, it is used for receptions.

With respect to the Roman Amphitheater: Is a short walk from the Greek theater. However, unlike the Greek theatre, which is well preserved, the Roman theater is all ruble in a grassy field. At its prime, the theater measured about 150 yards in depth and about 120 yards across. That rectangular pit was an entranceway that led to tunnels under the Theatre to allow gladiators and animals, etc., to enter the "stage." Roman remnant's of an old water tank still exist. These tanks held water for the Roman nautical games and water fights. They were fed by the Galermi aqueduct, parts of which are still standing.

Parts of the Triumphal Arch of Augustus remain. It is located in the southern part of the Roman amphitheater. It was a large arch of about 35 feet wide, about 19 feet deep, and about 40 feet in height. This arch was the entrance to the area during the Augustan period. In and around the area, there are remains from the Hellenistic period. Again, only bases remained while most of the blocks were removed (yes, again) by the Spanish to build a fort in the 16th Century.

An Alternative to the Escorted Tour

The Mill's of Galerme were a complex of water mills. These were located above the caves of the Greek Theatre. However, they only date from the late medieval period. Today only the millers' house remains visible. These mills ground grains, i.e., Amaranth, Kamut, Spelt, etc., so they could be baked into bread.

As for Pantalica (also a UNESCO World Heritage Site), if you are into history or archeology, this is the place to explore. It's free. But don't expect lots of ancient ruins here. What is left is an ancient cemetery. There are 4000-5000 tunnels built into rocky outcrops. This place dates from the 13th Century BC to the 7th Century BC. That's pretty old, about 3500 years. This place is a catacomb built into the rocky walls as opposed to underground tunnels. The actual town ceased to exist sometime around the 12th Century AD. Archeologists believe the town had a population of about 1,000.

After you have spent a minimum of two full days (suggested) in Syracuse, it's time to move on to Taormina.

** DAY 10 & 11 TAORMINA

If you are visiting the eastern side of Sicily, this is one of the highlights. You can also come down from Rome for the day via an early flight to Catania (CTA) and then fly home in the evening. Please pack an overnight bag, fly down, and return to Rome the next day.

If you are driving from Syracuse, it will take you about 90 minutes (70 miles). The taxi ride from the CTA airport is about one hour. It will cost you about 80Euros to get directly to your hotel. The drive from Palermo is a hike. The 175-mile run will take you 3.5 hours without any stops. I wish I could have stayed several days on my last trip to Taormina. A drink and some olives at the five-star Grand Hotel Timeo Belmond didn't work for me, even though I nursed my Pina Colada with the A-List people.

Taormina dates back to when Ancient Greece established its first colony on Sicily in 734BC. Taormina is also as old as some of the other ancient sites you probably have been visiting in Sicily. Taormina ranked as one of the essential towns in Sicily and followed its history of being ruled by foreign monarchs.

ITALY NO TOUR NEEDED
You Can Do It Yourself

After the Italian unification in the mid 1800s, it began to attract tourists from northern Europe. Taormina received a lot of notoriety when the 43rd G7 summit was held here in May 2017. When strolling around Taormina, like Capri, keep your eyes peeled for the "A-List" people and the Paparazzi.

The town of Taormina lies on a massive outcrop at the end of a large hill that extends along the coast from Cape Pelorus. The old town lies about 820 feet above sea level. About 500 feet higher than the actual town, you will find a Norman castle. There are still ancient walls around the town. Numerous pieces of old buildings are scattered about.

If you are driving, those switchbacks which take you to the top of Taormina are extremely challenging. If you are driving, you will find paid parking in a massive concrete structure where there is a capacity for almost 1,000 cars. There are other paid parking areas. They are all government run and charge the same price. Depending on the parking area, shuttle buses are available.

>>>TIP<<<
The best way to visit Taormina for the day, is to park at the base of the Funivia (lots of parking spaces), then take the Funivia to the top of the hill. The Funivia is on the main seaside road. If you are staying at a hotel or a BnB, you must take a taxi to the top as it is pretty challenging to take a 40-pound luggage bag in a cable car; see the above paragraph about parking garages.
>>><<<

QUICK HISTORY AND WHAT TO SEE AND DO:
The only remnant of the Greek/Roman era, remaining and still used, is the Ancient theatre of Taormina. Originally it was a Greek theatre. The Romans later rebuilt it in the 2nd Century. It is very impressive, with a span of 358 feet. You will find the walkway down to the theatre on the left side of the Grand Timeo Hotel. It is best to have a drink, and some olives at the Timeo, first.

Other sites to be visited are the 14th Century Palazzo Corvaj, a 1635 Baroque fountain, the Church of San Domenico, and the

An Alternative to the Escorted Tour

municipal gardens. Below Taormina lies the seaside resort of Giardini Naxos. You will see the Isola Bella nature reserve and beach in the bay.

The church above the town is the Santuraio Madonna della Rocca. If you have the energy, you can climb steps on the path leading to the church. If you are physically challenged, you should be aware that there are a lot of steps. If you are inclined to visit the church, you will enjoy superb views of Mount Etna.

There are several other churches perched high on the slope overlooking the town, in addition to some castles.

So what's the draw with Taormina? Simple, it is highly romantic. Many Europeans consider this an excellent place for a honeymoon. In addition, there are incredible views of the sea. There are numerous shops and cafes on the main boulevard, the "Corso Umberto." About halfway down this boulevard, which spans about 15 blocks, is the Piazza IX Aprile. Late in the day, a pianist is playing the classics on a baby grand piano.

I cannot tell you how much I enjoyed the shopping, or should I say the look. There are great places for a honeymoon. There is a superabundance of hotels and BnBs. You can figure the count is at least a hundred. However, you will have to find a beach. The best thing is to stay in Taormina Mare for part of your stay. You might also consider Giardini Naxos or the Letojanni beach area. As for dinner or Pranzo (lunch), you will find an abundance of restaurants. However, it is best to ask the locals where they go.

>>>TIP<<<
If you are going to stay at a BnB, you should be aware that off the Corso Umberto, there is a slight slope to your right as you walk with the sea on your left. The best idea would be to check it out on Google Earth before you make your booking. You won't have a problem with the 3, 4, or 5 star hotels as they are all in flat areas.
>>><<<

After you have enjoyed your visit to Taormina, it's time to depart to Catania or Palermo for a flyout. If you are going back to Palermo, I suggest one or two nights in Cefalu (pronounced Chef-a-loo.) Cefalu is only a four-hour run from Taormina instead of nine hours to the PMO airport. So you can easily leave Taormina at about 3PM and head for dinner in Cefalu. Please see my next section on Cefalu's beautiful village and seaside town.

CATANIA AND MOUNT ETNA
No question, the draw to this area is the drive around Mount Etna. Also, remember that Etna is still an active volcano.

If you are overnighting in Catania before a flyout to one of the European hubs or have an additional night in Taormina, I strongly recommend a day trip circumventing Mount Etna. If you don't have a rental car, you can take the train down to Catania, then catch the special train which goes around the volcano completely. However, you must remember that it is an actual "U" and not a true circle. It returns to a different location in Catania, where you can get the train back to Taormina. It's definitely a nice day trip.

If you are not in love with volcanos, there are several sites worth visiting in the old section of Catania. They are the ruins of the Greek and Roman theatre, the Castello Ursino, which dates to the 13th Century (it's a castle), and the Cathedral di Sant' Agata. The Cathedral was built 1078-1093 but needed to be rebuilt several times because of eruptions from Mount Etna and earthquakes. The lastest rebuilding was in the Baroque style.

** DAY 12 & 13 CEFALU
Cefalu pronounced (Chef-a-loo) is just the town you want to stay in before you leave Italy. It's not touristy! So don't expect to buy coffee mugs, snow globes, and refrigerator magnets (made in China, of course) in this quaint seaside town.

The best place to stay is at the Hotel La Calette and Bay, about four miles east of the town. It is a five-star hotel on the ocean, modern and very reasonable. And please book a room with a view of the sea and the pool if you are visiting during the season.

An Alternative to the Escorted Tour

>>>TIP<<<
If you are overnighting in Cefalu and visiting the town, do not repeat; do not attempt to drive in the city. Some of the streets are too narrow, and you risk getting stuck in one of them. Don't laugh, I did! Please take it from my experience. If you are staying at the Hotel La Calette or any hotel outside of the village itself, my advice is to take a taxi for no more than eight Euros to the center of the town, walk around, shop and then return to your hotel after lunch.
>>><<<

Cefalu is a resort town. However, sitting on the small beach won't be in vogue if you are there in the off-season. The village itself is great for local shopping. And, further, I love mixing in with the locals. The main drag is called Vittorio Emanuele (named after the first king of unified Italy). It's all cobblestone. After you go through the portal at the end street, you will emerge at the sea. Just turn around and take those great pictures.

La Rocca, called the castle, is a fortified cliff about 820 feet above the sea. Rocca has ridges facing east, west, and south. Scaling the cliffs is impossible since the lower half is fortified. The path fortified in the middle ages allowed climbing to the top.

Note, climbing "Rocca" is NOT advisable. You need to be skilled at hiking on steep paths. It is best viewed at sunset with the Rocca di Cefalu in the background behind all those houses.

There are numerous churches in the village. My suggestion is not to stay in the village but to stay in one of the lovely beach resorts. It is best to visit the town from 11AM- 3PM. You should note that many shops will be closed 1PM-4PM for siesta.

The following day it is a fast run of about 60 miles (a little over an hour) to PMO airport to drop that rental car and fly home to Rome or drop into one of the hotels in Palermo centro. And remember you won't need a car in Palermo.

ITALY NO TOUR NEEDED
You Can Do It Yourself

** DAY 14 & 15 PALERMO (THE CAPITAL OF SICILY)

Palermo is famous for its history, culture, architecture, churches, and gastronomy. With four major outdoor markets in the city, you might want to rent an apartment and consider self-catering. You can broil a piece of fresh fish every day but still not sample all the fish from the Mediterranean. You can always have dinner out and breakfast in your apartment with goods purchased from the four outdoor markets. Shopping at these markets is part of the Palermo experience.

What comes to mind when people say "our cruise will be stopping in Palermo for the day?" Is it the Sicilian Pizza that is so different than the pizza we enjoy so much? Perhaps it's because Palermo is synonymous with the Sicilian Mafia? Or is it because of how quaint and Italian (or should I say Sicilian) the Old Town is? Most of us know that Palermo is the capital of Sicily. However, like Sicily, Palermo doesn't get the tourist traffic it deserves. There are lots of reasons. A week here would be best, but three days will do the highlights.

From early May to late September you might want to consider staying in the beach resort of Mondello, about seven miles from Palermo. I discussed this earlier in the chapter. There is frequent muni bus service #806 into the heart of Palermo (takes 30 mins.)

>>>TIP<<<

If you want to try your hand at driving in Palermo, drop your luggage off at your hotel. Then, proceed to the PMO airport. Once at the airport, follow the signs to the new (Metro) subway and take it back to the last stop, which is the Palermo Central rail station. It takes almost one hour and has about 16 stops. If you are flying into PMO, it is best to take a taxi to your hotel.
>>><<<

Palermo is made for walking. Using a car becomes a pain between the traffic, small streets, and the parking. If you are bushed after a day of walking, the best is to take a taxi back to your hotel. I also suggest that you stay at a hotel near the central rail station if you make any day trips to Agrigento, Trapani, the cathedral, or the

275

An Alternative to the Escorted Tour

waterfront. Buses depart near the main rail station for many points in Palermo and the abutting towns.

A SHORT HISTORY OF PALERMO

Palermo was founded by the Phoenicians in 734BC almost 2700 years ago. Palermo then became a possession of Carthage. Subsequently, the Greeks established two colonies here. They were called Panormos after the 5th Century BC. Panormus became part of he Roman Republic and Roman Empire for over one thousand years. From 831AD to 1072AD, control of what we know as modern-day Palermo passed on to Arab rule, becoming the Emirate of Sicily. The City was known as Balarm. The Normans took over in 1130AD until 1816AD, when it became the Kingdom of Sicily. In 1860, it became part of the Kingdom of Italy. The influence of the Roman, Arab, Gothic, and Baroque cultures made their mark on the churches, palaces, and other buildings throughout the City. The inhabitants of the City speak Italian and Palermitano, a dialect of the Sicilian language.

WHAT TO SEE AND DO IN PALERMO

I strongly suggest that you spend the first full day exploring Palermo. In other words, an orientation. See your front desk clerk and obtain a mappa (plan) of the city. Have him/her circle the four markets. Then, set out by visiting them. You can have a late lunch in Old Town. I would suggest you also visit some of the famous churches en route to the markets.

The most famous is the Ballaro Market. It is located on Via Ballaro. It is the largest of the four major markets. The del Capo Market is located on Via Cappuccinelle in the Capo neighborhood. It is known for fresh fish. There is also a fish market near the marina. The Vucciria Market can be found in the Piazza Caracciolo. This place is ancient! It is located in the very old quarter known as Castellammare. Small alleys with buildings falling apart and graffiti all over make this place a real "gotta see" for the tourists. There are hawkers all over, and shouting is an added attraction. In addition to the food markets, you will find other smaller markets throughout the city selling everything from antiques to shampoo and houseware.

276

ITALY NO TOUR NEEDED
You Can Do It Yourself

>>>TIP<<<
Visiting street markets in any city (even Paris or London) is a hangout for pickpockets. They sometimes work in teams. Ladies, don't put your handbag down on those lovely grapes! See my write-up under security in chapter 21. You should be extra vigilant.
>>><<<

All the street markets which usually sell food are closed on Sunday. There are some markets which sell antiques and sundries which open on Sundays for a few hours.

THE CHURCHES AND ARCHITECTURE OF PALERMO
Most of the churches and historical buildings of Palermo were built during the Baroque Period (1600-1750). You would need at least three full days to visit them all. Keep in mind that many of them do charge minimal entrance fees. Check to see if they are open on Mondays. Here is an overview:

The Cathedral di Palermo was built in 1185. It is definitely not Baroque. The Cathedral is a complex of several buildings built over 500 years. It appears to be a castle as it has a crenelated roof. The Church was built over the remains of a Muslim Mosque. The front entrance appears definitely to be Moorish. You need at least two hours to take in the entire complex.

The Cathedral at Monreale can be visited in a half day. But you should plan for a whole day. It's located about an hour away. It is also a complex mostly of Moorish and Norman design. The vaulted painted ceilings are incredible. If you have a rental car, no problem; otherwise, it is best to take the #389 bus. If you take other buses with connections, you will be forced to walk about a half mile. Allow extra time to have lunch at about 2PM in the village of Monreale. It is best to see your concierge. The church closes at about 3PM, so don't plan on getting there too late.

Santa Maria dell'Ammiraglio is best known as "La Martorana." It is part of the Byzantine Eastern Orthodox Diocese, as opposed to the Western Roman Catholic Church based in the Vatican. Since WWII, it has been home to the 15,000 Albanians who lost their

An Alternative to the Escorted Tour

church during the bombing of Sicily in World War II. La Martoran is a must see because of its painted and frescoed ceilings and walls. You will need about 1-2 hours here. There are many more churches. However, here are two interesting places that are must to see:

The Piazza Pretoria (also known as the Grand Square) contains a large fountain erected during the Inquisition. It contains statues of nymphs, nudes, and more. Other places worth a visit are the Palermo Opera House and the Museum of Tiles.

>>>TIP<<< DAY TRIP TO AGRIGENTO
There are several trains a day to Agrigento, home of the Valley of the Temples. It is a fast two hour run and only $30 round-trip. Trains from Palermo Centrale run every hour to Agrigento. For more information, consult www.omio.com.
>>><<<

Want something really different? If you did not know it, Palermo and parts of Sicily used to be home to the Mafia and the Cosa Nostra. Don't laugh, but there are several Godfather tours. It is best to query the internet with your favorite browser.

I hope you enjoy your visit to Italy and Sicily as much as I do.

>>>TIP<<< STOP PRESS - ITALY TOURIST TAX
As of April 1, 2024, many tourist locations in Italy have invoked a TOURIST TAX to control the number of tourists on peak days of the year and peak hours of the day. This is not to raise funds for the municipality but to control the flow of tourists. In essence, if you visit, say, Venice during the "off hours" or "off days," you won't have to pay the tax. But get off that train on July 8 at Noon, you will need to pay a tax and get a wristband. The taxing authorities are still working out all the details. The best suggestion I can offer is to check the internet using the search terms "Venice tourist tax" or "Italy tourist taxes," etc.
>>><<<

CHAPTER 21

HOTEL SELECTION
TELEPHONES/INTERNET
SECURITY/DINING
CUSTOMS/EURAIL

HOTEL SELECTION PROCESS

Did you know that even five-star famous hotels, such as The Waldorf Astoria in New York, The Savoy in London, etc., all have some negative reviews? So how do you choose a hotel? It's quite simple. First, convince yourself that you will do the best you can. Once you arrive, if there are any issues, resolve them at once. And as a seasoned traveler, remember, nothing is perfect.

First, find the hotel on Booking.com or Hotels.com. Spot them on the map and see if they are close enough to where you want to stay. Pay attention to hotels that are on a main boulevard or a busy drag. Then go to Tripadvisor.com. and read some of the reviews. Pay attention to the bottom two ratings, i.e., Poor and Terrible. Tick them off and read some of them. Discount comments like "the martini at the lobby bar was warm," or the desk clerk defined the word "grumpy." Pay close attention to the bad ones, "throughout the hotel, there was a musty odor", especially if the review was recent. Now, add the Poor and Terrible count. Then, add up all the categories, see the example:

Excellent	980
Very Good	1287
Average	390
Poor	330
Terrible	400

The ratio would be: $(330+400)/(980+1287+390+330+400)=.21$

An Alternative to the Escorted Tour

In summary, 21% of the total reviews were made up of either poor or terrible. You can rationalize that one out of five (20%) will have bad a "not so favorable" experience. If you can tolerate this, choose this hotel. It is best to compare three hotels. Also, remember, if you are using "points," it probably doesn't matter since who wants to pay cash when you can use points. If the ratio is far above 20%, explain this well to your traveling partner to seek a mutual decision.

Secondly, do consider other critical items. Will you have to pay for parking? Is breakfast included? Many five-star hotels do not offer breakfast. I was in a five-star hotel in Seville, and the breakfast was $36 per person. Great buffet, but I could have done with a slice of frittata and a coffee for $5 at a café down the street. You need not worry about any resort fees of $25 per person unless you stay in resort areas, e.g., Portofino in July.

Once you choose your hotel, you are ready to make the reservation. What you don't want to do is book it through the OTA, i.e., the Online Travel Agents (hotels.com, etc.). There are lots of reasons. You need to make it directly through the hotel's official website. The hotel's official website (URL) may appear on page 2 or 4 of your Google search. The official website of the Rialto Hotel in Venice is Rialtohotel.com. It is not "thehotelrialto.reservations.com/." Make sure you go to the official website to make your booking. Also, note that many hotels pull their listing from OTA's once they are up to perhaps 60% occupancy. So even though it says "no rooms left on our website," it doesn't mean the hotel is sold out. Also, don't hesitate to ask for multi-night discounts or multi-room rates. The hotel usually will want a credit card guarantee for the first night. Also, you can request special arrangements e.g., "we would like a room opposite the gardens," etc.

In their return email, make sure they state "Breakfast included with private bath" and 20Euros (or whatever) per night for parking, if not included. Do request a room NOT on the ground floor (zero floor) or next to the elevator. The rooms tend to be noisy. Finally, make sure they state their cancellation policy.

ITALY NO TOUR NEEDED
You Can Do It Yourself

CHECKING INTO YOUR HOTEL

On check-in, always ask to see the room first. Leave your bags in front of the reception desk. If the room is too small or faces the main street, ask the clerk if they have a nicer room facing the courtyard and perhaps larger. Another 10Euros may get you a better room. Turn on the heat or air-conditioner, and make sure the fan does not rattle. If you have a noisy mini-bar fridge, you can always unplug it, assuming you do not use it.

>>>TIP<<<

If the garage is too small to navigate (which it usually is), ask the front desk to have the bellman park your rental car. This way, you will avoid damaging your rental as you squeeze it between two other cars or one of those concrete posts. Have the bellman bring your rental out of the garage. Inspect your car when leaving to ensure no damage.

>>><<<

And one final point: once the lights go out, there is very little difference between paying $150 per night or $500 per night. You will still get a good night's sleep! All I ask is that it is clean and comfortable and that plaster does not fall off the ceiling. It is best to read those "current" comments on Tripadvisor.

TELEPHONE AND INTERNET CALLING

If you haven't learned by now, cellular calling while traveling abroad is quite expensive; secondly, you don't get a lot of minutes or data. The best approach is to use WIFI from your hotel room in the evening to make calls. There are many apps, such as WHATSAPP, FACETIME, ZOOM, MESSENGER, and GOOGLE VOICE, to name a few. These apps allow you to call over the Internet using your smartphone or tablet with the hotel's WiFi system (not a carrier, i.e., Vodafone, etc.). If the call is made to another cell phone using WiFi on the Internet, there is no charge. However, if you need to go off the Internet to a landline or another cell number, i.e. 555-555-1982 (at the far end), not on WiFi, you will pay a few cents a minute for what is known as the termination charge. On Google Voice, you will have to open an account and put $20 on it as a drawdown, as with Skype, etc.

An Alternative to the Escorted Tour

Currently, Verizon has a $100 (per month) plan offering 180 minutes of calling and some data. They also have a plan that charges you $10 for the day once you answer the call; see below.

Check with your carrier on rates for 5G, etc., if you must answer calls "on the street." Texting with Verizon while in Europe is still quite cheap. As of this writing, you don't need a plan at all. You will be charged $.20 to receive a text and $.50 to send a text. But don't start calling without a plan from Italy. It will cost you about $2 per minute. However, there is no charge for the $10 plan. In other words, you just sign up, and then when you call for the first time, Verizon charges you $10 for unlimited calls that day.

>>>TIP<<<   ** SURPRISE *
This is critical. Many cell phone users return home and find a staggering bill from their mobile carrier in a few weeks. Sometimes, it can be as much as $200-600 for that trip to Italy. Yikes, what happened? Simple. You must deny using 3G, 4G, and 5G services from the Roaming Carrier, i.e., Vodafone, etc. If you are on a very limited data plan, perhaps 250Mbs, you will exhaust that with 2-4 evenings on Facebook or sending photos back home. The best is to avoid these high data transfer applications unless you are strictly on WiFi in your hotel room. In your SETTINGS, you must DENY MOBIL DATA or MOBIL ROAMING in Mobile Networks, Data Roaming.

It's quite easy to do. All you need to do is go into your smartphone's settings and deny your phone the ability to use the cell carrier (as opposed to WiFi). I won't go into all the details since it varies by carrier and type of phone. However, it is best to just call your carrier and find out exactly how to DENY ROAMING. This way, you will not be charged any expensive roaming fees for calls or data. In summary, the best is to use WiFi from you room, café, internet bar or whatever.

It is difficult to control inbound calls. It is best to look at the number calling you and determine if you should take it. There is no charge if you do not answer the call. Since I don't sign up for any travel plans and make all my calls over WiFi from my room, internet café, or restaurant, I refuse to answer any call. Most people will text me, and if I have to make a long call, I duck into a standup bar or internet café and use their complimentary WiFi while having my double espresso with Sambucca or Amaretto.

>>><<<

SECURITY

Comparing Italy to the USA, crime in Italy is non-existent. There are no mass shootings every day. Very few, walk around with or even have guns. Police are well respected. It has to do with their culture. To repeat, turn on the TV in your hotel room. You will only see programs that fall into four categories: Soccer (or some other sport); game shows, e.g., Wheel of Fortune; Entertainment, e.g., "America's Got Talent" or better, "Dancing with the Stars," and finally, news, BBC or RAI. The only violence you will see is a re-run of a John Wayne Wild West movie (probably in black and white from 1955) or Italian or world news.

In Italy and most European countries, crime is called "Petty Crime." It can take the form of everything from scams to handbag snatching. Now, before you come to any conclusions, I can tell you that petty crime is rare. So there is no need to be concerned, especially if you follow my rules.

1. Don't bring anything you can't afford to part with. Ladies, leave the diamond cocktail ring home. Men, don't wear your Rolex; you don't need to impress anyone.

2. Men should purchase a money belt. The best is Amazon B015HXS2KY or equivalent. They are only $20 or less. I suggest this and not the pouches. However, both work. There is also another unit which goes across your chest.

3. Ladies, and also men, should purchase a handbag with a zipper and a wide strap which fits over the shoulder. Wear it across your chest and always walk with it away from the curb. In other words, NOT toward the gutter where it can be easily snatched by someone on a motor-scooter. Always zip it up after you take something out.

An Alternative to the Escorted Tour

4. Always take your wallet and smartphone to breakfast with you. While the staff at all the hotels is honest, you never know who will slip into the room when the maid is cleaning and tell the cleaner that he forgot something.

5. When leaving for the day, take that Ipad or tablet, bury it with your soiled underwear and zip up your luggage. Also take the charging unit and bury it with your soiled stuff.

6. Italian law requires that you always have your passports in your possession. Make copies and keep them in your luggage.

7. Purchase a cheap "sacrificial" wallet. Place a five-euro note in it with an expired library card (redac your name with a black marker) and keep it in your back pocket. Put your real wallet in that large front pocket where you can easily put your hand on it as you walk around that large outdoor market. If they want your wallet in that back pocket, all they will get is 5Euros and an expired library card, good.. ha, ha.

8. Beware of setups. If someone sits next to you on a park bench, consider getting up and moving. Watch out for people wanting to take your picture on the Rialto Bridge. While distracting you, the "partner" may bump into you and remove that wallet from your back pocket. Ha, once again, they only get that sacrificial wallet as they run down the street.

9. Beware of people willing to help you with directions or show you to your hotel (this is a big thing in Mexico City).

1. If you need to look at a map or your smartphone, back yourself up against a building where no one can come from behind and pick up that sacrificial wallet; it's better to slip into a stand-up bar or a café.
2. Don't use the ATM when it is dark. Have someone accompany you to the ATM. Or, better yet, use the ATM inside the bank instead of the one out on the street.

ITALY NO TOUR NEEDED
You Can Do It Yourself

3. One more item, don't let anyone who offers to help you with your bags, help you, unless he is the doorman at at your hotel.

DINING

Dining, whether dinner (cena) or lunch (pronzo), is a ritual with most Italians. Most of you will probably have a light lunch because of all your touring. So, I will skip lunch and proceed to dinner. First, most places will open at 8PM. You may be able to find a few places that open at 7:30PM; however, don't expect that. You can figure you won't eat anything until a half hour after you are seated. If this presents a problem, the best is to have a snack after you wake up from that snooze. The place will usually be packed by the time you leave the restaurant at 9:30. Second, there is a cover charge for all dining. This is usually about 2-4 Euros per person. The cover includes the tablecloth, utensils, bread, and olive oil (for dipping, they don't use butter) and may include olives. You can always ask.

>>>TIP<<<

Before you go out to dinner, ask the desk clerk where he goes. You can bet the prices will be better, and they will not have a menu but a chalkboard. They may only take cash. So before you sit down, check out the menu. If you do not want to dine there, go to your selected restaurant. I should note that most restaurants post their menus outside, so you can decide. Do walk in and ask the owner if there are any specials tonight. If you are near the coast, expect the specials to be fish.
>>><<<

Wine by the glass, usually of the region, is pretty inexpensive. So expect to pay about $3 a glass for Chianti in Florence or $3 for cold Frascati in Rome. Don't ask for exotic mixed drinks like a Pina Colada unless you are at a resort or a high-end hotel; they will not know how to make it. So it is best just to stick with wine and straight mixed drinks, e.g., a Martini, a Gin and Tonic (the Brits enjoy this), or an Italian aperitif (Aperitivo) like Compari and Soda. Also, you will find Coke, Sprite, and all that other stuff expensive at about $4 a can. You can buy it in the Supermercato

285

An Alternative to the Escorted Tour

for a lot less and stow it in your frigo bar in your room. So it's best to have your "Coke" or a glass of wine before you go out for dinner with some crackers and cheese, or better crusty bread and Olive Oil. Now, on to dinner.

When you walk into the restaurant, greet the matre 'd (usually the owner) with a "Buona Serra" (just Serra will also do) and smile. If there is a non-smoking area, ask for it. Remember, Europe smokes, and Italy does not have a Surgeon General.

After you are seated, the waitperson will present you with a menu. It's usually in Italian and English. The waitperson will ask you if you want bottled water. As far as I know, all of the tap water in Italy is fine. However, I usually order a liter of bottled water. They will ask you if you want natural, without gas (sin gas), or with gas (con gas.) It's usually ice cold and great with a piece of lemon. All water is inexpensive and costs about $2-$4 per liter.

Most restaurants that cater to tourists will offer you a Tourist Menu, or you can dine ala carte. The best deal is always the Tourist Menu. It includes an appetizer (the starter), a pasta dish, a main course, and dessert. If they offer a salad, it will be served before dessert. Many Tourist Menus also include a glass of house wine. Take it from me. It's always a good deal. If you don't want that full-course dinner, ordering some appetizers and a main dish is okay. Don't feel embarrassed to ask the waiter if you will share all with your partner. It is perfectly acceptable.

Two things you should realize. Dinner is slooooo. Expect to wait between courses. Better, as soon as you order dessert, ask for the bill. In the USA I always figure 90 minutes for a dinner. In Italy, it is best to figure two hours. And don't think the service is slow. It is no reflection on the establishment. They are all slow. It is their way of life. Take it easy and enjoy it. Order some garlic bread and have another glass of wine. And one final point. You won't find spaghetti and meatballs on the menu. It's not Italian! So enjoy the antipasto and the Osso Bucco with the sautéed broccolini (a contorni, a side dish) or the spinache (spinach). One more item: you must always ASK for the bill (il conto per favore), which means the count, please.

ITALY NO TOUR NEEDED
You Can Do It Yourself

CUSTOMS

Italy has some strange customs. Here are just a few. There is no such thing as salad dressing. So don't request creamy Italian, Ranch, or Blue Cheese. They only use oil (EVOO, extra virgin olive oil) and vinegar (Balsamic of Modena).

Pizza is only eaten with a knife and fork. You don't pick the slice up and try to bite off a piece like we do in North America. Also, it is ordered only for dinner unless you find a slice in a street shop, bakery, or a standup bar for lunch.

Cappuccino is usually consumed up to 12Noon. However, after dinner, an expresso is served. Most tourists will, of course, have a Cappuccino. You will find that most Italians will finish their dinner off with a "pony" of limoncello or grappa. Limoncello is lemon liquor from the Naples area and grappa is made from the leftovers of wine fermentation.

When you leave the restaurant, you are required to carry the receipt for 100 meters with you. This keeps the Financial Police on their feet, making sure that you paid all those VAT taxes. In the USA, many restaurants take the cash and destroy the handwritten bill; no can do in Italy!

TIPPING

Also, remember restaurants include the service charge (what we call the TIP) in all their pricing, in addition to all those VAT taxes. However, if the meal was really good, most patrons will leave a few coins (about one Euro per person) on the table. And, taxi drivers do not expect a tip. However, most tourists will tell the taxi driver to keep the change (just the coins, under one Euro).

EURAIL

Most of your friends who probably have never been to Italy will suggest that you get Eurail passes for unlimited travel through Italy; WRONG! The *Italian* Eurail pass only allows travel for a few days during the period. In other words, you can take the train, say, five days in a 14-day period. It only pays off if you are doing some "long haul" routes, e.g., Venice to Palermo in a day, Genoa to

An Alternative to the Escorted Tour

Brindisi, etc. The 2024 rates for five days of travel in a 30-day period will cost you $212.00 for second-class travel. That is just the pass. You still have to convert this to a ticket and pay a reservation fee. In addition, you cannot use it on Italo trains. At $212, that's $42/day for the five days of travel, which is about break even with a regular ticket. And further, why would you use a rail pass and spoil a day of travel when the round trip from Florence to Pisa for the day is about $25? The best thing to do is figure out your long-haul travel days, i.e., Rome to Florence or Naples, and see what the total will cost you. Then compare this with an Italy Rail Pass.

If most of your travel will be rail, it is best to get my companion book *ITALY The Best Places to See by Rail,* which explains the rail system in detail. A simple suggestion at this point is just to purchase point-to-point tickets.

PAYING IN DOLLARS
When presented with an option on a credit card charge to pay in Dollars or Euros, ALWAYS pay in Euros, never Dollars. You will get the true bank rate and not the establishments rate.

APPENDIX COMMENTS
You will find in the Appendix which follows, several "logical" maps of the itineraries I have discussed. I often read several of the Italian travel sights on the internet. I find that some people don't have the foggiest idea where some of these towns are located. These maps, or better diagrams, will give you a feel for their location and the distances between them.

CLOSING REMARKS
I thank you for reading this book and hopefully, your travels through Italy will be as enjoyable as mine have been. If you enjoyed this book, and purchased it through Amazon, please be kind enough to write a short review. And, thank you!

You are always welcome to email me for "tech support" or to seek my advice. Ciao for now..

Bob Kaufman, thegelatopress@gmail.com

ITALY NO TOUR NEEDED
You Can Do It Yourself

ROME – FLORENCE – VENICE – MILAN

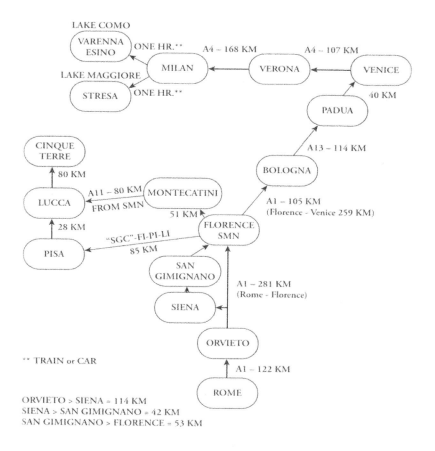

LAKE COMO
VARENNA ESINO — ONE HR.**
MILAN ← A4 – 168 KM ← VERONA ← A4 – 107 KM ← VENICE
LAKE MAGGIORE
STRESA — ONE HR.**
40 KM
PADUA
CINQUE TERRE
80 KM
A13 – 114 KM
A11 – 80 KM
LUCCA ← MONTECATINI
FROM SMN
BOLOGNA
28 KM
51 KM
A1 – 105 KM
(Florence - Venice 259 KM)
PISA ← "SGC"-FI-PI-LI — FLORENCE SMN
85 KM
SAN GIMIGNANO
A1 – 281 KM
(Rome - Florence)
SIENA
** TRAIN or CAR
ORVIETO
A1 – 122 KM
ORVIETO > SIENA = 114 KM
SIENA > SAN GIMIGNANO = 42 KM
SAN GIMIGNANO > FLORENCE = 53 KM
ROME

An Alternative to the Escorted Tour

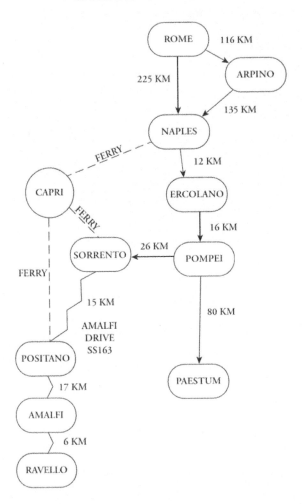

AMALFI & NAPLES AREA

ROME — 116 KM — ARPINO

225 KM

135 KM

NAPLES

FERRY

12 KM

CAPRI

FERRY

ERCOLANO

16 KM

SORRENTO — 26 KM — POMPEI

FERRY

15 KM

AMALFI DRIVE SS163

80 KM

POSITANO

17 KM

AMALFI

6 KM

RAVELLO

PAESTUM

ITALY NO TOUR NEEDED
You Can Do It Yourself

TUSCANY / UMBRIA HILLTOP TOWNS

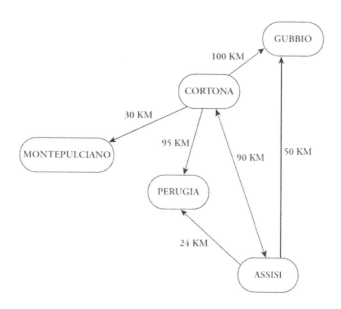

An Alternative to the Escorted Tour

APULIA & SALENTO

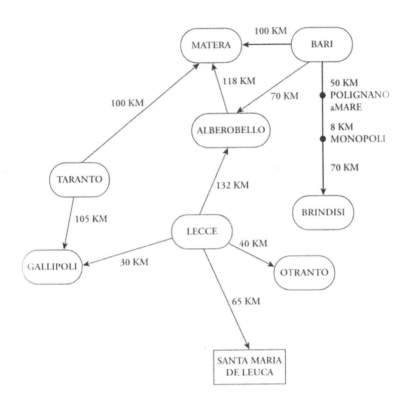

ITALY NO TOUR NEEDED
You Can Do It Yourself

SICILY - AROUND THE ISLAND

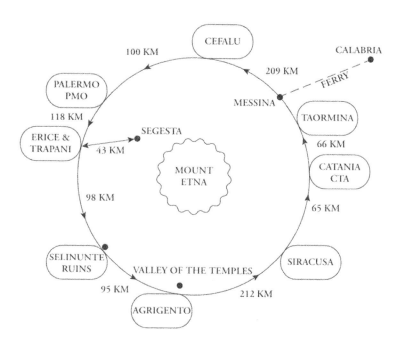

Made in the USA
Monee, IL
25 November 2024

71062770R00167